THE **COMPLETE** **IDIOT'S** **GUIDE** TO

Numerology

Second Edition

by Kay Lagerquist, Ph.D., and Lisa Lenard

ALPHA

A member of Penguin Group (USA) Inc.

This book is dedicated to all of you who long for meaning and want to understand how to live your life with consciousness and move with the flow. As our greatest spiritual journey is to "Know Thyself," as mandated by the Oracle of Delphi in Pythagoras's time, I offer the wisdom of numerology as a light on the path. May you be guided to the highest and best expression your soul's purpose, through the numbers.

Kay
April, 2004

ALPHA BOOKS

Published by the Penguin Group

Penguin Group (USA) Inc., 375 Hudson Street, New York, New York 10014, USA

Penguin Group (Canada), 90 Eglinton Avenue East, Suite 700, Toronto, Ontario M4P 2Y3, Canada (a division of Pearson Penguin Canada Inc.)

Penguin Books Ltd., 80 Strand, London WC2R 0RL, England

Penguin Ireland, 25 St. Stephen's Green, Dublin 2, Ireland (a division of Penguin Books Ltd.)

Penguin Group (Australia), 250 Camberwell Road, Camberwell, Victoria 3124, Australia (a division of Pearson Australia Group Pty. Ltd.)

Penguin Books India Pvt. Ltd., 11 Community Centre, Panchsheel Park, New Delhi—110 017, India

Penguin Group (NZ), 67 Apollo Drive, Rosedale, North Shore, Auckland 1311, New Zealand (a division of Pearson New Zealand Ltd.)

Penguin Books (South Africa) (Pty.) Ltd., 24 Sturdee Avenue, Rosebank, Johannesburg 2196, South Africa

Penguin Books Ltd., Registered Offices: 80 Strand, London WC2R 0RL, England

Publisher: *Marie Butler-Knight*
Product Manager: *Phil Kitchel*
Senior Managing Editor: *Jennifer Chisholm*
Senior Acquisitions Editor: *Randy Ladenheim-Gil*
Book Producer: *Lee Ann Chearney/Amaranth Illuminare*
Development Editor: *Lynn Northrup*

Senior Production Editor: *Billy Fields*
Copy Editor: *Susan Aufheimer*
Illustrator: *Kathleen Edwards*
Cover/Book Designer: *Trina Wurst*
Indexer: *Brad Herriman*
Layout/Proofreading: *Ayanna Lacey, Donna Martin*

Contents at a Glance

Contents

Foreword

Numerology, the study of the spiritual qualities of numbers and letters, has been one of the greatest gifts in my life. Using the guidance of this ancient knowledge, I changed my life forever in 1972 when I selected a new last name for myself after my divorce. In one of those amazing synchronicities upon which you reflect years later, I was guided to make the acquaintance of a woman named Ruth Drayer in Santa Fe, New Mexico. In a casual conversation, I mentioned to Ruth that I had had a persistent thought for the last few months that I ought to change my name. I didn't want to take back my maiden name and had not made any real move to find a new one. Ruth said, "Oh, if you're going to change your name, you ought to use numerology to harmonize the new name with your birth date in order to create the best Destiny for that birth date."

I had never heard of this system, but I was eager for Ruth to work out my chart. We started with my birth name and birth date, and when I saw her simple, handwritten chart, a light literally went on in my head! I was fascinated to see that there is a blueprint of our destiny hidden within the energies of our name and birthday. I selected my last name, Adrienne, because I had always liked the sound of it, and I had given it to my daughter as a middle name. Spelling it Adrienne instead of Adrian happened to coincide to the total numbers in my birth date—so that was the best choice.

Without a doubt, the name I now have, Carol Adrienne, which totals to the number 11—has opened up my life path in ways I could never have believed possible. Little did I realize then—being a novice to the system—that the 11 put me on a path, while very challenging, that has given me my livelihood, success, and insight into the mysteries of the spiritual quest. For this I am forever grateful.

Throughout the years, the accuracy of the numbers has been astounding. Numerology, I found, explains the various personalities within different families. It can also highlight the possible attractions and conflicts between couples.

For me, numerology has provided confirmation of life decisions about when to move, change jobs, start new projects, buy property, be patient, and even find a mate or get pregnant. Over the years, I've received many letters and phone calls from people who report that events unfolded right in line with the advice of the numbers.

I am delighted to be able to recommend *The Complete Idiot's Guide to Numerology, Second Edition*, by Kay Lagerquist and Lisa Lenard because it is one of the clearest and easiest books on numerology that I have read. They obviously love their subject, and this book is so well written and well laid out, that the reader will have no trouble immediately putting the information to use. I didn't want to put it down, even though I know the subject well! I felt as if the authors were chatting with me by the fireside.

Without a doubt, numbers influence our lives. If we open our eyes to this hidden spiritual knowledge, we have within our grasp a priceless intuitive tool. For example, one of the most fun uses of numerology is to add up the numbers in your house or apartment. I'll never forget one day during a very, very challenging part of my life when I was being treated for breast cancer, going through a divorce, starting a full-time counseling practice, moving, and having financial problems.

I was standing in the shower and realized that my house number, 2078, not only added up to 8 (money and legal matters), but also represented every number of my karmic lessons (karmic lessons are the missing numbers of your name—I had no letters for the numbers 2, 7, or 8 in my name). No wonder, I thought, that things were a bit dicey here!

My next house number was 1015, which added up to 7. This new house gave me a time of healing, a good place to write in solitude, and a simple life. I then moved to 6641, adding again to 8, but also representing my 6 Soul Number, 6 Destiny, and the 41 of my birth year. I had incredible success in that house, and have since moved on to another 8 house (314), which continues to provide me a space to work at home, work in publishing (as a writer), enjoy success, and make good money—all characteristics of the number 8.

It's all in the numbers. Read on and find out what you came here to do.

—Carol Adrienne, Ph.D.

Carol Adrienne, an international workshop facilitator and master numerologist, is the author of the best-selling *The Purpose of Your Life*, *The Numerology Kit*, *Find Your Purpose, Change Your Life* and co-author with James Redfield of *The Celestine Prophecy: An Experiential Guide*.

Introduction

Every number tells a story—and the story it tells is the story of you. And the best thing about numerology is that all you need to know is your birth name and your birth date—it's that simple. From those two pieces of information, you'll create your Numerology Profile.

Basically, your Numerology Profile consists of five Core Numbers: your Life Path Number, your Destiny Number, your Soul Number, your Personality Number, and your Maturity Number. Taken together, these five numbers paint a singular portrait of who you are—both the secret you and the you who everyone else sees.

The energy of the numbers is all around us, and we'll show you how to find the numbers for your Personal Years, Personal Months, and even Personal Days, as well as how to live in the house that's right for you, figure the numerological synergy of your relationships, or choose a name. With numerology to guide you, you can direct your life by the numbers.

How to Use This Book

You don't need a thing to go with this book except for the two pieces of data we've already mentioned—your birth name and birth date. We know you won't read this book cover to cover at first, but will instead figure out your five Core Numbers and go straight to those chapters. That's fine with us, but we'll bet you'll want to learn more about the other numbers once you read about your own.

This book is divided into five parts:

Part 1, "The Intuitive Power of Numbers," introduces you to numerology and how numerology works. We show you how you can use spiritual numerology to help you live in the flow—in harmony with the universe. You'll also learn how to convert letters into numbers and methods for adding and reducing for accurate calculations.

Part 2, "The Energy of 1 Through 9, Plus Master Numbers and Karmic Numbers," takes an in-depth look at the numbers 1 through 9 and shows the higher and lower energetic vibration of each number as well as its interpretation. We also introduce the Master Numbers, 11, 22, 33, and more, and the Karmic Numbers, 10, 13, 14, 16, and 19.

Part 3, "Your Five Core Numbers: Life Path, Destiny, Soul, Personality, and Maturity," is where you'll learn how to calculate the five Core Numbers of your

Numerology Profile with accuracy. Each chapter also includes detailed interpretations and insights into the meaning of *your* Core Numbers.

Part 4, "Divining the Future with Numerology," reveals how to calculate and interpret your own Personal Year, Month, and Day numbers. We also introduce numerology's Pinnacles and Challenges: your potential for achievement and difficulty in each spiritual growth cycle of your life.

Part 5, "Living by the Numbers," shows you how to apply numerology in your everyday life—from your relationships, to choosing a name, to understanding the energetic vibration of your house or apartment number, to deepen the metaphysical understanding of your numbers and their meaning.

Extras

In addition to all this, we've scattered boxes throughout the text with definitions, tips, warnings, and fascinating tidbits to help you understand and learn more about numerology. Here's what to look for:

Merlin's Notes
Merlin the Magician used numerology for character analysis as well as foretelling the future. We chose Merlin as a symbol of a wise wizard who used metaphysics to harness the energy of the universe and to understand its mysteries; in these boxes you'll find insights and explanations to improve your understanding of numerology.

Easy as 1-2-3

With these simple tips, learning numerology really *is* as easy as 1-2-3!

By the Numbers

These boxes define numerology terms so that you can speak the language of numbers.

Sixes and Sevens

Take care when you come across one of these cautionary boxes—it can help you avoid making numerological errors.

Acknowledgments

From Kay: I want to thank Carol Adrienne for her wonderful foreword, her friendship, and her continued inspirational work in helping others to get to the heart of their life's purpose.

Thanks to Lisa, the consummate supportive writer, for her encouragement, for without her sense of humor and spark, this book might have been as dull as dirt. I, too, thank Lee Ann Chearney of Amaranth Illuminare for her courage in producing this book and bringing the sacred information of numerology out in a user-friendly format to mainstream audiences to read, enjoy, and, hopefully, be inspired to put it to use.

A special thanks to my daughter Anna-Stina for choosing to incarnate as a 3 soul and a 3 personality so that I might learn the true essence of the creative spirit, to say nothing of an unquenchable enthusiasm for life.

Further, I want to acknowledge all those who have gone before us to blaze the metaphysical trail, especially the women of the Numerical Institute of California, Dr. Juno Jordan, and the many authors who have contributed to the current body of literature that now exists about this fascinating subject.

Also, I would like to acknowledge the Sparkle Sisters: Kate Calhoun, Connie Dawson, Ph.D., and Paula Pugh who supported me through the writing of this second edition.

I owe a tribute to two unique groups of numerology students who studied with me for six years. As a group they willingly examined all aspects of numerology. For the Seattle, Washington group, I would like to thank Susie, Beth, Cherie, Jeanne, Theresa, and Judy. From the Whidbey Island, Washington group, I want to thank Nancy, Betsy, Andy, Cynthia, Paula, and Charlene. They have funded me with a vast reserve of stories and experiences about living with the numbers.

Lastly, to my friends, clients, and family who have been patient and understanding while I essentially "vanished" for months to write this book, I extend a heartfelt thanks.

From Lisa: Thanks, as always, to book producer Lee Ann Chearney of Amaranth Illuminare for her vision and masterminding, and to the editors and production staff at Alpha Books—for everything. I cannot imagine having co-authored the first edition of this book without the wisdom and patience of Kay Lagerquist, who taught me not only about numerology, but about faith and trust. Once again, I also give love and thanks to Bob and to Kait.

Special Thanks to Carol Adrienne

We were thrilled and delighted when Carol Adrienne, numerologist and co-author of *The Celestine Prophecy: Experiential Guide*, the best-selling *The Purpose of Your Life*, and *Find Your Purpose, Change Your Life*, agreed to write our foreword. We were still more thrilled when she e-mailed us about her delight with our book—and attached the fabulous foreword you see here. We've since both begun intriguing correspondences with Carol. But then, numerology, as you'll soon discover, is often the beginning of beautiful friendships. Carol—thanks.

Trademarks

All terms mentioned in this book that are known to be or are suspected of being trademarks or service marks have been appropriately capitalized. Alpha Books and Penguin Group (USA) Inc. cannot attest to the accuracy of this information. Use of a term in this book should not be regarded as affecting the validity of any trademark or service mark.

Part 1

The Intuitive Power of Numbers

Have you got a favorite number? Does one certain number keep popping up in your life? There is a reason. Numbers have meanings. Did you know that each number has a vibration as well as a distinct energy pattern? Even your birthday and your name have meaning. Your life is made up of numbers which tell the story of the journey of your life. Your numbers tell how you can intuitively get the most out of life. It's time to learn exactly how numerology works, and why it can help you live successfully, happily, and in harmony with others.

The Wisdom of Numerology and Your Birthday Number

In This Chapter

- What numerology can tell you about transition and change in your life
- The origins of numerology
- Your five Core Numbers
- Numerology and your energetic cosmic code
- Finding your Birthday Number

Trying to figure out your life? Curious about your future? Who isn't? There are many ways to wisdom—and numerology is one of the most intriguing. You may have already heard of astrology, the Tarot, or palmistry, which, like numerology, are methods of knowing yourself and your future.

Numerology is one of the metaphysical sciences. As an accurate, easy-to-use system for self-study and divining the future, numerology may prove an easy way for you to find some wisdom of your own. What, for example, if we told you your birthday means something? Or that your name will reveal your destiny?

The ancient metaphysical science of numerology has unlocked the mysteries of life for over 2,500 years. Today, numerology continues to be a profound tool for discovering who you are, where you're headed, and who you might become.

The Intuitive Power of Numbers

Numerology is a symbolic language of numbers, as well as a system of relating numbers and names to teach us about the human condition. With numerology, you can enhance your intuitive power.

By the Numbers

Numerology is the study of the significance of names and numbers.

You can think of numerology as the science of number energies, with each number having its own vibratory influence. Based on the belief that a person comes into this life on a certain date, with a certain name, numerology uses numbers to tell who a person is and what the map is for his or her life.

What Numerology Can Do for You

Not only does numerology tell us about ourselves, it gives us information about the people around us. Numerology can help you …

- Understand endings and change.
- Learn more about the psychological conditions at work.
- Make sense of the cycles in your life.
- Identify your challenges.
- Enhance your intuition.

Plus, numerology is easy—there are no theorems, equations, or difficult calculations. All you'll ever have to do to learn what your numbers are is add (and, occasionally, subtract).

Predicting by the Numbers

According to Juno Jordan, the "grandmother" of modern numerology, "Everything is named or numbered, but few people are conscious of the degree to which names and numbers influence their experience, progress, and communication."

Numerology is the study of what names and numbers mean and is based on the idea that your birth name and birth date paint a detailed portrait of who you are and what your potentials and challenges are.

Once you've learned what your numbers have to say about you, you'll have a convenient map for your life—both to show you the best road and to keep you from ending up on a dead end.

A Plan for Life

You play a unique role in the scheme of things and numerology is a system for knowing the path for your time here on Earth. We've all been given a choice—to go through life aware and conscious, or to live this life unaware and unknowing. With numerology, you can discover gems of wisdom so that you can live consciously—aware of the plan.

Whether it's an architectural blueprint or a *Feng Shui* floor plan, we look to symbols to add meaning and vision to our lives. Numerology, as a system of symbols, is as simple as the numbers in your birthday and the letters of your name.

By the Numbers

Feng Shui is the ancient Chinese art of placement, based on the belief that a home or building is a definable map of energy influencing our daily lives.

Not So Ancient History

The science of names and numbers, as numerology has been called, has its origins in the ancient cultures of Greece, China, Rome, and Egypt, and it also has ties to Jewish, Christian, and Islamic traditions. Even Plato accepted that certain keys for solving nature's mysteries are held in the numbers.

As we move forward in the *Aquarian Age*, the astrological era that corresponds with the new millennium, numerology emerges as an important tool for understanding intuitive and psychological self-knowledge, as you will see. But let's start at the beginning.

By the Numbers

Astrologers refer to the **Aquarian Age** as a time of heightening our awareness to a broader perspective and awakening us to great change. This Age of Aquarius, as it's also called, is thought to cover the next 2,000 years and began approximately at the new millennium.

The Father of Math—and Numerology

Pythagoras, a sixth-century B.C.E. Greek mathematician and mystic, is considered the father of Western numerology. Based on his precepts that nature is a set of numerical relationships, divine law is defined and accurate, and that all of this can be computed through numbers, he developed the "science of names and numbers." His central thought was the idea of order: All of life has a system and an order—a mathematical, musical, ethical, social, and cosmic order.

Merlin's Notes

Pythagoras didn't explore only numerology. He's also considered the father of modern mathematics (remember the Pythagorean theorem?) and is responsible for the first known exploration of musical harmony. Interestingly, he connected his two main interests in a concept called "The Music of the Spheres." According to this theory, everything vibrates to its own special harmony which then in turn blends into one great sphere of "celestial music."

Pythagoras's Idea of Numbers and Vibration

Pythagoras's philosophy goes something like this: The higher an object's vibration, the more spirit force it contains, hence the more positive its nature. When the rate of vibration is lower, however, the object contains less force, and so is more negative in its action. When taken all together, the vibration of everything great and small creates an absolute, undivided unity.

It is said that the first to use Pythagoras's ideas extensively were the Brethren of Purity, a tenth-century proto-Ismaili group from Basra. Annemarie Schimmel, author of *The Mystery of Numbers*, comments that "for the Brethren of Purity, numerology was a way to understand the principle of unity that underlies everything. It is a science that is above nature and yet is the root of all other sciences."

It was Pythagoras's belief that numbers are the measure of form and energy in the world, which led to his system of numerology. One of the main contributions to numerology given by Pythagoras is the theory that the numbers 1 through 9 are symbolic representations of the nine stages of the human life cycle.

Mrs. L. Dow Balliett

In early 1900, an ardent student of the Bible, Pythagoras, Plato, and other philosophers, Mrs. L. Dow Balliett introduced her own unique teaching of the system of numbers. Credited with originating Western numerology, Mrs. Dow Balliett pioneered teachings that were spiritual in nature, and focused on awakening people to the knowledge of themselves as divine beings.

Mrs. Balliett (back in the days when this was how "ladies" preferred to be addressed) was an influential speaker in the New Age Thought Movement and was a profound influence on one Dr. Julia Seton (who was also the mother of Juno Jordan—we get to Juno in a minute). While Mrs. Balliett is credited with westernizing numerology, Dr. Seton is credited with modernizing the name of the study of numbers into "numerology." As a result, this 2,500-year-old system was integrated into the movement toward enlightened thinking. Not surprisingly, Mrs. Balliett's teachings were rooted in the Pythagorean theory.

Dr. Juno Jordan

In the early twentieth century, a group of women in southern California began to explore Pythagoras's theories in earnest. These women, led by Dr. Juno Jordan (the daughter of the esteemed Dr. Julia Seton), formed the California Institute of Numerical Research and studied every aspect and nuance of numerology for 25 years. According to Dr. Jordan, they studied "every phase of the science of names and numbers: testing, proving, and disproving." Dr. Jordan herself (a doctor of dentistry from Denver Dental College in 1905) continued to teach and write about numerology until she passed away, two months before her one-hundredth birthday, in 1984.

Every authority on numerology today is grounded to one degree or another in these women's findings, especially in the writings of Juno Jordan. Some authorities try to "liberate" themselves from the teachings, some are straight "party line," and some just flat out change them, saying their information was "channeled" from higher sources.

We believe that Juno Jordan, along with her California Institute of Numerological Research colleagues, as well as a number of modern-day numerology experts such as Carol Adrienne—who wrote the foreword for our book—have much to offer us, and we've found their information to be both straightforward and reliable.

Easy as 1-2-3

One of the most important things to remember about numerology from the outset is that it's a symbolic system. This means that the numbers, in and of themselves, do not make things happen. At the same time, however, as Dr. Juno Jordan herself pointed out, "Numbers do not lie."

Numerology Today

Numerology enjoys a renaissance today, and that should be no surprise—it has much to offer in the way of personal knowledge we can use *right now.*

Here, in the twenty-first century, many have become aware of their own personal power—to visualize, create, and manifest—and in the desire to expand these powers, they continue to search for intuitive systems of knowing oneself. It's no wonder the science of numbers is experiencing a rebirth. After all, much wisdom and insight can be gleaned from the knowledge of your personal numbers.

Today's scientists tell us everything in the universe vibrates and has energy, and that somehow all of this energy is connected. So is it any surprise then that a system that is about the energy of numbers is finding its way into our lives? We think not. Numerology fits our time.

While today we look to a therapist to solve the mystery of relationships, or consult a financial advisor to guide us to a secure plan for our lives, there's not really anyone to tell us about ourselves. Where, for example, can we get insight into who we really are, or the purpose of our life, or why we feel drawn in a certain direction, or find out if we're on the right track? Eventually, nearly every one of us comes to wonder if we're missing something. Is there more meaning to this life than the daily grind?

If you've ever asked if there's a plan for your life, or if there's a way to know what the future holds, our answers are yes and yes: Numerology holds the key. Numerology can help you place the story of your life into a larger picture.

Easy as 1-2-3

You are a set of numbers—energies that together create your own special light.

Once you know your own numbers, you will be able to understand how you fit against the backdrop of the harmonic universe as a special source of light.

Looking for the Light

Your own personal story is important—and your numbers help to interpret your story. Further, it's not one number alone that will allow you to see the beauty and power of your being; it's the cluster of numbers that reveals the singular brilliance of who you are. In the next two chapters, we'll show you the first step toward discovering your own special light.

Your personal set of numbers symbolically represents the vibration that comprises your essence. Not only is your name filled with numbers, your birthday reveals a whole set of numbers telling of the themes of your life. You might think of these numbers as components of your "light," or, the full spectrum of light you put out. When your "light" is on, you express the positive aspects of a number. When your "light" is off, you may have the tendency to live in fear and express the negative (possibly because you don't know that you have numbers and that they can help you!). We'll show you the meanings of each of the numbers in your life, and discuss in depth the interpretation of each number. Then, it's up to you to let your light shine!

Your Five Core Numbers: Five Points of Light

Your Numerology Profile, as your personal set of numbers is called, is made of many numbers. The most significant ones are called Core Numbers. There are *five Core Numbers* in anyone's Numerology Profile. Some numerologists say there are four Core Numbers, but we say there are five.

That's because we are including the Maturity Number, a number some other numerologists simply ignore either because they aren't aware of it or perhaps they discount its significance since its full impact isn't fully operative until after age 35. However, we feel the Maturity Number, the summation of your name and birth date, is part of your original blueprint for life and has its rightful place as one of the Core Numbers.

By the Numbers

The five Core Numbers of a numerology profile are the life Path Number, Destiny Number, Soul Number, Personality Number, *and* Maturity Number.

You can think of your five Core Numbers as five points of light—your "light," or five energies that make up the unique vibration called "you."

The Five Core Numbers of Your Numerology Profile

Number	Formula
Life Path Number	Your birth date numbers
Destiny Number	Letters of your birth name
Soul Number	Vowels from your birth name
Personality Number	Consonants from your birth name
Maturity Number	Life Path Number + Destiny Number

Your Cosmic Code

Once you learn your five Core Numbers you'll see you've got a special set of numbers that are the cosmic code for your lifetime on this Earth. Your own vibrational pattern is composed of this unique set of numbers. We discuss both the calculation and meaning of each of your Core Numbers in Part 3.

Easy as 1-2-3

What are your numbers? Unlike a complex computer program or a difficult math calculation, your number code is simple. All you need comes from two things:

◆ Your birth name

◆ Your date of birth

Your personal cosmic code might look like this:

4 3 7 5 7

Or your code might look like this:

Life Path Number	4
Destiny Number	3
Soul Number	7
Personality Number	5
Maturity Number	7

In Appendix B of this book you will find blank numerology worksheets to create your own Numerology Profile. As you learn your numbers, record them on one of the worksheets we provide for you. Photocopy the worksheets to figure and create Numerology Profiles for those dear to you.

Your Birthday Number

Throughout this book, you'll find many exercises to help you put the numbers to work for you. You'll probably want to begin a notebook journal for this purpose, although we've provided spaces for you as well.

We know you're eager to get started, so we're going to begin with an easy number you can find right this minute: your Birthday Number or the number of the day you were born. This number, quite simply, is the sum of the digits of the day you were born.

Let's say you were born December 4. Your Birthday Number is 4. This one is easy because it's already a single digit; in numerology, remember, we reduce numbers to their single-digit *root* numbers by adding them together. If you were born on December 13, your Birthday Number also is 4; 1 + 3 = 4. Were you born on December 22? This, too, is a 4 Birthday Number (2 + 2 = 4). The 4 is the root number for all three of these birthdays and is called the *Birthday Number*.

July 24 = 6
Nov 20 = 8

Or what if you were born on the 28th? That's easy, just reduce the 28 by adding the 2 and 8 together to get 10. Now reduce again to a single digit. Add 1 + 0 = 1. You have a 1 Birthday Number. Got it?

To put it simply, you want to look at two elements when considering the meaning of your day of birth: the actual number(s) of the day you were born, like the 4th or 28th, and the Birthday Number (the sum of the numbers of the day you were born.)

By the Numbers

In numerology, a **root** number is the result of sequentially adding numbers together until the result is a single digit. **Birthday Numbers** are reduced to a single digit by adding the digits together. The number 26, for example, would reduce as 2 + 6 = 8.

If you were born on the 11th or 22nd, your birthday has special significance. These two birthdays are Master Numbers and there is much energy associated with them. When calculating for the Birthday Number, a Master Number birthday is still reduced to a single digit, but you will want to read about these Master Numbers in Chapter 7 as well as the brief description of the 11 and 22 birthday here in this chapter.

Okay, what's *your* Birthday Number? Let's do one more example to clarify the guidelines for figuring this number. Simply use the day you were born: only the day! If it is a single number like 6, that is your Birthday Number. If the day you were born is a number like 18, add the 1 and the 8 together to get 9—then 9 is your Birthday Number.

Write your Birthday Number in the cake in the following illustration.

Now read on to discover the meaning of the day you were born.

Write your birthday number here

Your Birthday Number is a great number to start getting you into Numerology and what it can tell you about you.

What Your Birthday Number Reveals About *You*

It's important to remember that, in spiritual numerology, the belief is that your soul chose your birthday because that day reflected what you need in this life to help you achieve your destiny. To find the hidden meaning in your Birthday Number, look for the date of your birthday.

Birthday Numbers (1 Through 9)

Your Birthday Number is 1: If your birthday is the 1st, 10th, 19th, or the 28th day of the month. You have an independent spirit, a desire to lead the pack, to be original, and usually are known to have courage. More than anything else, people whose birthdays add up to a 1 are pioneers.

◆ *A 1 birthday* indicates you want to be first … and here you are, leading the month! Individuality is number one with you, and you are both forceful with your ideas and good at giving orders—but not at receiving them. If your Birthday Number is 1, you already know that "Innovation" is your middle name. Film director Ron Howard was born on March 1, 1954.

◆ *A 10 birthday* indicates you are ambitious, original, determined, and have an enterprising nature. Independent and courageous, you love start-up projects but will not want to be saddled with managing the details. You will have difficulty taking orders and don't like second-place positions of any kind. You have a compelling nature and will. An unchecked ego may lead to fanatical leadership. Osama bin Laden was born on March 10, 1957.

◆ *A 19 birthday* indicates a tendency to be self-centered (a trait shared with most 1 birthdays) and an inability to see yourself in relation to others. In this lifetime, you will be tested to respond with compassion and sympathy and to contribute to the betterment of others. You have executive ability, although often unconventional, an excellent mind, and your public and private life will vary greatly. You do not give up easily and usually will have to overcome obstacles before reaching the strongly desired leadership position. Bill Clinton was born August 19, 1946; Ted Turner was born November 19, 1938.

◆ *A 28 birthday* indicates that like the 1 birthday you're determined and independent. The 28 birthday can indicate that you're often fighting yourself when it comes to playing by the rules, but your sense of determination never allows you to stay down for long. In fact, as a 28 your ability to lead stems from clear thinking, and you are courageous in the way you approach life. Actor Alan Alda was born January 28, 1936; computer whiz Bill Gates entered this life October 28, 1955.

Your Birthday Number is 2: If your birthday is the 2nd, 11th, 20th, or the 29th day of the month. You do best in partnership, like to work in a team, and are a natural peacemaker. You are considerate, sensitive, supportive, cooperative, and need an aesthetic lifestyle. You love to be with others and prefer to work behind the scenes.

- *A 2 birthday* indicates you seek balance and harmony. You're a natural mediator in any situation. Adaptable and sensitive to others, your 2 Birthday Number means you'll always be the peacemaker. Nobel Peace laureate Mikhail Gorbachev, last president of the Soviet Union, was born March 2, 1931.

- *An 11 birthday* indicates an intuitive, high-energy person. You have a kind of nervousness that requires balance as the key to a harmonious life. Idealism, inspiration, and innovation are the gifts of the 11, a Master Number. Master innovator Steve Wozniak, co-founder of Apple Computers, was born on August 11, 1950.

- *A 20 birthday* indicates adaptability and understanding. Tact is a byword, and you're always considerate of others. The 0 suggests you're intuitive as well. Apollo astronaut Buzz Aldrin was born January 20, 1930; actress Nicole Kidman was born June 20, 1967.

- *A 29 birthday* indicates you have both personality and potential to spare. You're intuitive and a dreamer in the real sense of the word, and so should be careful not to let your moods swing too far in one direction or another. You strive for inner peace. Former U.S. president John F. Kennedy was born May 29, 1917, and talk show icon Oprah Winfrey was born January 29, 1954.

Your Birthday Number is 3: If your birthday is the 3rd, 12th, 21st, or the 30th day of the month. You are noted for your creativity, enthusiasm, good sense of humor, and a capacity to bring joy. Your sense of fun and friendliness is contagious and you are blessed with a childlike happy spirit.

- *A 3 birthday* indicates blessings. If you are born on the 3rd day, lucky you. The 3 is considered the luckiest number of all! Talented professional football quarterback Fran Tarkenton was born February 3, 1940. The 3 is also the number of the entertainer. Actor Tom Cruise was born on July 3, 1962; home and garden maven Martha Stewart was born August 3, 1941.

◆ *A 12 birthday* indicates friendliness, enthusiasm, and a desire to establish an individuality of your own. Creativity is the name of the game here. You are also emotional, sociable, and affectionate. Gymnast Cathy Rigby was born December 12, 1952, and rocker Ozzy Osbourne was born December 12, 1948.

◆ *A 21 birthday* indicates being social is second nature. You have many friends and interests, and you enjoy people immensely. At your best, your creativity is an inspiration to others. Opera singer Placido Domingo was born on January 21, 1941; actress Goldie Hawn was born November 21, 1945.

◆ *A 30 birthday* indicates that you're charismatic, creative, and outgoing. You attract people from different walks of life, and have a fine sense of art and harmony. The 0 in your birthday gives you tremendous power with words and the ability to inspire others. Writer Truman Capote was born September 30, 1924, musician Eric Clapton was born March 30, 1945, and golf pro Tiger Woods was born December 30, 1975.

Your Birthday Number is 4: If your birthday is the 4th, 13th, 22nd, or the 31st day of the month. With a strong desire for stability and security, people who have a 4 birthday number believe in strong foundations and are both practical and reliable, as well as honest and fair. Self-discipline is the key word here, you are known to be hardworking and practical.

◆ *A 4 birthday* indicates you appreciate both form and order. You won't find the words "sense of humor" are the first quality often associated with the 4. (Forgive us, 4s, we know you like a good time, to rest, and relax and have fun, too!) Famed feminist Betty Friedan was born on February 4, 1921.

◆ *A 13 birthday* indicates a great lover of family and tradition as well as a natural organizer. Creative and energetic, you are self-disciplined and a very practical manager as you often insist on accuracy. This birthday suggests there may be health problems, and the challenge is to be willing to work hard and apply yourself, in spite of any limitations. The genuine "beautiful mind," scientist John Nash, was born June 13, 1928.

◆ *A 22 birthday* indicates you will be called to plan, organize, and lead large projects. 22 is a Master Number and it says you are very competent and must use your intuition and practical solutions to manifest things that benefit humankind. Master assignments don't get much bigger than the one undertaken by the first U.S. president George Washington, born February 22, 1732.

◆ *A 31 birthday* indicates that you are strong-willed and determined as well as fortunate and blessed with original ideas. You have artistic talent, too, but must search for concrete form to express it. At your best you're both practical and grounded, a builder through and through. Building her own *Harry Potter* literary universe is author J. K. Rowling, born July 31, 1965.

Your Birthday Number is 5: If your birthday is the 5th, 14th, or 23rd day of the month. You have an innate sense of adventure and a desire for constant change and stimulation. Patience is not your forte, but having your freedom is. Commitments can be hard to make with a 5 Birthday Number. Communicative and magnetic, the 5 can be highly attractive to the opposite sex. You are forward thinking, resourceful, highly curious, and love movement. You've got to be quick to keep the attention of a 5.

- *A 5 birthday* indicates risk taking is second nature. We'd say risk taking is *first* nature to these folks. Quick and clever, number 5 birthdays are excellent salespeople, nontraditionalists, and sometimes the resident rebel. Batter up! Baseball great Hank Aaron was born February 5, 1934.

- *A 14 birthday* indicates you are a *calculated* risk taker, are somewhat erratic, and can get yourself into trouble when you shirk responsibility. You might have a tendency to overindulge in food, drugs, alcohol, and sexual pursuits and will need to work hard to break these tendencies. Genius and master of the bad hair day Albert Einstein was born March 14, 1879 and the ultimate risk taker, Donald Trump, was born on June 14, 1946.

- *A 23 birthday* indicates a person who's emotionally sensitive, creative, and intuitive. Quick thinking and versatile, you learn quickly and are both adventurous and restless. You want both good communication and a lot of excitement. Leonardo da Vinci was born on April 23, 1452; musician Bruce Springsteen was born on September 23, 1949.

Your Birthday Number is 6: If your birthday is the 6th, 15th, or the 24th day of the month. As a 6 you are devoted to creating harmony for your loved ones. Artistic and idealistic, number 6 birthday people want to comfort, nurture, and provide, and have a humanistic nature with a love of animals and children. You are extremely responsible and family-oriented, as well as romantic.

- *A 6 birthday* indicates you are emotional and sensitive, and you love deeply and seriously. You are creative and artistic, and you put a high value on your home and nest. Sharing July 6 birthdays are artist Frida Kahlo (1907), George W. Bush (1946), and author of this book, Kay Lagerquist (1944).

- *A 15 birthday* indicates you're responsible but independent at the same time. Sympathetic and adaptable, you can facilitate change in difficult situations. You

---

Merlin's Notes

Your Birthday Number influences the middle years of your life. The number under which you were born plays a special role from the approximate years 28 through 56. We discuss the influence of your Birthday Number during those years in Chapter 16.

---

want to settle within the family structure but commitment is a struggle and restlessness is part of the bargain. Actor Ben Affleck was born August 15, 1972.

◆ *A 24 birthday* indicates a pragmatic approach that comes from your unique blend of hard work and fairness. You are determined, which sometimes shows as stubbornness, but are creative and love your home. You might be better at continuing rather than starting and will pick up responsibilities where others falter. Apple Computer co-founder Steve Jobs was born on February 24, 1955.

Your Birthday Number is 7: If your birthday is the 7th, 16th, or the 25th day of the month. You look for depth and meaning in all that you do. Analytical by nature, you take longer than most to make a decision. Thorough, reflective, and private, you need to go to natural settings for rejuvenation. Solitude and silence are desired surroundings for the 7 Birthday Number.

◆ *A 7 birthday* indicates you may appear to others as aloof but are really very loving and often shy. However, you most likely will withdraw in conflict. People with 7 birthdays need to guard against skepticism, as well as a tendency to be secretive. You will do well when you trust your well-developed intuition. Russian president Vladamir Putin was born October 7, 1952; television journalist Katie Couric was born January 7, 1957.

◆ *A 16 birthday* indicates you may find your life brings sudden (even traumatic) events that are really wake-up calls to look at your life more honestly. You insist on independence, need time to rest, meditate, and contemplate. You may have an unusual interest in the technical, scientific, metaphysical, or spiritual subjects. Like all the 7 birthdays, you may be a perfectionist and may be seen as unusual or different. Tennis great John McEnroe was born February 16, 1959, and pop diva Madonna was born August 16, 1958.

◆ *A 25 birthday* indicates a unique or unusual approach to solutions. You have good intuition, can be extremely sensitive, and are introspective. You have a cautious yet curious side and may be drawn to spiritual or psychic exploration. The 25 birthday is perceptive and good at dealing with people. Actor Christopher Reeve was born September 25, 1942.

Your Birthday Number is 8: If your birthday is the 8th, 17th, or the 26th day of the month. You are capable in the business world, can handle money and large projects masterfully, and are eager to have success, especially with material wealth. Ambitious, confident, and authoritative, others may be intimidated by your power. Needless to say, you will want to be the boss in most situations—even in your marriage and personal relationships.

♦ *An 8 birthday* indicates strength of character, good judgment, a solid value system, and the ability to handle large projects. You're ambitious and have a desire for both material success and security, so being in charge goes with the territory. The 33rd president of the United States, Harry S Truman, was born May 8, 1884.

♦ *A 17 birthday* indicates you are very capable in the business world. You will often take an original approach, are ambitious, and can be self-centered. Introspective and sometimes remote, you have a good mind and intuition. Politician Newt Gingrich was born on June 17, 1943; actor Robert de Niro was born August 17, 1943.

♦ *A 26 birthday* indicates practicality, responsibility, and a solid sense of business. You feel strongly about home and about supporting those around you, though you need to learn to be a source of strength to others without taking control of the situation. Former first lady and current U.S. senator Hillary Clinton was born October 26, 1947.

Your Birthday Number is 9: If your birthday is on the 9th, 18th, or the 27th day of the month. You are broadminded, tolerant, generous, sensitive, creative, and have a unique approach or solution to problems. With a philanthropic, humanitarian nature, you have a soul-aching desire to make the world a better place.

♦ *A 9 birthday* indicates the humanitarian impulse. This is the number of the dreamer, a compassionate heart, and broad-minded thinking. You are idealistic and can inspire others, yet can be a bit of a dramatist. Musician John Lennon was born October 9, 1940, and astronomer Carl Sagan was born November 9, 1934.

♦ *An 18 birthday* indicates you can work well with others but must preserve your independence. You are broad-minded, tolerant, and generous. Creative, imaginative, and idealistic, you inspire others. You have excellent potential for achievement and financial success. A born leader, you attract money from the service-oriented work you do. Musician Paul McCartney was born June 18, 1942.

♦ *A 27 birthday* indicates someone who is both analytical and intuitive. Others will find you original and creative but you may also appear detached or secretive because you like to keep your deepest feelings to yourself. This number embraces an element of sacrifice; you are concerned for the planet, and universal love is paramount to you. Diplomat and Nobel Peace laureate Henry Kissinger was born May 27, 1948.

A Birthday Message for Friends, Family, and Special Loves

Are you getting a sense of interpreting the meaning of your Birthday Number? Your Birthday Number is a good place to begin your study of numerology, and it's a number that is easy to discover for your friends and family as well. You may want to include a Birthday Number description with the next birthday card you send to someone.

One of the first things to put in your numerology journal is a list of Birthday Numbers for those nearest and dearest (or just closest!) to you. Then make a few notes on their special talents and tendencies—you will gain new wisdom and insights into the birthday energy for these people.

The Least You Need to Know

- ◆ Your numbers are a vibrational energy pattern showing your essence.

- ◆ You have five Core Numbers in your Numerology Profile.

- ◆ Your Birthday Number reveals your unique talents and tendencies, and especially influences the middle years of your life.

- ◆ Numerology's wisdom gives new meaning to your life, and insights into the people around you as well.

The Philosophy of Numerology

In This Chapter

- The philosophy behind numerology
- Understanding the number energy for yourself
- Numbers have meanings
- A spiritual approach to numerology
- The nine-year growth cycle

Everything's got a philosophy behind it, and numerology's no exception. Once you understand why we use numbers to explore ourselves, you'll be ready to learn how to add some of your own numbers together. We like to think of numerology as a way of exploring all the various aspects of your self and your environment.

Just as your wall mirror reveals your outer image, the mystical mirror of numerology can disclose your inner self.

Numerology Works Like Feng Shui

No, numbers don't have power over you. However, it's important to realize there's more at work in a person's life than just what you see. Numbers, vibrationally and symbolically, contain two major elements:

◆ A vibrational frequency that attracts certain energy—like a magnet

◆ A potential for spiritual attraction and connection

Just as Feng Shui shows a map of the natural flow of energy in the living spaces of your house and the things you place in it, your personal numbers create a template for the energy in your life. And just as the principles of Feng Shui give you the ability to change the energy in your home or office, and thereby change your life, numerology can help you understand how to live in accordance with your own natural energy or how to change it.

Easy as 1-2-3

Your personal numbers are a source of strength and healing that invite you to step up to a higher level of awareness. The study of numbers is one key to interpreting the forces of your outer world in order to better understand your inner self.

This means that once you become aware of the principles of numerology and the meanings of the numbers, you'll have a code to change the energy surrounding your life to a harmonious vibration that allows you to be more successful and reach your highest potential.

Numbers and Our Lives

The universe is based on the fundamental reality that all things are related, and within that underlying notion of unity, all things are energy. It's our relationship to this energy that defines our lives. Numerology is about the relationship of numbers and their influence on our lives.

The act of giving something or someone a name isn't a superficial act; it comes from our intuitive feel or connection to this person or object. Numerologists maintain that each of us carries the perfect name—a name that reflects our inner nature. Even if you argue that your name or date of birth are a matter of chance, or even that they were an accident, you'll most likely agree that your name and your birthday have an effect upon your life.

Numerology, as one of the metaphysical sciences, is a search for understanding. Even though ancient in its origin, numerology is enormously useful in its application to the search for direction in everyday life today.

PDG
DM

Different Strokes for Different Folks

As we mentioned in Chapter 1, we all have five Core Numbers. If you pick up any of the numerology books in a bookstore today, you'll find the authors calling these five Core Numbers by other names. What's important is that even though there may be different names for these five Core Numbers, all of them are figured the same way. We're all really talking about the same thing—some folks just call them something else.

Numerology Rule: The most important numbers in numerology are the Core Numbers. There are five of them: The *Soul Number*, *Destiny Number*, *Personality Number*, *Life Path Number*, and *Maturity Number*.

So that you don't become confused by all the different names for the Core Numbers when you are consulting other numerology books (and we do encourage you to use at least three resources to get a full understanding of your numbers), we've devised a handy chart to sort this out. Here's a list of the five Core Numbers, what they've been called in various numerology books, and a quick reference for how to get them.

Core Numbers and How to Figure Them

Core Numbers	Other Names Used	How to Figure It
Life Path Number	Destiny Number; vocational number; birth force	Month + day + year of birth
Destiny Number	Expression number; self-expression number; mental number; outer self	Vowels + consonants of name
Soul Number	Heart's desire; motivation number; soul urge; self-motivation number; individuality number; the inner self	Add together the vowels of name
Personality Number	Self-image number; heart self; quiescent self	Add together the consonants of name

continues

Core Numbers and How to Figure Them (continued)

Core Numbers	Other Names Used	How to Figure It
Maturity Number	True-self number; reality number; realization number; ultimate goal; power number	Destiny + Life Path Number + date of birth

One thing that has remained consistent is the name for the Birthday Number: Everyone seems happy to call the number of the birthday just that! When we talk about the Birthday Number, we're referring to only the day of the month of your birth—such as the 6th or the 29th.

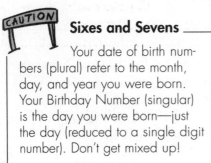

Sixes and Sevens

Your date of birth numbers (plural) refer to the month, day, and year you were born. Your Birthday Number (singular) is the day you were born—just the day (reduced to a single digit number). Don't get mixed up!

Just as there are different views about what to call the five Core Numbers, there are different philosophical approaches to the study of numerology. Numerology as a study might be approached from a variety of angles. However, because it's called the "science of names and numbers," we shouldn't be too surprised to find a large part of what goes on to be focused on name analysis.

Here are some of the different specialties found in the study of numerology:

◆ Names analysis

◆ Biblical numerology

◆ Character analysis

◆ Spiritual numerology

◆ Predictive numerology

◆ Numerolinguistics (the language of numbers)

Spiritual Numerology—It's Our Way

Spiritual numerology is based on the premise that we're more than the physical manifestation of our collective gene pool—we are spirit. Spiritual numerology suggests that the interpretation and analysis of numbers emphasizes growth of higher consciousness, and shows how to use the numbers to grow in your awareness and advance spiritually.

Spiritual awareness means being tuned to the larger picture, to the idea that there's a greater plan, awareness, and source than ourselves, and that the numbers hold symbolic information that spell out a path of spiritual guidance.

Spiritual numerology embraces the idea of reincarnation; that is, that the soul is ongoing, while the physical body is temporary. The idea, then, would be that you are a soul having a physical experience in this lifetime. It also suggests that your soul was somewhere else before it came here to this lifetime (incarnation).

By the Numbers

A way to frame an individual's journey on Earth as one of meaning and purpose, **spiritual numerology** is based on the idea that each of us carries a set of vibrations, a blueprint for our life. This blueprint can be discovered from a Numerology Profile.

Now, if your soul was somewhere else before, what was it doing? Spiritual numerology would say that your soul was learning and growing, getting ready for your time on Earth now. This information is revealed in the Soul Number.

In spiritual numerology, we also look to see what karmic debts you came into this life with. These would be lessons you didn't learn in past lives, or even lessons you refused to learn, and represent unfinished business you've come back to finish. We look to the Karmic Debt Numbers, specifically 13, 14, 16, and 19, for the nature of the karmic debt and information about how you might relearn or finally learn what your soul needs to grow and advance. The number 10, while also a Karmic Number, is not about a karmic debt to be paid back, but instead indicates that karma has been completed.

By the Numbers

The Karmic Number 10 is not really a debt. It is referred to as a karmic number but no debt is owing. In fact, it is the opposite: The 10 indicates that karmic debt is complete. It is a good karma number, so to speak.

When working with Karmic Debt Numbers 13, 14, 16, and 19, a person is given another opportunity in this life to complete any debt owed with regard to relationships, health issues, previous abuses of love, and power. These numbers give insight into previous abuses you have committed (failure to do the right thing) from a time before—or, as we like to say, your karma "in another life." We'll be covering the Karmic Numbers in more detail in Chapter 8.

Spiritual numerology is only one approach to this fascinating subject, and, as there are different approaches, there are differences of opinion about how to figure the numbers. If you're interested in exploring other approaches, you can check out some of the books listed in Appendix A.

More Than Mere Numbers

Numerology is concerned with the primary numbers 1 through 9 and their symbolic meanings, which we'll explore in depth in Part 2 of this book, where we'll also discuss the unique Master Numbers 11, 22, 33 and the Karmic Numbers 10, 13, 14, 16, and 19.

The science of numerology shares certain beliefs with other metaphysical sciences, including astrology, Tarot, palmistry, and handwriting analysis. Some of those shared beliefs include …

- ◆ Your birth date has a definite effect on your life.

- ◆ A person is born into a certain life at a certain time with a certain name, all of which influence his or her life.

- ◆ Nothing happens by chance.

- ◆ People have *reincarnated* into this life for spiritual growth.

- ◆ You have a destiny for this lifetime.

In addition to all that, numerology can help us discover what lessons we came to learn in this lifetime—and when it's best to take action and when it's not.

By the Numbers

As with all the metaphysical sciences, numerology subscribes to the concept of **reincarnation,** which is the belief that the soul is reborn into different physical incarnations, all of which are interconnected karmatically.

Not only does numerology tell us about ourselves, it can illuminate our understanding of others in our lives as well:

- ◆ For parents, numerology can help you understand why your children are the way they are and the best ways to encourage their growth.

- ◆ For mates, numerology explains personality quirks, what your partner truly desires in life, his or her soul vibration, and how best to achieve harmony in relationships.

♦ For teachers, numerology is a way to understand your students as unique individuals.

♦ For businesses, numerology gives insight into employees and partners and offers counsel about productive periods as well as slowdowns.

We think the value of numerology is how well it works. But we'll let you be the judge as you try do the numbers for yourself, and the people in your life.

> **Merlin's Notes**
>
> The beauty of numerology is that you don't have to study long before insights begin to come. That's because, of all the metaphysical sciences, numerology is the easiest to learn! As you will come to see, numerology's beauty is in its straightforward simplicity.

The End All—Be All

It's our belief that no one science of this nature gives the whole picture, and so, numerology need not be studied alone. Each metaphysical science offers a unique, specialized focus of self-discovery, and, while numerology can stand alone, it can be enhanced when used in conjunction with other disciplines. All that you are or anyone is, and how any two individuals will do as mates, is told only in part through one of the metaphysical sciences. Numerology is an excellent resource if you want insight into the five Core Numbers that represent core parts of yourself—illuminating your challenges, and giving you insights for living intentionally, fully conscious of who you are, and the direction for your highest potential.

Numbers as Mirrors

Numerology gives us a mirror into the soul. In the numbers 1 through 9, we find all the experiences life can present. We become privy to the *Soul Number* of each individual, as well as each individual's *Destiny* and *Life Path Numbers.* Such information is considered sacred knowledge and tremendously valuable to those who wish to make the journey. These numbers reveal a direction, a map for achieving happiness and success in your life.

We study numerology to become aware of who we are and to understand a time of change. The numbers affirm who we are and where we are in time. One of numerology's greatest gifts is

> **By the Numbers**
>
> Your **Soul Number** reveals what you long for in your heart of hearts. Your **Destiny Number** refers to your purpose and direction in life. Your **Life Path Number** reveals your natural gifts and talents that will allow you to fulfill your destiny.

that it teaches us tolerance and acceptance of others, as well as an explanation of the timing of events. As your self-awareness increases, you'll achieve a more objective view of your life, and from this you can make better choices for how to live it.

Numerology is a comprehensive system from which you will learn the following:

- **Your Life Path Number:** The special path that you walk in this lifetime. This number shows the natural gifts and talents that will allow you to fulfill your destiny.

- **Your Destiny Number:** The purpose and direction of your life. This number represents your calling and mission in life.

- **Your Soul Number:** This is your heart's desire and your inner motivation, what feeds your soul, and reveals what you long for in the depths of your being.

- **Your Personality Number:** This number shows how others see you. It is the outer look you wear, your preferences, and how others define you.

- **Your Maturity Number:** This number shows the direction for the second half of your life. It represents the "true you," as you begin to live in harmony with your inner and outer selves.

- **Your Life Lesson Numbers:** These are the numbers which are *not* present in your name. They tell of the lessons you're meant to learn now to advance your personal and spiritual growth.

- **Your Pinnacles:** These are the four phases of your life that point the way to your highest achievements.

- **Your Challenges:** These are the four doors through which you must pass to reach your highest attainments. The numbers representing the four doors define the difficulties and challenges you must confront.

- **Your Major Cycles:** These are the three divisions of your life that tell of the major themes governing your time here on Earth. These three numbers help to give meaning and focus to your *Pinnacles* and *Challenges*.

- **Your Personal Year:** This number tells you where to focus your energy for each year. The Personal Year Number indicates what you must face and accomplish to live in harmony with the natural flow of the year.

- **Your Personal Months and Days:** These numbers tell you what to expect and how to organize around coming events, and identify the theme for each month or day.

- **Your Birthday Number:** This number indicates a special talent you possess. It also shows a particular lesson you're trying to learn in this lifetime.

The Nine-Year Growth Cycle

We'll be using numbers 1 through 9 through-out this book. Why? Because numerology is based on the prime numbers 1 through 9. A nine-year-cycle rhythm is very important to the *numerological cycle* you are currently in. The philosophy behind this is that all the experiences we can have in a lifetime are symbolized in the numbers 1 through 9.

By the Numbers

A **numerological cycle** is a nine-year cycle that happens again and again in one's life-time, but with a different theme ruling the cycle each time. **Pinnacles** and their corresponding **Challenges** define four major phases (and themes) of a lifetime—in nine-year cycles.

Western Numerology Numbers 1 Through 9

In this book, we're using Western numerology, in which the numbers 1 through 9 have definite, unique, symbolic meanings that correspond to the evolution of a person's life. All of us experience this nine-step evolution and the only variation is the level of consciousness with which we do it. The steps are basically very simple: *over and over throughout our lives*

1. Beginning
2. Connecting
3. Creating
4. Building
5. Changing
6. Nurturing
7. Reevaluating
8. Expanding
9. Completing

Right now, you are somewhere in this nine-step cycle. If you want to learn where you are right now, you can go to our exploration of your Personal Year in Chapter 17. The thing to remember is we all move through the cycle of numbers, from 1 to 9, over and over again, throughout our lives.

Nine-Year Cycles

Numerologically, your life is operating on repeated nine-year cycles. Every year has a number, and each number has a particular meaning. This meaning is your theme for

By the Numbers

Your **Personal Year** identifies which year in the nine-year cycle you are in now. It's figured by adding your birth month and day to the current year.

By the Numbers

The **Universal Year**, the reduced number for any given calendar year, is the energy under which the entire Earth is vibrating for that year.

that year (called your *Personal Year*). In nine years you will have completed a specific cycle, which also has a specific lesson to be learned. In addition to the Personal Year, there are four Pinnacles to a lifetime, and four Challenges, that are figured in nine-year cycles.

The Universal Year

In the larger scope, besides the Personal Year Number, we want you to be aware of the Universal Year Number. The *Universal Year* is the actual year we are in, like 2004, which vibrates to the nurturing energy of the 6, or 2006, which vibrates to the expansive energy of the 8. The Universal Year is, quite simply, the calendar year. If the year were 2012, all of the planet Earth would operate under the 5, indicating a time of change.

To figure the Universal Year, just add the numbers together. For example, let's look at the year 2008, or 2 + 0 + 0 + 8 = 10. Reduce 10 and you will find it is a 1 (1 + 0 = 1). This means that the whole planet is functioning under the vibration of the number 1 Universal Year. Actually, because this 1 Universal Year number came from 10, we are reminded again that the 10 is a Karmic Number (see Chapter 8 for a discussion of Karmic Numbers), and is written as 10/1, representing both the full value of the 10 and its reduced number 1 (1 + 0). Therefore, we might say the Universal Year 2008 is a 10/1 year, a year of karmic rebirth and a time of a new beginning without the burden of previous karmic debt.

What does it mean to be in a 1 Universal Year? It's a time of new beginnings, a time for starting over and planning for the future. It's a time to stand up, to feel confident, persevere, be assertive, take charge, and get results. We would say, then, that this is what would influence all of us at a collective level, globally and locally, in a 1 Universal Year, and represents the energy that would surround us. However, don't confuse this with your Personal Year, because that's another story.

Zero Ain't for Nuthin'

The number 0 shouldn't be ignored. It represents an energy that's unformed and pregnant with potential: After all, it's full and empty at the same time. The 0 is the symbol of an open channel to higher forces.

We see the zero in numbers like 10, 240, and even 2000. When you have a 0 behind a number, the idea is that this magnifies the number ahead of it. If, for example, you have a 30th birthday, the 0 magnifies the 3. This birthday might emphasize learning to speak your truth, to express yourself, make good friendships, or to use your creative energy and all of these will be magnified by the 0's vibration.

Easy as 1-2-3

Remember, the 1 Universal Year is the first year of a nine-year cycle. Any 0s amplify the effects of the numbers they accompany. So you can't have a 0 Universal Year or Personal Year, even if it feels like it!

The year 2000 had *three* 0s. Humanity won't see three 0s for another thousand years. The presence of the tri-fold energy of the 0s in year 2000 heralded the ominous new beginning of a new vibration. The 0s, three in succession, emphasized that this new time of living under the influence of 2 energy is yet to be formed and is open to the influences of the great mystery of life and its unseen forces.

All through the years 2001 through 2009, and in subsequent years 2010 through 2090, the presence of 0s enhances and magnifies the qualities and challenges of the 2 vibration: resolution of duality; peaceful, unified co-inhabitation of planet Earth; a deeper sensitivity and loving kindness for all; living a slower rhythm that is more in tune with nature; honoring the feminine; and highlights the need for cooperation, relationship, and connection. The 0 in any number signals an intensification of the vibration and energetic properties of the number it follows.

In the next chapter, we will take you through how to calculate numbers and a closer look at the meanings of numbers 1 through 9, Karmic Numbers 10, 13, 14, 16, and 19, and Master Numbers 11, 22, 33, and beyond.

The Least You Need to Know

- You can learn to understand your own energy through numerology.

- Spiritual numerology emphasizes growth of higher consciousness.

- Numerology is based on numbers 1 through 9 and their symbolic meanings.

- You have a nine-year growth cycle.

- The Universal Year is a number that everyone on Earth vibrates to.

Chapter 3

Numbers Have Meanings, Plus Calculating the Numbers

In This Chapter

- ◆ How to add those numbers together
- ◆ Quick reference guide to the numbers
- ◆ Learning the reducing plan that's best for you
- ◆ Letters have meanings, too
- ◆ Your Numerology Profile

Enough history and philosophy! We know you really want to know what numerology can do for you. Numerology can teach you a secret code for unlocking the mystery hidden in the numbers surrounding your life.

In this chapter, we'll be showing you how to do just that by performing the simple calculations you'll need to discover what your numbers are. We'll show you how numerology works and discuss different methods of adding and reducing the numbers, and then we'll look at your birth name and begin the process of compiling your personal Numerology Profile.

Pick a Number, Any Number

Calculations for numerology are really quite simple: You either add or subtract.

The main idea behind the manipulation of the numbers is to find the single base number. This base (root) number is usually a reduced number that comes from a double-digit number, but the single number will tell the story—unless of course, it's a Master Number. (We'll get to that in a few pages.) The method for adding the numbers is indeed the most controversial question in numerology. The trick is *how* you add the numbers together.

Numerology Rule: Reduce numbers to a single digit. Add the numbers together to get a single root number.

You've already calculated your Birthday Number in Chapter 1 by using numerology's rule of reducing. For example, if your birthday is on the 14th day of the month, add 1 + 4 together to get the reduced number 5. You've got a 5 Birthday Number.

Numerologically, there are essentially four ways to add the numbers:

1. Add across.

2. Reduce as you go.

3. Add down.

4. Add double digits.

Let's look at each of these individually, so you can see the differences for yourself.

Addition Method #1: Adding Across

One way to add the numbers is to add straight across. Here's a quick example.

Let's use the birth date example of July 6, 1944. If you're adding the Date of Birth Numbers (we're talking about *all* of your birth numbers), you might think to add them like this:

$$7 + 6 + 1 + 9 + 4 + 4 = 31$$

$$3 + 1 = 4$$

The single number 4 is the root number (also called the reduced number). The reason we don't like to use this method for using Date of Birth Numbers is that when the add-straight-across method is used, you lose the chance of finding Master Numbers, which is the case in our example, as you'll see.

> **Numerology Rule:** Don't add all the numbers straight across! The numbers within a number are important as well, as you'll find out when we calculate your five Core Numbers in Part 3.

Let's look again at the July 6, 1944 birth date when *reduced* before it's added. When we do this, it reveals a Master Number! To do this for July 6, 1944, you'll reduce 1944. (July is a 7 and the day is a 6, so no reduction is necessary for calculating the numbers of the month and day—only the year needs reduction in this birthday.)

To find the year's reduced number, add the numbers together: 1 + 9 + 4 + 4 = 18. Now, you'll reduce again, to arrive at the single-digit number 9 (1 + 8). Once you have reduced the year number, add all the reduced numbers together (but remember, in this example, 7 and 6 can't be reduced). Add: 7 + 6 + 9 = 22. Our new way of writing the sum of this date of birth will be 22/4.

Easy as 1-2-3

We endorse Addition Method #2, reducing as you go. It ensures the discovery of Master Numbers.

Voila! 22/4 reveals a Master Number. You would have missed it using the add-straight-across method.

Addition Method #2: Reducing First, Adding Together

Another method for adding numbers is to reduce as you go along. Here's an example to illustrate this method. The date of birth December 16, 1972, might be written like this: 12 + 16 + 1972. If reduced first, it looks like this: 3 + 7 + 1 = 11/2.

Reducing before you add is fast. Some numerologists swear by this system, and it's certainly the easiest method for beginners. Notice in our example that we have uncovered yet another Master Number, the 11. We'll be explaining what that means in a few paragraphs.

We recommend reducing as you go. It's faster—and you carry less weight (something we all desire!).

> **Numerology Rule:** Watch for Master Numbers when reducing to a final number. Remember, the Master Numbers 11, 22, and 33 have special meanings.

Addition Method #3: Adding Down

A third method for calculating numbers is to set it up like a simple math problem. For example, to figure composer, singer, and songwriter Paul Simon's date of birth, October 13, 1941, we would write it like this:

$$
\begin{array}{r}
1941 \\
+\ 13 \\
+\ 10 \\
\hline
1964
\end{array}
$$

Then, we'd reduce 1964 to the root number 2 (1 + 9 + 6 + 4) = 20; 2 + 0 = 2). This method reveals that the Life Path Number (the sum of the birth date numbers), one of the five Core Numbers, for Paul Simon is 2, intensified by the presence of the 0, the eternal circle of life. (See Chapter 12 for everything about the Life Path Number.)

We use this method as a tie breaker when trying to determine if we are really dealing with a Master Number. We would use Method #2 first, then try Method #1, and last of all try Method #3, to see if two of the three methods give us the same answer.

Here is an example: Angela thinks she might have a Master Number birthday. Her birthday is February 12, 1941. Let's see how to use the different methods to determine whether her birthday numbers add up to a Master Number.

Using Method #1, adding straight across for Angela, we find:

2 + 1 + 2 + 1 + 9 + 4 + 1 = 20

2 + 0 = **2**

Not a Master Number, though the presence of the 0 intensifies the energy of the 2 for Angela as it does for Paul.

Using Method #2, reducing first, then adding together, we find:

2 + 3 (1 + 2) + 6 (1 + 9 + 4 + 1 = 15, or 6) = **11/2**

11/2 *is* a Master Number.

Using Method #3, adding down, we find:

$$1941$$
$$12$$
$$+\ 2$$
$$\overline{\hspace{2cm}}$$
$$1955$$

$$1 + 9 + 5 + 5 = 20;\ 2 + 0 = \mathbf{2}$$

Again, not a Master Number for Angela.

Therefore, we would conclude that Angela doesn't have a Master Number after all, and neither does Paul Simon.

Adding across for Paul Simon, October 13, 1941:

$$1 + 0 + 1 + 3 + 1 + 9 + 4 + 1 = 20;\ 2 + 0 = \mathbf{2}$$

Reducing first, then adding together for Paul, we find:

$$1\ (1 + 0) + 4\ (1 + 3) + 6\ (1 + 9 + 4 + 1) = 11,\ \text{or}\ 2) = \mathbf{11/2}$$

We can only be sure of a Master Number result if we use all three methods to verify. Remember—*you want two out of three methods to agree to get a true Master Number.*

Going back to our original example of the July 6, 1944 birthday, let's try the third method to confirm our Master Number result of 22/4:

$$1944$$
$$7$$
$$+\ 6$$
$$\overline{\hspace{2cm}}$$
$$1957$$

$$1 + 9 + 5 + 7 = \mathbf{22/4}$$

> **Merlin's Notes**
>
> The nature of Master Numbers is such that those who carry them are usually extremely sensitive to extrasensory perception, intuition, and Higher Guidance. They also carry a special responsibility to mankind to leave the world a better place by helping the race to evolve to a higher consciousness.

Of course, it's necessary to try all three addition methods only if you're working to confirm a Master Number result.

Method #4: Double-Digit Adding

This method is almost the same as Method #2 because it reduces first, then adds together. When doing numerological interpretations that involve adding your Date of Birth Numbers or Name Numbers, hold onto the double-digit number when adding. For example, let's look at the birthday for Josh Groban, the young singing phenomenon known for his spectacular operatic tenor/romantic balladeer voice who was discovered at the 1999 Grammy Awards dress rehearsal while singing a duet with Celine Dion. Josh's birthday is February 27, 1981.

In the double-digit method, we reduce all double-digit numbers to their single digits and then add each single-digit number together for the combined number total. The combined number total will be two digits, or a double-digit number. In this method, we hold onto the double-digit numbers for additional information.

To start, we need to reduce two numbers in this birthday to single-digit numbers before we try to figure out the total, double-digit number. First, we reduce the year number in this birthday: 1981 to 19 (1 + 9 + 8 + 1), and continue to reduce 19 by adding 1 + 9 to 10 and reduce a final time for the single-digit number: 1 + 0 = 1. Next we reduce the day of birth number, 27, because it has two digits: 2 + 7 = 9. The month in this birthday doesn't need to be reduced because it is only one number, 2. Finally, we add all of the single-digit (reduced) numbers together for our final total: 2 + 9 + 1 = 12. The number 12 is the double-digit total for Josh Groban's birthday. To make things more clear, it might help to write out the steps like this:

2 + 27 + 1981

2 + (9) + (19)

2 + (9) + (10)

2 + 9 + 1 = 12

If we were to reduce the 12, we will find a single-digit total of 3. In using this double-digit method, it is important to consider both the double-digit number and the reduced total number, so we would write the total 12 separated by a / and then write the 3. The birthday total will then look like this: 12/3. We can then say Josh's Date of Birth Numbers add up to a 3.

By holding onto the double digits, we can see what numbers lie behind the total (the 1 and the 2 are what are influencing the reduced number 3, in other words). In our example here, it's pretty important, because Josh has a 3 Life Path, the path of entertainment, drama, and expressing oneself in a creative way. However, the double-digit influence suggests that he will have to assert his independence and strong principles

(1) in using his natural artistic, rhythmic gift (2) to overcome tendencies of shyness, sensitivity, and the desire to please others (2) as he pursues a lifetime path of entertainment and creative self-expression (3). So here we can see that the double-digit numbers (12) tell more of Josh's story than just the 3.

Reducing Is Not a Diet Plan

No matter which method of addition you choose, you'll have to add your numbers together and then reduce. The reduced number gives the simple, root number from which an interpretation can be made.

Choose the method that feels right for you. Try them all and see which one gives you the most information. Don't be dismayed by all of these choices. Your method of calculation is one of the most important decisions you'll make in your study of numerology.

If you're not sure, start with Method #2 and reduce first. It's our favorite method. The more you work with the reducing methods, the easier it will be to find the one that works for you. Just like diets—sooner or later, you find one that reduces perfectly!

The Lowest Common Denominator

You've already seen us refer to Master Numbers using two numbers: for example, 22/4 or 11/2. When writing a Master Number, you'll have two numbers to consider: the Master Number and the reduced number. Therefore, it helps if you write Master Numbers like this so you will be conscious of working with both of the numbers involved:

- 11/2 for the Master Number 11
- 22/4 for the Master Number 22
- 33/6 for the Master Number 33

The same would be true for all of the Master Numbers. In a Master Number, the lower, or reduced, number is equally as important as the higher number and it is important to read the meaning of both numbers. If you see a Master Number written as 11 or 22 or 33, it is still a Master Number, you just aren't as conscious of both numbers and their vibrational quality when it is written as 11/2, 22/4, 33/6.

Whether you're working with a Master Number or any other double-digit number, you'll be interested in the meaning of both numbers—it just gives you more information. If your result is the Master Number 22/4, for example, you'll want to interpret both the 22 and the 4. In the advanced study of numerology, you might want to consider interpreting the meaning of other double-digit numbers in your chart much like we did in the example of Josh Groban's birthday.

Working with Double Digits

Some numerologists give a lot of credence to the double-digit number. This is because a number with two or three digits gives added information to the root number in consideration. Double or multiple digitizers write these numbers as 21/3, 17/8, or 103/4. Both the single root number and the double number are considered for numerological analysis. For example, let's look at the 15.

When we reduce 15, we add the 1 + 5 to find the root number 6. Now, let's say you wanted to know the Life Path Number for your son. You would add up the numbers of his date of birth, say, February 18, 2002, and, reducing as you go, find that it adds up to a 15/6.

$$2 + 9 (1 + 8) + 4 (2 + 0 + 0 + 2) = \textbf{15/6}$$

The number 6 tells us that this young man will have a path to walk in this life that brings responsibility, duty, nurturing, and care for others. However, if you look at the 15, you note that both the 1 and the 5 are to be considered; they show how he'll go about his Life Path 6 duties. In other words, he may be facing responsibility and duty, but will want to be independent (the 1) about the way he goes about these duties, and will also demand freedom from time to time (the 5).

Easy as 1-2-3

You'll gain insight into the underlying concerns or the direction that is given to the numerological interpretation of a single root, or reduced, number, by looking at the double-digit numbers as well. In this way, you can see the full energy motivating the base number.

Getting the full numerological energy of the root number is actually much easier than it might appear at first glance. First, look to the reduced number for your interpretation. Then, look at the double-digit number to see what other influences are involved. If working with the double-digit number is too much, too soon, and you're not ready for it, just concentrate on the single root, or reduced number—there's plenty there!

Now that you've got the basics of how to figure your numbers, it's time to see what these numbers can tell you.

> **Numerology Rule:** Don't reduce Master Numbers! They tell of special attributes.

The Meaning of Numbers

The key to numerology is: Each number has a specific meaning. We introduced you to the numbers in Chapter 1 and we'll give our in-depth analysis of the distinct meaning and message of each number in Part 2 of this book, as well as the special meanings of the Master and Karmic Numbers. For now, though, here's a detailed handy guide you can use for quick reference to the meanings of the numbers.

The Meaning of Numbers Quick Reference Guide

Number	Key Words and Concepts
Numbers 1 through 9	
1	Beginning, independence, innovation, leadership, masculine principle
2	Harmony, unity, relationships, cooperation, feminine principle
3	Saying one's truth, imagination, optimism, playfulness, creative expression
4	Building, formation, hard work, endurance, seriousness, practicality
5	Change, transition, progressive thinking, resourceful, freedom, versatility, promotion
6	Balance, nurturing, service oriented, responsibility and duty, family focus, marriage and divorce number, domestic and work issues
7	Analysis, research, science, technology, solitude, wisdom, spiritual focus, investigative, mystical, metaphysical
8	Authority, power, finances, business, success, material wealth, organization, self-mastery
9	Endings, vision, tolerance, transformation, spiritual consciousness, cosmic, teaching, global awareness, perfection
Master Numbers	
11	Master of Illumination, the inspirational messenger, the number of light; one who raises consciousness, reformer of world problems, wants to uplift others, inspires by teaching own truth

continues

The Meaning of Numbers Quick Reference Guide (continued)

Number	Key Words and Concepts
22	Master Builder, visionary; knows how to plan and execute large projects; wants to further consciousness of humankind—especially feminine consciousness; powerful skills of manifestation; the humanitarian
33	Teacher of Teachers, master of compassion, master of healing through love, use of creative energies to serve others
Karmic Numbers	
10	Renewal rebirth, karmic completion, mastery, beginning again with consciousness
13	Reworking karmic laziness through discipline
14	Reworking karmic abuse of freedom through order and stability
16	Reworking karmic abuse of responsibility and love through spiritual rebirth
19	Reworking karmic abuse of power through learning to show compassion and sacred use of cosmic wisdom for the greater good

The most important numbers to know are your five Core Numbers, which we introduced to you in Chapter 2, and are the subject of all of Part 3 of this book. You can find the meaning of your name and date of birth using numerology. Your *birth name* alone is composed of three of the Core Numbers: the Soul Number, Destiny Number, and Personality Number.

Your Date of Birth Numbers give you a wealth of information. As you will see, they tell you what lesson you're working on at a particular age, what your potential is for achievement, what the theme is for each year of your life, and what's influencing you as you live out each year. To understand this information about yourself, all you have to do is add!

Next, let's look at the name and see how it adds up. How, you ask, can I add up my name? There are no numbers in my name! Ah, yes, but there are.

Alphabet Soup: Letters into Numbers

In Western numerology or Pythagorean numerology, whenever we calculate a word, such as your name or the name of the street you live on, or when we want to discover the meaning of a word, we assign numerical values to letters of the alphabet.

Remember that when Pythagoras first devised the system of numerology, he noted that everything in the world is made up of numbers, and so applied numbers to the Arabic alphabet. Using the numbers 1 through 9, he came up with a chart that allowed him to decipher the meaning of any name.

Letters and Their Numbers

Here is a handy conversion chart you'll find useful as you calculate the numerical energy of letters and words.

Letters and Their Numbers

1	2	3	4	5	6	7	8	9
A	B	C	D	E	F	G	H	I
J	K	L	M	N	O	P	Q	R
S	T	U	V	W	X	Y	Z	

You may want to tab this page to refer to as you read this book. But, hard as it may be to believe right now, eventually, you'll memorize the number for each letter. It just takes practice!

Once Pythagoras had the numbers to figure a person's name, he had a tremendous tool for seeing into the hidden essence of that person, and so it was thought that anyone who knew this method of decoding a name could see into the soul. That's why this numerological information was carefully guarded and taught only in the Mystery Schools to devoted students sworn to secrecy. But now *you* know the secret!

Easy as 1-2-3

As you know from English class, the letter "y" may be considered a vowel or a consonant, depending on the word or name. For a full discussion of the use of the letter "y," refer to Chapter 11.

Merlin's Notes

In ancient times, esoteric schools, called Mystery Schools, initiated leaders of humanity into ways of knowing the laws of Universal Principle. These schools trained initiates in the hidden meaning of the mysteries of life. It was an intense spiritual training. Pythagoras founded his Mystery School in approximately 500 B.C., where he taught self-perfection, philosophy, science, social reform, music, astrology, astronomy, numerology, nutrition, hygiene, medicine, and leadership—all mysteries of the time.

Oprah Is a 4

An easy way to start is to look at how to calculate a first name. Do we know any Oprah's? Let's say your first name is Oprah. Using the letter chart, we find the corresponding numbers for each letter of her name:

O = 6

P = 7

R = 9

A = 1

H = 8

_____

31 = 3 + 1 = **4**

When you add up all of the numbers, you will see that 31 is the total for Oprah.

Unless you arrive at one of the Master Numbers, as we've said before, you reduce any two-digit sum by adding the numbers together. In this case, the sum for Oprah is 31, or 3 + 1 = 4, so the name Oprah is a 4. In numerology, it's thought that a person's first name reveals her or his most personal lessons. We will discuss more about the meaning of names in Chapter 10, when we talk about your full name as your destiny. Now let's look at the meaning of the name Oprah.

The name Oprah adds up to a 4, so we know that certain things are true about this name. For example, because the 4 is symbolic of the builder, you can expect that a woman with the name Oprah will want to build her life around security and permanency. All that she undertakes is done to build toward something. She can work hard, but has a high need for security, and sometimes can be more controlling and rigid than she would like to be. She has excellent abilities to organize and manage projects and as a 4, she will use a practical, honest approach to anything in her life. You can turn to Chapter 5 for a detailed analysis of the number 4. We get to know all that—and more—from just one number! Sound like an Oprah we know?

The Name You Were Born With

Later, when you will be figuring four of the five Core Numbers of your Numerology Profile—your Destiny, Soul, Personality, and Maturity Numbers—you'll be working with some aspect of the name you were born with. We're talking about the full name appearing on your birth certificate, even if you don't like it or never use it.

Numerology is working with your very essence, which means your original, pure vibration. We can get that only with your original name.

There are a lot of wonderful stories about names given out at birth, such as Carol vs. Carole, where the "e" was left off the birth certificate and she went through 50 years of her life thinking she was someone other than who she really was; or a baby in a hospital given another baby's name.

The philosophy behind using the name given at birth is that there are no mistakes. It follows that the name given to you at birth was not a mistake. However, clerical errors do occur and if this is the case for you, use the original birth name that was intended for you when you are doing numerological calculations. Just be sure to check the spelling on your birth certificate!

The numerology school of thought goes something like this: You were given the very name you got because it is the correct set of vibrations you will need to achieve your destiny, to work on your karmic lessons, and for your soul to express itself fully in this lifetime.

It's also thought that you selected your parents when you were back in "soul land," and they agreed to be a channel for your birth and life on Earth. The name decided for you was meant to be—existing as an intuitive moment for your parents. Even if you were named after your great uncle Leopold III, the point is: Your name is not a mistake.

> **Universal Law:** All things happen according to a Master Plan or Master Design. We all have free will to make choices for how we live the Master Plan.

Adopted Names and Name Changes

When you don't know your original name, you'll figure the numbers of your Numerology Profile with the name you were given at adoption, because this name is the essence or vibrational pattern you grew into.

So what if you don't know your birth name? You will simply figure a profile for the adopted name. However, if you should have both a birth name and an adopted or changed name, then use the original name for the pure essence of

Sixes and Sevens

Even if you've changed your birth name, dropped it, or gone to great lengths to have the "correct" name put on your birth certificate, you'll still need to use your original intended name— if you have access to it—to figure your Numerology Profile.

your numbers. Then figure another profile for the name you came to live by. This second profile will show who you have become.

Not surprisingly, the question of a married name is often brought up. The married name is figured separately from your original birth name, and shows what energy or lessons you added to your life during the period you carried that name.

All of your five Core Numbers remain the same as they were at birth. The married name is what energy you drew to you—that you needed to learn the next step. Always figure your married name separately from your birth name. It is not part of your original Numerology Profile. You'll find out more about all the ramifications of naming by the numbers in Chapter 20.

What Your Birthday and First Name Numbers Say About You

As you learned in Chapter 1, your Birthday Number is the number of the day of the month you were born. Like the name on your birth certificate, it cannot be altered, although you can choose to go by a different name or age in your public life. Perhaps your birth name is Alice but you always go by Ali, and yes, you give your birth year as 1969, *not* 1959—and most of the time, you actually get away with it! But that won't work in your Numerology Profile, where you need to use the name and date recorded at your birth.

Note that your Birthday Number is not one of your five Core Numbers, but its influence is potent all of your life, and it's particularly potent between your 28th and 56th birthdays. The number for your first name is only one piece used to interpret the whole energy of your Destiny Number.

So what are the numbers for *your* Birthday Number and First Name Number? Let's begin the process of revealing your numbers and what they mean. We'll start with your Birthday Number, which you identified in Chapter 1.

My Personal Information

My first name as it appears and is spelled on my birth certificate is:

_____Kent_____.

The date of birth on my birth certificate is:

Month:__11__ Day:__15__ Year:__51_____.

My Birthday Number

The day of the month upon which I was born is (circle the appropriate number for the day):

1 2 3 4 5 6 7 8 9 10 11 12 13 14 (15) 16 17 18 19 20 21 22 23 24 25 26 27 28 29 30 31

From calculations you did in Chapter 1 to determine your Birthday Number, fill in your Birthday Number.

My Birthday Number is: ___6___ .

My Birthday Number reveals (turn back to Chapter 1 to learn each number's significance and write in a few key words here):

Idealistic Independent Responsible family harmony Creative change

My First Name Number

Write the letters of your first name, as it appears on your birth certificate, using the spaces below. If there aren't enough spaces, write in more (and what a long first name you have!).

Letters of your first name:

K e n t _ _ _ _ _ _

Corresponding number for each letter:

2 5 5 2 _ _ _ _ _ _

Sum of the numbers for the letters in your first name: ___5___ .

My First Name Number reveals (use The Meaning of Numbers Quick Reference Guide in this chapter to get an initial interpretation) transition/Resourceful/promo about my personal lessons.

Now, you're on your way to understanding how numbers can reveal so many things about you, leading to insights about your core essence and life purpose. Before we continue to help you use numerology to further illuminate your path, let's look, in Part 2, at the energies of each number, the 1 through the 9, as well as the special import of the Master and Karmic Numbers.

The Least You Need to Know

- ◆ Numerology believes that all things are related.
- ◆ Remember to reduce the numbers first, and then add them across.
- ◆ The letters in your birth name and the numbers in your birthday have meaning.
- ◆ Use the name you were born with and your precise birth date to figure your Numerology Profile.
- ◆ It's easy to create a Numerology Profile of your own.

Part 2

The Energy of 1 Through 9, Plus Master Numbers and Karmic Numbers

Numerologists believe that each number has its own special meaning. The number 1, for example, being first, naturally likes to lead, while the number 5—smack in the middle—is often a turning point and change catalyst, while the 9 signals completion and the end. Then there are the Master Numbers 11, 22, and 33 that resonate to still higher frequencies, and the Karmic Numbers 10, 13, 14, 16, and 19 that present some lessons all their own.

Chapter 4

The Numbers 1, 2, 3: Independence, Harmony, and Joyful Self-Expression

In This Chapter

- Number 1 is self-sufficient and wants to lead
- Number 2 is sensitive and gentle and wants to support
- Number 3 is enthusiastic and energetic and wants to create
- The spiritual essence of the 1, 2, and 3
- The energy of numbers 1, 2, and 3

If you want to light a fire under a project, get a 1 on board. If you want a patient, supportive, detailed team player, get a 2 on your staff. If you want a quick, clever, contagiously fun person to lighten up the scene, get a 3. Each of these three numbers has clearly identifiable qualities and is unique in its energy. The 1, 2, and 3 reveal a sacred cycle: 1, the number of creation; 2, the number of assimilation; and 3, the number of expression. This triad creates a three-stage action of the mind or way of thought formation: 1, the number of impression; 2, the number of re-impression, and 3, the number of expression.

In this chapter, we examine various facets of the numbers 1, 2, and 3 including the energy of each number, a peek at life with each of the numbers (should you be living with one of these three), as well as the spiritual essence, special abilities, and places of growth for each number. We also thought you would want to know some key words associated with each number, as well as the astrological equivalent, the matching Tarot card, the letters, and the polarity, colors, gems, and flowers, so we've created a chart for each number that shows its correspondences.

Number 1: Leader of the Pack

What makes a leader? Knowing what one wants, having the courage to go to the head of the pack, having strength of will, and having the wit, intelligence, and quickness to execute the plan.

Independent and headstrong, the 1 is both ambitious and determined. Never afraid to try something new, the 1 will "boldly go where no one's gone before"—but seldom "goes with the flow."

He or she will begin it with flare and a burst of enthusiasm. The 1 assesses what needs to be done with the speed of light and then executes the plan in about the same amount of time, all the while ordering everyone around. He or she means no harm— he or she is just into the power of his or her 1 energy. The drive and focus he or she will bring to the job—any job—are hallmarks of the number 1.

Easy as 1-2-3

The 1 is the number of initiation and action, the self-motivated leader.

Maybe you won't be able to tell a 1 what to do—but you won't find him or her waiting for anyone to tell him or her what to do either. While you may still be talking, the 1 will be long gone, already into the thick of the action.

The Number 1: Independence	
Key Words	Pioneering spirit, strong-willed, innovative, courageous, determined, and symbolizes the beginning
Astrological Equivalent	Aries
Tarot Card Equivalent	The Magician and the Aces of each Minor Arcana suit

Letters	A, J, and S
Polarity	Yang
Colors	Red, flame, cardinal, burgundy
Gems	Ruby or garnet
Flowers	Lily for purity, purple lilac for first emotions of love, sage for esteem, all red flowers for boldness

Merlin's Notes

Tarot cards, another metaphysical tool, present a symbolic picture of the elements of life. The Tarot deck is divided into two parts: the Major Arcana and the Minor Arcana. The Magician card, card 1 of the Tarot's Major Arcana, has the ability to create his or her own reality, and sometimes represents the need to find a new direction in life. Similarly, the act of creating one's own reality is very much in the domain of the independent, self-directed 1. The Aces in all four of the suits of the Tarot are represented by a perpendicular Cup, Wand, Pentacle, or Sword. The meaning remains the same for all four: A new beginning is foretold.

The Energy of the 1

The energy of the number 1 is intensely active, with a driving determination to get ahead. There's a mental vigor here, and it results in the goal-oriented, masculine expression of active, forceful, courageous energy. It is a direct and directed energy.

The basic meaning of the 1 is energy in a state of perpetual motion. The 1 has the power to create, develop, and govern all things pertaining to this earthly life, like the Tarot card, The Magician. The 1 however, requires a complete overcoming of self before it attains its highest success.

The Timing of the 1

The 1 is the number of new beginnings. It always signals a new time is about to begin, that new opportunities can be expected, and that all will be done with courage and the intent to get the job done. This is the number of initiation. In it's drive to get things done, the 1 will initiate, "move on it," and is often impatient to get going. Waiting isn't the 1's forte, unlike the 2.

You can think of the 1 as energy that begins all action, who leads the way to a new direction.

Life with the 1

As with all the numbers, life with the 1 can bring both blessings and challenges. The 1's insistence on action can mean it won't tolerate any dillydallying, and its strong opinions can sometimes make it contrary. A 1, however, won't care much if others find him or her contrary or forceful, because both of those are very much a part of who a 1 is.

The Blessing of the 1

The blessings of the 1 are its confidence, creativity, and vital energy, as well as its feisty, self-starter spirit. People with strong 1 influence in their Numerology Profiles will find it easier than any other number to initiate things and to get results. It's this independent spark of the 1 that's so inviting.

The Challenge for the 1

The weak side of the 1 is lack of self-esteem, self-consciousness, and the struggle to believe in the higher self. The 1 needs to learn to believe that he or she is capable of meeting the challenges of life, to have courage, and to be determined—even when there's doubt within.

The Lesson of the 1

The lesson of the number 1 is that this person will be required to overcome the negative expressions of self to attain his or her highest success. This is most prominently seen in the opinionated 1 who offends everyone with tactless, strongly stated opinions.

The 1's aggressiveness, for example, is often a cover for its aloneness and lack of self-confidence. The lesson for the 1 is that it must seek the right environment in which its strengths can thrive. You've got to put the 1s in with the grounded 4s, or the head-honcho 8s, rather than the timid 2s, or the idealistic dreamer 9s. Not patient themselves, 1s need to learn to surround themselves with people more patient than themselves (6s have a lot of patience), who at the same time will not be afraid to stand up to the 1 when necessary.

Individualistic, innovative, and original, nothing's going to get by the 1. Understanding the 1's need to be first goes a long way toward understanding its tendency to push everyone else out of the way to get there. Similarly, understanding all the nuances of the 1 can help you learn to live with its forcefulness—whether you're the 1, or someone you love (or don't!) is.

Relationships with the 1

Despite its ability to stand alone, the 1 can make a good friend, and often uses its sense of humor to get over the rough spots (quickly!). The 1 is also a good conversationalist, often using wit, intelligence, and insight to spice up favorite topics. Like the 7, one-on-one relating is its preference. However, in groups, the 1 will stand apart, it doesn't really like people it doesn't know. In the end, the 1 remains a loner at heart, because the 1 considers him- or herself different from the others.

When seeking relationships, the 1 looks for attractiveness in others, as well as a strong personality, strength of character, and a self-confidence that can match its own. The 1 doesn't like boredom, anything ordinary, or anyone who demands too much of it—the 1 likes to be the person doing the demanding!

At the same time, the 1 is very sensitive to other's approval or criticism, and if it senses any disapproval, no matter how minor, it may become angry and resentful. A little praise will go a long way with a 1—but the 1 needs to remember that praise is a two-way street, not a one-way alley!

The 1 likes to be in charge, so it can appear bossy, and it needs a mate of a strong character who's warm, patient, and capable of standing on his or her own. Love and affection are very important to the 1, and in fact the 1 won't reach its potential unless it's understood at home.

> **CAUTION**
>
> **Sixes and Sevens**
>
> As people with a 1 Life Path Number will tell you, 1s tend to jump first—and then check to see if there's water in the pool. If you're a 1, you probably know about bungee jumping into new projects, commitments, or investments.

What's Important to the 1

Approval, activity, and ambition are of primary importance to the 1. In addition, the 1 prefers to work alone and likes to be the one exploring and trying out new things. The 1 needs to be creative and is often the trendsetter or future forecaster. The 1 also values obedience, the new, independence, and matters of principle.

Not a physical laborer, the 1 lives on the mental plane. The creative 1 strives for originality in its thinking and has the courage to be original—the "pioneer." Action-oriented 1s are also good in business, and can do well with finances when it's about the good of others rather than personal prestige.

The 1 is especially qualified to head up just about anything—as long as there are others there to keep the ball rolling once the 1 has got it started: 1s like to start it, but not to stick around and manage it.

As a high-powered vibration, the 1 is the thinker and planner, quick-witted and ready to start *now!*

Cosmic Connection

Once we know what a number's energy translates to, we're also aware of the numerological "vibe" we're getting from someone or something. The vibes you might pick up from a person with strong 1s in their five Core Numbers (we discuss the Core Numbers in Part 3); or from a 1 house number (we discuss the numbers for your house and apartment in Part 5); or in a 1 Personal Year (we discuss the Personal Year number in Part 4) are as follows:

- ◆ Individualistic and innovative
- ◆ Strikes out alone
- ◆ Headstrong, impatient, impulsive
- ◆ Symbolically denotes a new start

Spiritual Essence of the 1

Spiritual numerologists believe that each number represents a universal principle, which is a step in the cyclical evolution of all things. Every number vibrates to an inner meaning, and it should be no surprise that the 1 vibrates the spirit of all things, as if the 1 were the "spirit" of the organization, or something was done with the right "spirit."

Higher Ground

The number 1 symbolizes the spirit at the center of all things. It stands for "spirit," which, we should note, is not the same as the "soul": Spirit is the masculine spiritual principle, the fire, or the spark; and soul is the feminine spiritual principle.

Easy as 1-2-3

In numerology, odd numbers as considered to be yang, while even numbers are considered to be yin.

The French say it is *l'esprit de coeur,* or "the spirit of the heart," and in America we say he or she is a "spirited one." The 1 is the essence of the vital, pulsating imprint of beginning energy, which penetrates all things which are about to be brought into reality. This new beginning comes complete with a spark of spirit.

The 1 represents the prime masculine principle, the *yang*, which in turn signifies the law of polarity. Masculine, active, forceful, courageous, and powerful are aspects of yang polarity.

The yin/yang symbol represents the oneness of all (the 1) through duality (the 2), creating wholeness and unity.

Raising the Vibration for the Number 1

The cosmic vibration is the energy a number gives off. The energy of any given number can be expressed positively or as a higher energy. The higher energy of the number 1 is seen as leadership, strength, courage, keen perception, and establishes a strong identity. When the 1 is positively expressed it is tough, forceful, determined, knows its mind, and self-aware.

On the other hand, when the 1 is expressed with a lower vibration it is aggressive, pushy, willful, demands its own way, wants instant gratification, is opinionated, egotistical, can be domineering, and acts as a know-it-all.

We could go on, of course. The point is: The 1 doesn't like to be told what to do, so leadership is a natural channel for the 1. In addition, when the 1 doesn't understand itself or isn't self-aware (or when others aren't understanding), it can become shy, vacillating, self-conscious, or even reticent to express its opinion or resonate to its more natural bold, decisive, and confident self.

The 1 will have trouble with anything that seems haphazard. Carelessness, lack of logic, inattention to order—all of these are contradictory to the 1's natural need to go straight from point A to point B.

Whether expressed as either consciously or unconsciously, the 1 is a potent vibration.

A Meditation for the Number 1

Sit quietly in a room where you won't be distracted or disturbed. Close your eyes and take three deep breaths, exhaling slowly. Begin to visualize yourself as a radiant being of light. Your light is becoming brighter and brighter. You are strong, vibrant, perceptive, and aware. Your light is strong.

Think of something you would like to begin. Let your mind bring in ideas for this new beginning and focus on the energy rising as you think about it. Once you have a strong sense of this new beginning, state your intention. You might want to say to yourself, "I am beginning this (name what you are beginning) with clarity, strength, and purpose." You might want to begin to repeat an affirmation to crystallize the vibration of this new beginning. You can create one of your own, or use ours, "I am confident, clear, and determined as I begin this new venture." Repeat this affirmation, or your own affirmation, at least three times slowly, breathing deeply with each statement.

When you are ready, open your eyes, let yourself refocus, and then write your statement of intention for this new beginning in your journal. Stay focused on your intent for your new beginning; know that it is part of your life purpose.

The Number 1 in Your Numerology Profile

A number 1 person will mingle with the world, but is never really one of "them." If you vibrate to the 1, whether it's your Birthday Number, Pinnacle, Challenge, Personal Year, Soul Number, Destiny, Life Path, Personality, or Maturity Numbers, you must learn through personal experience that as we have indicated, a 1 has to overcome self-absorption, self-interest, and selfish focus. To do this the 1 has to realize that to love without thought of holding out for what one gets in return is what allows the 1 to become a happy individual, rather than a separate, lonely one.

By the Numbers

If a number is repeated many times in a name, that quality is a marked trait in a person, and a possible talent. At the same time, it can present a challenge to have an over-intensification of a number.

It's time to use your journal. As you work with your Name Numbers, keep in mind that the letters, A, J, and S are the "1" letters. For example, the name Sara has 3 letters that are the "1" energy: S, A, and another A. It is considered normal to have 1–3 in a full name, so Sara has all of hers in her first name, and if she has other 1s in the rest of her name she will be working with a lot of the assertive, driven 1 energy. If you have more than four of these in your name you are considered strong and independent.

If you have six or more, or an over-intensification of 1s, you are considered head-strong, and too independent and might be prone to headaches, as some numerologists believe.

If you have no 1s in your name, you most likely will lack confidence and courage and will be learning how to gain these traits as you move through your life. Go ahead and count your 1s in your birth name and record these in your journal. You'll want to do the same for the 2s in a minute.

Number 2: Two Heads Are Better Than One

The saying, "Two heads are better than one" neatly sums up the basic principle of the 2: It's at its best when relating and working with others. Cooperation is the hallmark of the 2, and, not surprisingly, it's the number of the diplomat and the mediator, as well as the joiner (the neighbor who belongs to Habitat for Humanity, the dedicated PTA parent, or care-giving physicians who staff Doctors without Borders).

While the 2's patience may sometimes look like laziness to non-2s, the 2 knows that "slow and steady wins the race." Whether it's through patience or its unique ability to see both sides of any situation, the 2 will be noted for its capacity for giving comfort to all.

Easy as 1-2-3

The number 2's astrological equivalent, Libra, is represented by the scales, which weigh balance, and strive for equality and fairness in relationships.

The Number 2: Harmony	
Key Words	Sensitive, feminine, receptive, patient, loving, cooperative, relationship conscious
Astrological Equivalent	Libra
Tarot Card Equivalent	High Priestess (intuition, balance, duality); the 2s in each Minor Arcana suit
Letters	B, K, and T
Polarity	Yin
Colors	Orange, peach, salmon, gold
Gems	Moonstone, gold
Flowers	White jasmine for amiability, white lilac for modesty, mimosa for sensitivity, pansy for shyness

The Energy of the 2

Where the 1 is aggressive, the 2 is passive, waiting rather than forging ahead. Similarly, where the 1 exudes energy, the 2 is calm and patient, and, unlike the 1 who needs to be dominant, the 2 is content to stay in the background. The 2 is gentle, quiet, subtle, and supportive in its expression.

Easy as 1-2-3

The **2** gravitates toward living in peace, finding harmonious solutions, and, most important, finding sensitive partnerships. It seeks to live without discord.

The Timing of the 2

The 2 has an excellent sense of timing, knowing just when to bring up that delicate issue. Blessed by an innate sense of rhythm and harmony, the 2 has natural musical ability as well, and seeks a harmonic rhythm to life for all.

Life with the 2

As it is with all the numbers, life with the 2 can bring both blessings and challenges. The 2's knack for arbitration can make it too considerate, and its consideration of others can result in fear of rocking the boat. You'll have to talk long and hard and then listen well to get the 2 to tell you what's wrong.

The Blessing of the 2

The 2 is much blessed. It possesses a finely tuned sensitivity, and is excellent at mediation and drawing people together for peaceful resolution. The 2 takes life slowly—soothing, arbitrating, mediating, and balancing as it goes.

As the first feminine number, the 2 naturally seeks the perfect balance between any opposition, and allows seeds to gestate until they're ready to form. The 2 will let things evolve, unlike the 1, who will push to make them happen.

The Challenge for the 2

The main challenge for the 2 is figuring out how to be seen as cooperative without ignoring its own independence and personal needs. A second challenge is that the 2 will always wait until the "right time"—and so sometimes misses opportunities. And finally, there's the challenge of not getting caught in indecisiveness.

Twos are so sensitive to the issue of cooperation that they often struggle against having to stand alone or having an opposing opinion. Standing alone is not a 2 strength—standing together is.

The Lesson of the 2

Because it's so sensitive, the 2 often places others first, and so the lesson for the 2 is to not be a doormat for others, to be true to itself, and to speak up with tactfulness. Until this lesson is learned, the 2 will find itself again and again in situations where this lesson presents itself, so it's important for the 2 to learn how to stand up for itself.

Relationships with the 2

If you're looking for a healthy relationship, you can't do better than a 2. The 2 is an excellent partner: faithful and affectionate, as well as careful with money. Not surprisingly, 2s like their partners to demonstrate love physically, and may constantly seek reassurance and encouragement.

The 2 is cultured, charming, and gracious, and so makes a wonderful host or hostess. On the other hand, the 2 can be shy and self-conscious, and is dependent by nature. Above all, companionship is essential to 2s, and they don't like to have to make decisions by themselves.

> **CAUTION**
>
> **Sixes and Sevens**
>
> The 2s can become possessive of people and/or things. They can be jealous (with their super sensitivity, they pick up on every vibe), but they dislike arguments, and are always the first to want to kiss and make up. Still, when a 2 is hurt by criticism, it may behave as if it's a mortal wound. When this happens, the 2 can become nitpicky and critical, because its world must be in balance for the 2 to feel right.

What's Important to the 2

The 2 loves all things beautiful, and this love of aesthetic appearance means not only that they adore the nicer things in life, but that they'll create this for others as well. The 2's love of beauty is just one more way they create harmony with the world around them.

Groups and organizations are important to the 2. There's also a desire for precision and exactness, and the 2s are often the tidy polishers of every last detail. Fastidious, orderly, neat, and clean, the 2 will see that every last detail and fact is gathered and placed into its proper position.

Cosmic Connection

Spiritual numerologists believe that each number represents a universal principle, another step in the cyclical evolution of all things. Every number vibrates to an inner meaning, and it should be no surprise that the 2 vibrates to the energy of the unity of duality.

Endowed with an inner light that loves peace, the 2 has a unique insight into right and wrong—because it understands the true relationship between human and spirit.

Spiritual Essence of the 2

The spiritual essence of the number 2 is unity. The 2 seeks unity with life's principles and laws. The 2 is the builder of all relationships, the unification of 2 opposites into a whole.

The 2 represents the prime feminine principle, yin, which in turn signifies the law of polarity. Feminine, gentle, receptive, sensitive, and spiritual are all aspects of this gentle number.

Other dualities native to the 2 are these:

◆ Masculine/feminine

◆ Youth/age

◆ Joy/sorrow

◆ War/peace

◆ Friends/enemies

The 2s will work to resolve these dualities, and any that show up in life, in an effort to bring a harmonic balance to their own lives and the lives of others, especially their loved one. Conflict and discord are not tolerated well with the 2.

Higher Ground

It should be no surprise that the cosmic vibration, or energy pattern of the number 2, vibrates to its own unique harmony. Slower and more subtle, the 2 wishes to merge, which makes it both receptive and supportive.

The 2 is patient and peaceful, yet has a heightened sensitivity to light, sound, and energy. The 2 finds the harmony in all things, and dwells in both beauty and things of the spirit.

Raising the Vibration for the Number 2

The cosmic vibration is the energy a number gives off. The energy of any given number can be expressed positively or as a higher energy. The higher energy of the number 2 is seen as the peacemaker, the loving companion, strongly intuitive, emotionally receptive, good at details, persuasive, blends opposites, and is noted for being kind and considerate. When the 2 is positively expressed it is understanding, poised, adaptable, artistic, and romantic.

When the 2 is expressed with a lower vibration it can be indecisive, divided, weak, self-deprecating, nitpicky, and fearful of what others say or think.

We have to remember that the 2 is dependent by nature and therefore needs partnership to fulfill its function. In our strongly assertive, aggressive American culture, this can be mistaken for frailty, when in reality, the vibration of the 2 is the much-needed sensitivity and gentleness that saves us from ourselves.

A Meditation for the Number 2

Sit quietly in a room where you won't be distracted or disturbed. Close your eyes and take three deep breaths, exhaling slowly. Begin to visualize yourself as a radiant being of light. Your light is becoming brighter and brighter. You are strong, vibrant, perceptive, and aware. Your light is strong.

Think of a relationship you would like to bring peace to. Let your mind focus on this relationship. Bring love into your heart center now. See a loving, glowing light encircling this relationship, radiating and warming each person. Now see this loving, glowing light enter the hearts of each person and expand, and expand once again.

Now focus on the energy rising as you think and feel this relationship. Once you have a strong sense of new light or energy, state your intention for this relationship. You might want to say to yourself, "I am patient and peaceful in this relationship. I know everything is happening in exactly the right order and exactly at the right time." Or you might want to say to yourself, "All is well in my world, all my relationships are harmonious." Repeat your affirmation to crystallize the vibration of this new energy for your relationship. Repeat this phrase, or your own phrase at least three times slowly, breathing deeply with each statement.

When you are ready, open your eyes, let yourself refocus, and then write your statement of intention for this relationship in your journal. Stay focused on your intent, and your peace in this relationship; know that it is part of your life purpose.

The Number 2 in Your Numerological Profile

Every number's got its plusses and minuses, and as you study the 2's, you'll notice how much they're really two sides of the same coin. Where's the line between cooperative and conciliatory, and when does "good at details" spill into nitpicky?

If you vibrate to the 2, whether it's your Birthday Number, Pinnacle, Challenge, Personal Year, Soul Number, Destiny, Life Path, Personality, or Maturity Numbers, you must learn through personal experience that, as we have indicated, not to sacrifice your self-respect while trying to avoid conflict and preserve the peace.

It's time to use your journal. As you work with your Name Numbers, keep in mind that the letters, B, K, and T are the "2" letters. The normal number of 2s in a name is one, indicating that you are considerate, helpful, and sensitive to others' needs. If you have two or more of these found in your full name, you have all of the traits mentioned, plus an ability to bring others together, you are good with details, and you have a fine sense of rhythm and timing. The more 2s you have the more sensitive you are, which can be both a good thing and a burden.

If you have no 2s in your name, you most likely lack consideration and patience with others and will be learning how to gain these traits as you move through your life. Go ahead and count your 2s in your birth name and record these in your journal. You'll want to do the same for the 3s in a minute.

Number 3: The Sunshine Number

Forever young, no number brings more joy than the 3. This is the number of creative self-expression, of the optimistic happy spirit, of enthusiasm and imagination. The 3 belongs to the concord of 3-6-9 (numbers with kindred energies), where the artistic, inspirational, and spiritual are its realm. The 3 is the most emotional of this concord, probably because of its emotive, dramatic flair. The 3 is the number of the trinity, represented, for example, in the cycle of birth, life, and death.

Easy as 1-2-3

The letters of the 3 are C, L, and U. Note that these letters together spell L-U-C, not surprising for this luckiest of numbers!

The Number 3: Joyful Self-Expression	
Key Words	Creative, optimism, gift with words, imaginative, dramatic, emotional, self-expression

Astrological Equivalent	Leo
Tarot Card Equivalent	The Empress (the ultimate creative force); the 3s in each Minor Arcana suit
Letters	C, L, and U
Polarity	Yang
Colors	Yellow, gold, lemon
Gems	Topaz
Flowers	Yellow jasmine for happiness, larkspur for lightness, lily of the valley for return of happiness

The Energy of the 3

The 3 energy positively bursts forth. The vibrational energy of the 3 is excitable, enthusiastic, and exuberant. Intensely creative, the 3 can sometimes be hyper, insisting on everything immediately.

Flooded with exuberance, bubbling with joy, the 3 can be a very intense energy when there's no appropriate channel for this effervescence. When the 3 has no outlet for its creative, engaging energy, it becomes chaotic, disorganized, involved in trivial matters, or depressed.

The Timing of the 3

Time for the 3 is *now*. The 3 is the poster child for instant gratification. It is spontaneous and doesn't like to plan ahead, after all, there are s-o-o-o many choices and there might be something more interesting to do in the next moment. Tomorrow is a long way off to the 3. Our advice is get out of the way of this fireball and don't count on a 3 for Thanksgiving dinner—even though the 3 would bring fun, joy and a lively pace to the celebration.

Life with the 3

As it is with all the numbers, life with the 3 can bring both blessings and challenges. The 3 is known for its tendency toward faddishness and its intoxicating love of luxury. It may be less well-known for its self-centeredness and laziness.

Still, nothing keeps this happy number down for long, as you'll see from its blessings.

The Blessing of the 3

The 3 is a happy spirit, blessed with humor, optimism, and enthusiasm for life—after all, its joyful energy sees a lot of opportunity for expression.

The 3 is lucky in both money and opportunity; so lucky that it takes luck for granted. The 3 will never wonder where its next meal, next dollar, or next job is coming from. When the 3 needs something, it will be there.

Blessed with an uncanny knack for being in the right place at the right time, luck favors the 3 in everything.

The Challenge for the 3

There are several challenges for the 3, mainly to find appropriate channels for its creativity, enthusiasm, and exuberance. The 3 is also challenged to keep the spirit of the inner child alive, and so of course needs playful, positive relationships and environments. No wet blankets for this number!

The 3 will be challenged not to scatter its energy. Because life is so fun, and there are so many things to do, imagine, and see, it's not unusual for this number to have three things going at once.

The biggest challenge for the 3 by far is to learn to communicate straight from the heart. The 3 needs to find the words to match his or her emotions, to find the courage to utter the words, and to slow down long enough to deal with the emotional situation.

The Lesson of the 3

The lesson for the 3 is to focus on the moment and not scatter its energy. The 3 must live in joy in order to create and inspire others. The 3 must learn that laughter is health for the soul and therefore seek a steady diet of wit and humor.

Relationships with the 3

The 3 dislikes being in subordinate positions and wants to be one jump ahead of everyone else. It can be shrewd, original, observant, and a hard worker, and this combo is what allows the 3 to rise in the world. Note, however, that the 3 can also have a sharp tongue. (After all, its forte is expressing itself!)

In relationships, 3s are warm, generous, impulsive, and loyal. They're extremely good company—witty, entertaining, and fun to be with. The talent to be a pleasing hostess or host, entertaining, a good conversationalist, and colorful with a touch of drama, all come together to make the 3's life exciting and lively.

Naturally playful and spontaneous, as a partner, the 3 is the most fun person imaginable. Still, you can count on those emotions to surface, and not in a predictable pattern. The 3 can be moody, emotive, euphoric—or anything in between. After all, this number is the pulse of life itself, so the current runs strong and full. There are those (like the 4 you'll meet in the next chapter) who will want to suppress this energy.

The number 3 is flirtatious, so watch out! It will more than likely have more than one interest—and more than one admirer. It's also very conscious of what's said, both to and about it—criticism is crippling to this number.

Because 3s have vivid imaginations, for children with 3s in their Core Numbers, it's important they not have their imaginations suppressed or be told of weaknesses, unlovely features, or handicaps. This helps to keep those active imaginations optimistic. Parents of 3s are well advised to protect this 3 spirit. The 3 energy is a joy and a gift.

Sixes and Sevens

The 3 and triangles go together. Watch out for those triangles in love, the office, and family. Such relationships are bound to be emotional—that's the nature of the 3.

What's Important to the 3

Nothing's more important to the 3 than to be free to use its imagination to beautify and create. Whether its energy is used to make handcrafted Valentines, have a stimulating conversation, or make an inlaid tile fire pit, the 3 needs to express itself.

Cosmic Connection

Spiritual numerologists believe that each number represents a universal principle, another step in the cyclical evolution of all things. Every number vibrates to an inner meaning, and it should be no surprise that the 3 vibrates to the energy of vision and creative imagination.

The 3 can be inspirational with its insights and feeling, and, while its strength is to be creative and incubate ideas, it depends on other numbers to put those ideas into form.

Spiritual Essence of the 3

The spiritual essence of the 3 is bringing that which has never been into being, the power of creativity in all its forms. The essence of the 3 is a natural sweetness, an inner beauty, and a bubbling enthusiasm that creates joy—a spiritual gift for all to share.

Higher Ground

In the Pythagorean system, the 3 represents the meaning of excellence, because it has a beginning, a middle, and an end.

The magical aspect of the 3 is often used in fairy tales, with three of something to make the happy outcome:

- Three rooms of flax in "The Three Spinning Fairies"
- Three tasks in "The Frog Prince"
- Three chances to discover the name in "Rumpelstiltskin"
- Many others where the mysterious answer is found in three doors, three riddles, or three wishes

Raising the Vibration for the Number 3

The cosmic vibration is the energy a number gives off. The energy of any given number can be expressed positively or as a higher energy. The higher energy of the number 3 is seen as inspirational, brilliant (as in shines brightly), and joyful. When the 3 is positively expressed it is enthusiastic, artistic, witty, humorous, with childlike playfulness.

When the 3 is expressed with a lower vibration it can be prone to exaggeration, gossipy, selfish, scattered, critical, lazy, and wasteful.

We have to remember the 3 learns quickly and has a keen mind, so changing the energy to a higher frequency shouldn't be hard. And we can always count on the 3 to bring in a light note, no matter how heavy the occasion.

A Meditation for the Number 3

Sit quietly in a room where you won't be distracted or disturbed. Close your eyes and take three deep breaths, exhaling slowly. Begin to visualize yourself as a radiant being of light. Your light is becoming brighter and brighter. You are strong, vibrant, perceptive, and aware. Your light is strong.

Now let your mind focus on a situation or a person where you would really like to speak your truth. Begin to focus on the feeling and words that come from your heart.

Without blame or judgment, focus on what is true for you. Now, visualize a ball of golden light forming in your heart. The light begins to warm you, the golden color glows and reminds you that you want what is highest and best for all. Let this light expand and move beyond your body, expanding further beyond the room you are in, expanding into the place where this person or situation exists. See this golden glow encircling this person or situation radiating warmth and love. Now see yourself speaking the truth of your heart lovingly, gently, and clearly.

Now focus on the energy rising as you think and feel this moment. Once you have a strong sense of new energy, state your intention for this person or situation. You might want to say to yourself, "It is my intention to lovingly say what is true for me as honestly and clearly as I am able to this person." Repeat your affirmation to crystallize the vibration of this new energy.

When you are ready, open your eyes, let yourself refocus, and then write your statement of intention for saying your truth in your journal. Stay focused on your intent, and your truth in this situation; know that it is part of your life purpose.

The Number 3 in Your Numerology Profile

Gifted as the 3 is with words and with abundant enthusiasm to deliver the message, it still can have its spirit dampened. But as we've said before, nothing keeps this happy number down for long. The 3 is the joyful, happy, sunshine in our lives.

If you vibrate to the 3, whether it's your Birthday Number, Pinnacle, Challenge, Personal Year, Soul Number, Destiny, Life Path, Personality, or Maturity Numbers, you must learn through personal experience that, living only for ease, the glitter, the luxury, or not making use of your considerable creative talent, will lead to unhappiness. There is much better use of your creative energy.

It's time to use your journal. As you work with your Name Numbers, keep in mind that the letters, C, L, and U are the "3" letters. If you have one or two of these, which is the normal amount, you have an ability to express ideas and feelings and you know how to have fun.

If you have more than two 3s in your name, you will have to work to stay focused so you can use your abundant creativity effectively. If you have no 3s in your name, you most likely will have trouble communicating your feelings to others. Usually, 3s in a name indicate an artistic, creative bent, a way with words, and an imaginative approach.

Go ahead and count your 3s in your birth name and record these in your journal. You'll want to do the same for the 4s in the next chapter.

In Part 3 you will have a chance to see where the 1, 2 and 3 show up in your chart when we show you how to work with your name and birth date numbers to find your five Core Numbers.

The Least You Need to Know

- The 1 likes to lead, but not to follow.

- The 2 likes to follow, but not to lead.

- The 3 likes to synthesize and create.

- You can change the energy of your name if you have too many or too few 1s, 2s, or 3s.

The Numbers 4, 5, 6: Stability, Change, and Responsibility

In This Chapter

- ◆ Number 4 is dependable and wants security
- ◆ Number 5 is the risk taker and wants freedom
- ◆ Number 6 is the humanitarian and wants to provide
- ◆ The spiritual essence of the 4, 5, and 6
- ◆ The energy of numbers 4, 5, and 6

The solid, stable 4 understands the value of good, honest labor, and isn't afraid to work hard to get the job done. When it comes to the number 5, change is the name of the game. Got a problem? Take it to the 6, who will give you sympathy and understanding. Each of these three numbers has clearly identifiable qualities and is unique in its energy.

In this chapter, we examine the numbers 4, 5, and 6, including the energy of each number, a peek at life with each of the numbers (should you be living with one of these three), as well as the spiritual essence, special abilities, and places of growth for each number. We also thought you'd want to know some key words associated with each number, as well as the astrological equivalent, the matching Tarot card, the letters, and the polarity, colors, gems, and flowers, so we've created a chart for each number and its correspondences.

Number 4: Stability Matters

Where the 3 may revel in "fun, fun, fun" and the happy spirit of joyous self-expression, the 4 is all about discipline and following the rules; it is serious and cautious. The 4 is steeped in tradition, practical, and respectable, a manager you can rely on, building a solid foundation on which you can always stand.

Stability matters to the 4, so it can't understand others' more frivolous ways. A 4 puts in a hard day's work, stays between the lines (all four of them), and respects both rules and convention. Sober and true, the 4 is both persevering and practical.

Easy as 1-2-3

Taurus, the astrological equivalent for the number 4, represents the pragmatic, grounded builder of solid, secure foundations.

Someone's got to be disciplined and dedicated, and the 4 handles these tasks like the solid character it is. The 4 is also efficient and well-organized, which is another aspect of its discipline and concentration. Trustworthy, honest, straightforward, the 4 is the symbolic version of an Eagle Scout.

The Number 4: Stability and Security	
Key Words	Hard work, planning, cautious, conventional, management and order, building, symbolizes putting things into form
Astrological Equivalent	Taurus
Tarot Card Equivalent	The Emperor and the 4s of each Minor Arcana suit
Letters	D, M, and V
Polarity	Yin
Colors	Greens
Gems	Jade, emerald
Flowers	Nasturtium for patriotism, bluebell for constancy

The Energy of the 4

The energy of the 4 is a grounded energy. This energy is methodical and plodding. It forms and reforms. It builds, endures, preserves, makes order, and systematizes. The 4 represents the principle that creates form and foundation for plans, dreams, ideas, patterns, philosophies, thoughts, and feelings, and gives form to things, as well as stabilizes and structures them. The 4 is a grounding energy for the other numbers, especially the 3, 5, 6, 9, 11, and 33. While these numbers are about ideas and emotions, the 4 brings a practical side to the idealistic and emotional.

The 4 carries a solid and stable energy, and those with this number give off the "vibe" of predictability and conventionality. No boat rocking here.

The Timing of the 4

The timing of the 4 is, quite simply, on time. Rarely late, a 4 is notoriously punctual, keeping appointments, arriving on time, if not early, and takes your time and theirs seriously. Wasting time is strictly verboten.

The 4 orders time and space into practical use. The 4 expresses the concept that things perceived only as a part of the realm of light—such as spirit, the 1, and creativity, the 3—move into the physical form represented by the 4 with its grounding in Earth time. The 4 is a heavier, denser form of energy, which means it takes more time to do things and to form things. The 4 is certainly not moving at the speed of light.

The 4 doesn't like to be hurried, and moves slowly and methodically. The 4 often needs to work to quicken its thinking, and to experience action to learn adaptability (from the 5, of course).

Life with the 4

As it is with all the numbers, life with the 4 can bring both blessings and challenges. The 4's discipline, for example, can cross over into rigidity, while its knack for organization sometimes can translate into control.

The Blessing of the 4

The 4 has endurance, dedication, and discipline, and so, can naturally bring order to chaos. It also has the know-how to manage a business or a home and create order in its life—or, for that matter, in anyone else's.

Well-organized, the 4 can always see the best ways to set up systems. In addition, the 4 keeps efficient systems, whether it's an appointment book, calendar, road map, or bookkeeping method. The 4 has great discipline, stamina, and "stick-to-it-iveness," as well as the gift of concentration.

The Challenge for the 4

The challenge for the 4 is to not be rigid but resilient, to see the need for structure but not be inflexible. Its best use is to help form something as a foundation for life, rather than a box that restricts growth. It's always a challenge for the 4 to *not* be controlling (after all, things must fit into the plan—read as, fit into the box).

The Lesson of the 4

Many 4s tend to see life as confined and narrow because they follow the rules and are bound by the policy, and so think that the plan is cast in cement. They forget that living in between the narrow lines, or living in the rut, is a rut of their own making. Hence, they're presented with this lesson over and over: The 4s are learning to look outside the box; get out of the rut, take a risk, take a chance (they need the 5s), and be creative with their options.

Those of us who don't have 4 as a Core Number can't understand this kind of dogged adherence to doing things. Besides the propensity for efficient order, the 4 can be stubborn as well, so most often will argue that it's not being inflexible. Most of the rest of us will give up and leave the 4 to its fixed ways, which is precisely why the 4 will remain stuck. When the 4 is able to see outside the box, it experiences the soul-song of the 5—freedom from restriction.

Relationships with the 4

Not surprisingly, 4s are devoted, thoughtful, faithful, and considerate partners. They're also home lovers, who manage financial affairs well, and usually don't live beyond their means. A 4 can always be counted on to be reliable, and, yes, predictable. A nice bonus is that the 4 always cleans up its own messes!

The 4 has been called both the "salt of the Earth" and the "pillar of the community" because it's the backbone of any organization, family, or marriage.

You can count on your 4 to be reliable, consistent, and punctual, and to manage the task at hand.

The 4 will tend to see things in a common-sense manner. Born to build, the 4 loves to create permanent and lasting things, whether it's a marriage, a system, a job position, or building a company from the ground up. Note, however, that the 4 is not an originator. It needs and depends on others, such as the 1, the 3, and the 8, for inspiration and vision. The 4 won't get carried away with emotion or imagination; we'll just leave that to the 3 and the 9. The 4 does, however, have high standards of honesty and courage, and succeeds in what it does through hard knocks and responsibility.

The 4 has a high need for security—in business, in marriage, and in the right to be itself. This number makes a trustworthy, dependable partner. Fundamentally, the 4 is serious and conscientious, has strong opinions about right and wrong, likes to plan, and looks forward to results. At the same time, the 4 doesn't like to be "ordered" or "told" what to do, but rather has the need to feel in control, so clear boundaries are important in a relationship. The 4 is willing to do the hard work with family, in laws, business tasks, and daily living, as long as it feels it's respected, and its own rights are honored.

Easy as 1-2-3

The 4 always needs something to build, construct, fix, mend, or arrange, and is able to conform to systems and establish patterns. For all those reasons, the 4 makes a good partner. Besides, 4s are neat and tidy (it's that need to make order!).

What's Important to the 4

Above all, the 4 values order and discipline. It values efficiency, whether it's with time or money, and will always have the most practical approach to a situation. It is important to the 4 not to waste things or time.

Cosmic Connection

It should be no surprise that the cosmic vibration, or energy pattern of the number 4, vibrates to its own unique rhythm. More grounded than the other numbers, the 4 will manifest the ideas of the 1 and the 3, order the details of the 2 and build a tangible plan for the outer world.

Universally, we see the 4 as …

- Four seasons: spring, summer, autumn, winter.
- Four directions: north, south, east, west.

♦ Four elements: fire, earth, air, water.

♦ Four aspects of self: physical, mental, spiritual, emotional.

♦ Four human functions: sensation, feeling, logical thought, intuition.

♦ Four aspects of matter: mineral, gaseous, animal, vegetable.

The 4 provides the elemental form and structure to things in nature and our daily lives.

Spiritual Essence of the 4

Spiritual numerologists believe that each number represents a universal principle, another step in the cyclical evolution of all things. Every number vibrates to an inner meaning, and it should be no surprise that the 4 vibrates to the energy of spirit made manifest into matter, or, putting things into law, system, and order.

Juno Jordan, the grandmother of modern numerology, says the 4 is "the foundation upon which all things stand to sustain life." The 4 is the number of forms, and brings everything down to Earth.

The essence of the 4, spiritually, is the point at which spirit is brought into matter, and the spirit of the 1 and the creative expression of the 3 (1 + 3) finally find form in the 4.

Higher Ground

The principles of honesty and integrity are inherent in the makeup of the 4. This serious, hard working, extroverted energy dreams of making things applicable and useful through planning, teaching, ordering, and careful management. This energy grounds other energies creating a practical reality for all.

The 4 might be considered rather dull, but what we have here is a down-to-earth, respectable, trustworthy, precise intention where life on the Earth plane is taken seriously. Through this 4 energy we can depend on problems to be dealt with systematically, with work hard, and the management of a situation—any situation—to be handled efficiently. Bet they didn't have a 4 managing things prior to the Northeast energy blackout of 2003.

Raising the Vibration for the Number 4

The vibration is the energy a number gives off. The energy of any given number can be expressed positively or as a higher energy. The higher energy of the number 4 is to establish order, bring ideas and plans into concrete form, and to maintain routine and systems. When the 4 is positively expressed it is steady, determined, industrious, calm, steadfast, and has strong standards of right and wrong.

When the 4 is expressed with a lower vibration it is stuck in a rut, fears change, is rigid and controlling, and lacks discipline.

A Meditation for the Number 4

Sit quietly in a room where you won't be distracted or disturbed. Close your eyes and take three deep breaths, exhaling slowly. Begin to visualize yourself as a radiant being of light. Your light is becoming brighter and brighter. You are strong, vibrant, perceptive, and aware. Your light is strong.

Think of a place where you are experiencing fear in your life at this time. Capture this fear and hold it in your mind. Let your mind gently surround this fear and wrap it in a blue light shaping it into a ball. Now see a radiant beam of light coming down through the top of your head and entering the blue ball of fear you are holding in your mind. See this bright light pierce the center of this blue ball and from its very center begin to glow with radiant white light. Let this white light expand from the center, filling the inner regions of the blue ball, and now breathe into the center of the light center. Take another breath and as you exhale, expand the white light to the outer edges of the ball. Now, with the next breath, see the white light absorb all of the blue ball and notice that all that remains is a radiant, glowing white energy. Your fear has been transformed into light. Focus on this light. Breathe again into this light. Once you have a strong sense of this light, state your intention. You might want to say to yourself, "I am willing to let go. I release this fear (name the fear). I let go of old limitations." You might want to begin to repeat an affirmation now to crystallize the vibration of this release. You can create one of your own, or use this one: "I am at peace with the process of my life. I am safe." Repeat this affirmation, or your own affirmation, at least three times slowly, breathing deeply with each statement.

When you are ready, open your eyes, let yourself refocus, and then write your statement of intention and your new affirmation in your journal. Stay focused on your intention of release throughout the day and know that it is part of your life purpose.

The Number 4 in Your Numerology Profile

If you vibrate to the 4, whether it's your Birthday Number, Pinnacle, Challenge, Personal Year, or your one of your five Core Numbers: Soul, Destiny, Life Path, Personality, or Maturity, you must learn through personal experience that, as we have indicated, a 4 has to overcome issues of control out of the need for security. To do this the 4 has to realize that everything happens in exactly the right method and at the exact right time. There is a larger operating energy at work and the 4's part is to find practical solutions for daily life thereby bringing stability to any situation.

It's time to use your journal. Look for the 4s in your name. As you work with your name numbers, keep in mind that the letters, D, M, and V are the "4" letters. If you have two 4s in your name you're considered practical, and have an ability to stick to things. With three to five 4s you have the ability to build and construct things of lasting nature. With more than five of these in your name you are considered too rigid, controlling, and stubborn.

If you have no 4s in your name, you most likely lack concentration and application and will need the help of others. However, few people lack in the qualities of this number and if you don't have 4s in your name, look to the Pinnacles, Core Numbers, and Birthday Number. Generally at least one 4 will be found somewhere in your Numerology Profile for this is the number of all endeavor. Go ahead and count your 4s in your birth name and record these in your numerology journal. You'll want to do the same for the 5s in a minute.

Number 5: Everybody Changes

All things in life change and the life of the 5 is no exception. Those who carry the number 5 in the Life Path, Destiny, Soul, Personality, Maturity, or Birthday position will be intimate with the notion of change—it's probably been the constant in their lives. Change brings with it the opportunity for adventure, risk taking, excitement, stimulation, and curious exploration—and these are all trademarks of the number 5.

Easy as 1-2-3

Changeable Gemini and the number 5 are "two of a kind"—one thing you can expect for certain with either is to expect the unexpected.

Magnetic, 5s will make sure to stir up the action if things seem to be getting a little dull, and, not surprisingly, you can count on the 5 to be the life of the party—so long as he or she sticks around.

The Number 5: Change Is the Name of the Game	
Key Words	Freedom, change, progressive, curious, investigative, rebellious, unconventional, sensual, resourceful
Astrological Equivalent	Gemini

Tarot Card Equivalent	The Hierophant (unorthodox, not accepting responsibility, rebelling against the status quo); the 5s in each Minor Arcana suit
Letters	E, N, and W
Polarity	Yang
Colors	Turquoise, green-blue
Gems	Aquamarine, turquoise
Flowers	Ranunculus for radiant charm, gardenia for sensuality

The Energy of the 5

The energetic number 5 is the principle of constant motion. It's a magnetic, pleasure-loving, impulsive energy. Sudden and unexpected, and often scattered, the impatient 5 energy can be disruptive or thrilling. The cosmic energy pattern of the 5 is that it frees up, changes, adapts, quickens, energizes, expands, and creates.

The 5 loves to travel, because movement is its operative principle. Of course, the 5 also loves physical activity of any kind (5 is the aerobic number), and prefers fast-paced living so it can use its quick, creative mind. Needless to say, monotony is death to a 5 and impatience is its Achilles' heel.

The Timing of the 5

The 5 is the middle point and it governs the time of transition. It also positions itself toward the progressive and futuristic; its movement is forward. This is the number of impulsive and restless action, so the 5 will not respond to things slowly like the 2 and the 4, but will act and think quickly, often in haste. The comfortable rhythm for the 5 is speeding.

Life with the 5

Folks with 5 are adventurers who love to try anything new. Not surprisingly, travel is especially exciting to the 5, whether it's meeting new people, visiting different cultures, or just living in different surroundings because it knows how to adapt. People with 5s are of many talents—clever, resilient, and creative. Their quick thinking and resourcefulness is particular to the number 5 and so is the fact that you can never tie them down. You might think of the classic movie *Out of Africa* and one of its adventurers, Denys Finch Hatton, played by Robert Redford, as the ultimate 5.

In business, a 5 is an excellent asset because he or she is a rapid thinker, has a fertile mind and a quick wit, and possesses a keen perception of public opinion and need. The 5 can also administrate or head up a company, not because the 5 has true executive ability, but because he or she is good at getting others to act. 5s are naturals in advertising, marketing, networking, sales, and promoting an individual's talent. They can sell anything to anyone because they're "good talkers." They're also good at giving speeches, like to help others, and are full of ideas for improvement.

Easy as 1-2-3

5s are lucky with future events, often getting that lucky break because they're not afraid to gamble on the future or take a risk—unlike the perfectly planned, security-conscious 4.

If 5 is your Destiny or Life Path Number, you may find yourself in lines of business that involve speculation, money-making schemes, or any line of work that is designed to get quick results. 5 is the gambler at heart—the one who's willing to take risks and shortcuts.

A 5 person is multitalented, and this number is often called the "Jack (or Jill) of all trades." With all these talents, the 5 will bring an abundance of opportunities; life can be very exciting with a 5.

The Blessing of the 5

The 5s are blessed with pep, energy, speed, enthusiasm, wit, and excellent powers of observation. They have a magnetism that stems from their enthusiastic, curious response to life and the people in it. People are just drawn to the 5, and it's thought that a 5 is forever young for these qualities.

The Challenge for the 5

The challenge for the 5 is to not get lost in physical desires or scatter its potential, ending up with nothing to show for the 5's many talents. The 5 must learn to focus and make a meaningful existence by using freedom in a productive manner.

Sixes and Sevens

Because this free spirit is often attracted to the glitz and multiple opportunities it finds in the world, the 5 can fail to incorporate the traits that give structure to its life: stability, dependability, and permanence. (Where is that 4 when you need it?)

Still, too many changes, too many interests, or too much freedom can bring chaos to anyone's life and so it is with the life of the 5. Chaos is almost always hovering around the 5. Too much chaos, whether it stems from a lack of discipline or an inability to apply the 5's talents to anything substantial, usually brings on the downside of the 5—uncertainty, unreliable income, possible failure, and loss.

The Lesson of the 5

The main lesson for the 5 is the constructive use of freedom, and it needs to learn to do things in moderation. The 5 also needs to learn from others' mistakes so that the 5 doesn't have to try everything for him- or herself. Basically, this number has come to learn how to stick to it, to establish structure, and to create stability, so that the 5 can truly enjoy the freedom he or she so desperately desires.

Relationships with the 5

Generally, you will find the "Don't make me commit" attitude lurking about in relationships with the 5. Fond of the opposite sex, you know that if you're a 5, you can expect that the opposite sex is attracted to you. However, making a commitment or being bonded in the bliss of holy matrimony may be a long time coming because, first and foremost, the 5 fears losing freedom. If you do manage to marry a 5, don't be surprised to find the marriage breaking up if it becomes dull or boring (just keep it hot, honey!).

Housekeeping or any domesticity is not the 5's gig, either. After all, it's not very interested in repeated routine or binding responsibility. Be sure to consider these things before signing on the dotted line with a 5 (and that includes business partnerships, too). If a 5 has 4, 2, or 8 in its Numerology Profile, the 5's freedom-loving traits will be more grounded and stable. When a 5 has an active, entertaining, useful life, he or she will be a happy and protecting companion.

5s are secretly afraid of failure but they're careful not to communicate their fear to others. Sensual, earthy people, 5s possess great elasticity of character, and, as born gamblers, they're always ready to take a chance. When being negative, 5s can be hurtful, conceited, promiscuous, lustful, irresponsible, or rebellious. Whew! It's a wonder anyone wants to have a relationship with this number—but they do, because they are usually quite sexy, among other things.

5s are affectionate, loving, and sympathetic. The 5 has more extremes of temperament than any of the other numbers (yes, even more than the 3). This is due to the 5's restless nature, and the idea that the grass might be greener somewhere else.

A 5 gets into hot water when its temper, impatience, and impulsive nature are without training or education, or are improperly channeled. The 5's haste, lack of discipline, and quickness with words can bring on quarrels, accidents, and legal troubles if the 5 hasn't developed the necessary patience, understanding, and discipline.

Another irritating little habit of the 5 is to take credit for something another has achieved, simply because the 5 once helped guide the other person. A 5 can be very unappreciative of all he or she has received and that others have done on the 5's be-half. A 5 is more dependent on others than he or she wishes to admit (you've gotta be if "Change" is going to be your middle name). Once the 5 learns to appreciate and share the responsibility, this lively, fired-up energy will delight you, but only until tomorrow, when things will change again.

What's Important to the 5

The 5 loves freedom, lack of restriction, and variety. As long as there's variety, the 5 is happy and challenged. It's when the going gets slow that the 5 gets going.

The 5 wants to feel free to change things, to be seen as flexible, to be known for and to find opportunity to be resourceful. And most of all, it is important to the 5 to never feel boxed in.

Cosmic Connection

The 5 causes each human life to mirror the laws of nature, to allow for change and adaptability in life. The energy of forward movement is what drives the number 5. Remember, too, that the 5 is the symbol of the five-pointed star, which is said to be the symbol of humankind as Leonardo da Vinci illustrated in his model of mankind.

The 5, the midpoint in the numbers 1 through 9, is the symbol of the transition and represents the vitality and energy of life itself. As the pivotal point between the 1 and the 9, the 5 allows change to take place in the original idea established by the 1, the beginning.

Spiritual Essence of the 5

The spiritual essence of the 5 is the free spirit, and it's meant to help us all bring about change, learn to live without fear, take risks, and break up old patterns. It should come as no surprise that we all experience the 5 at some point in our lives, either in our name, through one of the five Core Numbers, or through the Personal Year Number because change is not only inevitable, it is necessary.

Higher Ground

The higher ground for the 5 is discerning the path of responsible change. Two concepts clearly describe the heart of this particular path: "curious" and "freedom loving." Let's look more closely at these two traits of the 5:

Curious

◆ Unafraid of new experiences, lands, people, languages

◆ Intellectually curious

◆ Voracious reader

◆ Wants to be up on trends—to be "in the know"

Freedom loving

◆ The 5 abhors dullness and routine

◆ Desires freedom of thought and action

◆ Seeks freedom of worship—looking to the unconventional, unrestricted expression of spirituality

◆ Supports the law of change

Easy as 1-2-3

The 5 would make a great private eye or FBI agent. It's great on the investigative side, loves the adventure, and its innate curiosity would be well utilized in ferreting out information.

Taking all of this into consideration, "true north," or the correct navigational direction, for the 5 will be contentment and commitment.

Raising the Vibration for the Number 5

The vibration is the energy a number gives off. The energy of any given number can be expressed positively or as a higher energy. The higher energy of the number 5 is to be useful in promoting an individual or issues of public welfare, or helping to change the rules, the form, or the routine. When the 5 is positively expressed it is adaptable and effectively communicates; it is creative and quick thinking. 5s are drawn to metaphysics, the occult, and the philosophical as methods of investigating the mystery of life. These are, after all, just one more way to satisfy the 5's curiosity. At the same time, however, the 5 can be introverted and private about these matters in spite of its worldly interests.

5s are interested in all the latest health tips, diets, and psychological programs for improving emotional well-being, as well as yoga or meditation groups. The 5 needs to be up on the latest trend, thinking, or avant-garde approach.

When the 5 is expressed with a lower vibration it is hasty, impulsive, lustful, and unstable. We have to remember, that the 5 is the architect of change so moving the energy to a higher vibration shouldn't be hard. It's just the possibility of addictions that keep the 5 stuck.

A Meditation for the Number 5

Sit quietly in a room where you won't be distracted or disturbed. Close your eyes and take three deep breaths, exhaling slowly. Begin to visualize yourself as a radiant being of light. Your light is becoming brighter and brighter. You are strong, vibrant, perceptive, and aware. Your light is strong.

Think of something you would like to change in your life. Focus on what this change might mean. Breathe into this feeling. See a ball of golden light about one foot above your head. Breathe and notice that when you do this golden light expands. Now see this golden light begin to slowly move downward touching the top of your head, continuing down to cover your face and back of the head. See the golden light continue to slip over your entire body, front and back, side to side. You are now completely encompassed in golden light. Now focus on your heart area and see a rose-red light pulsing there. This is your heart light. Now state your intention for making this change. You might want to say to yourself, "I forgive myself for all the harm I may have caused myself, wittingly or unwittingly. I forgive (name the person or situation) for any harm he/she/they may have caused me, consciously or unconsciously. I am willing to allow this change to happen in my life. In my heart, I know change can happen." You might want to begin to repeat an affirmation to crystallize the vibration of this change. You can create one of your own, or this one: "I now choose to allow this change to happen at exactly the right time. I now choose to believe it is becoming easier and easier to make this change." Repeat this affirmation, or your own affirmation, at least three times slowly, breathing deeply with each statement.

When you are ready, open your eyes, let yourself refocus, and then write your statement of intention for this liberation in your journal. Stay focused on your intent for responsible, safe change; know that it is part of your life purpose.

The Number 5 in Your Numerology Profile

If you vibrate to the 5, whether it's your Birthday Number, Pinnacle, Challenge, Personal Year, Soul Number, Destiny, Life Path, Personality, or Maturity Number, you must learn through personal experience that, as we have indicated, a 5 has to recognize the difference between freedom and escape. To do this the 5 has to take responsibility for changing his or her life and curb overindulgences.

It's time to use your journal. Look for the 5s in your name. As you work with your name numbers, keep in mind that the letters, E, N, and W are the "5" letters. The average number of 5s in a name is,

Easy as 1-2-3

The letters of the 5 are E, N, and W. For a quick memory trick, remember these letters spell "new," the hallmark of the 5's love of change.

strangely, five, so if you have more 5s in your name than that it often suggests a restless nature, a tendency to not complete tasks, or being addicted to constant change.

If you have no 5s or only one 5 (we don't see this very often), it indicates that you have dislike of crowds and will lean more toward wanting to be alone. It is also usually an indication of one who is not easily adaptable.

However, if you don't have 5s in your name, look to the Pinnacles, five Core Numbers and Birthday Number. Generally this number will be found somewhere in your profile for it is the number of change and let's face it, everything and everyone has to change, sometime in some way. Go ahead and count your 5s in your birth name and record these in your journal. You'll want to do the same for the 6s in a minute.

Number 6: The Number of Love

Got a question? You can be sure the 6 will have some good solid advice. Generous, sympathetic, self-sacrificing, caring, and a good counselor: Sound like anyone you know? Whether you're looking for fresh-baked brownies or a shoulder to cry on, the 6 may be the number you need.

It's said that if you look carefully at the way the number 6 is written, you'll notice it has a fat little belly that is pregnant with love. The 6 represents romantic love, passionate love, mother love, and tender love. This number also rules marriage and domestic happiness, and represents the heart of things, where the love resides, and where love is nurtured. Whether it's a community project, tending to animals, or educating children, the 6 will see that it's all done with love.

The 6 is considered the number of the "Cosmic Mother." In family concerns, the 6 is the loving parent at the center who is the hub of the wheel, nurturing, loving, supporting, and nursing the family (and not always the mother—we know some fathers who are great at this). More important, the 6 loves its role—although the 6 can sometimes get a little too motherly for the 1, the 5, and the 7.

> **Merlin's Notes**
>
> The 6 is thought to be ruled by the planet Venus, the planet of love, which is very appropriate because 6s, with their love of beautiful homes and lovely objects, have a very Venusian outlook on life. 6s are artistic and imaginative, too, with excellent senses of color, and they're often known for their musical and vocal talent, with many having very pleasing voices.

The Number 6: Comforting and Responsible	
Key Words	Duty and responsibility, love of family, humanitarian, artistic, nurturing, balanced, community service, the marriage and divorce number
Astrological Equivalent	Cancer
Tarot Card Equivalent	The Lovers (making commitment in matters of love and romance, balance in relationships); the 6s in each Minor Arcana suit
Letters	F, O, and X
Polarity	Yin
Colors	Royal blue, indigo
Gems	Pearl, sapphire
Flowers	Rose for love, honeysuckle for devotion

Easy as 1-2-3

The number 6's astrological equivalent is Cancer. Cancer is the sign of the nurturer, who is caring and family focused and who loves to create a safe haven and cozy nest.

The Energy of the 6

With the 6 you'll find an energy that's nurturing, loving, and concerned. The 6 energy is the caretaker of what's already been formed, and this number is both humanitarian and service oriented. The cosmic vibration of the 6 is a warming, soothing, protective energy.

The 6's energy focuses best when it is ministering to the needs of others through teaching, counseling, nursing, healing, beautifying, and nesting.

The Timing of the 6

The 6 is slow and deliberate in thought and action, retreating when hurried into promises or action. Being hurried or rushed doesn't work for this conscientious service-oriented number.

Life with the 6

The 6 is romantically inclined and leans toward the ideal in matters of the heart, therefore the 6 is likely to have some ideal notions about marriage partners. For this reason, the 6 can find it hard to have a partner live up to his or her high standards about how the ideal partner "should" be—and we emphasize "should" because 6s are big on shoulds.

Everything in a 6's life must be harmonious, for this number, above all else, requires balance in its life. If there should be a quarrel or disruption, a 6 will have an urgent desire to put things right in the home. That's because the home is the nest for the 6, and if there's any discord there, trust the 6 to rush in to set it right. A 6 will spend much of his or her leisure time planting flowers, remodeling, or doing home projects, preferably with his or her spouse.

The 6 is one of the money numbers, where money flows toward the 6 through service to others, not from personally motivated gain. The 6 is a great business number, especially for a cottage industry or a home-based business—or for any service-based business. 6s will pour their hearts and souls into a business and nurture it to success as if it were a child.

When a wrong or injustice is being committed, trust the 6 to speak "the truth," in an honest, straightforward manner, which usually comes out bluntly. The 6 is the champion of the underdog—is it any wonder that we find 6s naturally drawn to social work, community restoration projects, and children's education? I suppose we shouldn't be surprised that Hilary Rodham Clinton has a 6 Destiny Number and has devoted much of her professional life to defending children's rights and education, her family, and her (sometimes) infamous husband as she explains in her best-selling book *Living History*.

Speaking of education, the 6 is always the teacher because the 6 has a natural propensity to instruct others—especially about the right way to do something, what you "should" be doing, and the important lessons of life. The 6 also has strong interests in reform and principles, or any kind of instruction along the lines of emotions. This number is a natural for homeschooling, and you may find, whether you want it or not, that in your relationship with the 6, you are the recipient of many a lesson.

The number 6 governs counseling and teaching and people will be drawn to the 6 for advice or problem solving—talents at which this number excels. It's not unusual to find a 6 with a home-based business, especially a therapist or counselor whose clients will not only get loving advice, but will be nurtured by the environment of the caring 6.

6s are very responsible, and are often responsible for other people's stuff where there's no need to be. It's this desire to put others before themselves, their nurturing nature plus their need to be responsible, along with a strong sense of duty that leads 6s to overcommit and then find they're out of balance in their lives and relationships.

The Blessing of the 6

The blessing of the 6 is that he or she is wise and lives according to guidance from the heart. The ability to make a full commitment, to take on great sums of responsibility, and to execute it competently and with love is the blessing of the 6. But the 6's greatest gift is his or her loving nature.

No other number holds a candle to the 6 in terms of loving and nurturing, and the 6's warmth and comfort can be felt in the simple rush to pour you a hot cup of tea, close the blind from the glaring light, or bring you a blanket to ward off the cold—all without your asking. The 6 will establish a cozy home, complete with good food and warm hearth, close, loving relationships, and beautiful working environments.

The Challenge for the 6

The challenge for the 6 is to not be the long-suffering martyr and to remain realistic in matters of the heart. If you're a 6, your challenge is to learn not to sacrifice so much of yourself that you have nothing left to give or no heart to love.

In the 6's desire to be loved and to love, to care for others and be responsible, the 6 may not be seen as the strong, resilient force it truly is. In fact, for those who do not understand "coming from the heart," the 6 may be seen as egotistical or weak. In the 6's desire for beauty and love, he or she can idealize romance and marriage, and find it hard to live in the realistic day-to-day life (of dreary burden, said the 6). The 6 may put unrealistic demands on his or her partner, or find it hard to have a marriage partner because of the 6's ideal standards.

The Lesson of the 6

Ultimately, 6s must learn to love themselves—to be loyal, thoughtful, sensitive, and caring toward themselves. Then they will not dispense love from a diminishing well, but become a well of love itself from which all may drink.

Relationships with the 6

The number 6 is also called the marriage and divorce number because the 6 brings deep matters of the heart to bear upon one's life. If 6 loves, it will be a deep, committed love, not the flirtatious love attraction of the 3, or the sensual love affair of the 5. It will be the deeply felt "real" love of the marrying type (well, as real as an idealized love can be, anyway). This is devotion at its best. If one's marriage has no "heart" left, however, the 6 becomes the number of divorce. It's not unusual to find people getting married or divorced in a 6 year—but more on that in Chapter 17, where we discuss the Personal Year.

To love and be loved is the 6's deepest desire. Without love, a 6 won't reach the soul satisfaction or the heights of success the 6 is capable of. 6s need approval and praise. They crave it: Feeling appreciated is essential to the 6. If a 6 isn't receiving appreciation, don't be surprised to see him or her looking elsewhere for companionship or work—count on it!

Even though 6 is the marriage number, sometimes we will see a 6 fail to marry. When this happens we might look to one of the following as the cause: high ideals about marriage and love; early disappointment in love; a deep sense of loyalty to father, mother, or family due to a well-established sense of duty and responsibility. However, love may come late in life for the 6 as a reward for a life of service and sacrifice.

Learning to receive is one of the hardest tests for the 6. 6s are so competent at giving to others and so busy giving that they often don't realize they have abdicated their own needs. It is not unusual to see them undervalue their own need for support, nurturing, and love. But don't be confused; in reality, the 6 needs you to love and to praise him or her!

 Sixes and Sevens

6s must learn not only to give but to receive, which will restore balance to the devoted life of the 6. While this won't substitute for the much-desired approval the 6 seeks from others, it will begin to bring back into the 6's life the equally needed balance.

However, the 6 can go blissfully off in the wrong direction just with a note of praise, which is a contradiction of character in this otherwise strong, responsible number. That the 6 already has an idealized notion of love isn't too helpful in this situation. We might find the 6 falling in love and devoting his or her life to someone who flatters and only appears to love him or her. But don't be fooled—the 6 longs for and can deliver heart-connected love.

As you might have guessed, the 6 is capable of sacrificing—so much so that he or she becomes a martyr, weighed down by the burden of responsibility, duty, and concern for others. After a long many years of living in this manner, the 6 may find health challenges moving into his or her life. We believe that the health issues of fibromyalgia and chronic fatigue syndrome belong to the 6-type of consciousness. After all, these are the caregivers of the world and usually go way beyond their limit in giving and carrying the burden of others.

6s have firm convictions, a strong sense of right and wrong and what is just and fair, and they don't like to be contradicted. The 6s also tend to worry a lot about all manner of things, most of it unnecessary. It's one way the 6 can feel responsible—just keep worrying about things as a way to keep the issue warm, protected, and cared for. We know it's crazy, but the 6 is crazed when it comes to being responsible. The worry is that someone might think he or she doesn't care!

What's Important to the 6

Some of the things that are important to the 6 include …

- Things being fair.
- Loyalty.
- Calm and harmony.
- A comfortable home as the family haven.
- Things must be adorned with grace and beauty.

Cosmic Connection

The 6 embodies the perfected sense of balance between the spiritual and love, as represented by the six-pointed star, which is made up of two triangles, one upright and the other inverted. The star symbolizes the unification of the spiritual world and the material world through love which is the mission and nature of the number 6. The 6 desires to bring harmony, justice, and truth to all experiences in life.

Spiritual Essence of the 6

The spiritual essence of the 6 is primarily focused on the energy of love as a transformative force. At its most spiritual, the 6 embodies service through love. The 6 is thought to be spiritually protected.

Higher Ground

As the energy of service and responsibility, the life of the 6 will be filled with giving to others. The 6 is called to be the humanitarian caretaker of the family and community, and the provider for humanity.

Raising the Vibration for the Number 6

The vibration is the energy a number gives off. The energy of any given number can be expressed positively or as a higher energy. The higher energy of the number 6 is the capacity to love, nurture, and serve others. When the 6 is positively expressed it is giving, loving, sympathetic, understanding, honest, comforting, and balanced in its giving and receiving.

But even the 6 has its downside, and it can be clearly seen in some of the 6's classic traits. The 6's willingness to give, for example, can lead to martyrdom, while the 6's desire to help his or her family can make the 6 meddlesome, or worse, interfering. Codependence, overprotection, and dominance can be seen as negative expressions of the 6 by other numbers when the 6 is only trying to help.

When the 6 is expressed with a lower vibration, knowingly or unknowingly, it is interfering, unforgiving, opinionated, stubborn, stern, argumentative, worries excessively, and is unreasonably set in its own ways.

We know the 6 is dedicated and responsible, so changing the energy to a higher frequency shouldn't be hard. It is just the myth of the ideal marriage, family, or child, and all those "shoulds," that keeps the 6 stuck.

A Meditation for the Number 6

Sit quietly in a room where you won't be distracted or disturbed. Close your eyes and take three deep breaths, exhaling slowly. Begin to visualize yourself as a radiant being of light. Your light is becoming brighter and brighter. You are strong, vibrant, perceptive, and aware. Your light is strong.

Focus on your heart area. See a soft rose-pink light surrounding your heart and chest areas. Take a deep breath and see this rosy light expand upward and downward in your body. Breathe again and see the rose-pink light enter your heart and notice a rosebud centered in your heart. Breathe again and as you exhale notice the rose opens slowly and fully. Feel this energy in your heart. Relax and breathe. Now, think of something or someone you are worried about. Draw your worry into the center of this open rose. See the rose close gently around your worry and notice the rose turns into a golden light. See this light become brighter and brighter until it dissolves into radiant white light which at its brightest moment disappears in a burst of light.

Now state your intention. You might want to say to yourself, "I willingly release (name the person or situation) to the highest good. I am willing to release my worry. I allow balance back into my life with the release of this worry." You might want to begin to repeat an affirmation to crystallize the vibration of this new sense of calm and peace in your heart. You can create one of your own, or this one: "I am at peace. I trust life to bring the highest and best for all my relations. It is sufficient for me to send my heartfelt love to (name person or situation), for love is the most formidable force in the Universe." Repeat this affirmation, or your own affirmation, at least three times slowly, breathing deeply with each statement.

When you are ready, open your eyes, let yourself refocus, and then write your statement of intention for this new sense of calm and peace in your heart in your journal. Stay focused on your intent for your releasing worry; know that everyone is on his or her life path and everything is happening at exactly the right time.

The Number 6 in Your Numerology Profile

If you vibrate to the 6, whether it's your Birthday Number, Pinnacle, Challenge, Personal Year, Soul, Destiny, Life Path, Personality, or Maturity Number, you must learn through personal experience that, as we have indicated, a 6 has to guard against idealizing family and marriage and martyring yourself in the name of caring, providing, and nurturing. (Read as, "don't be codependent.") To do this the 6 has to give love without condition and take responsibility for itself, meeting its needs, and creating balance in its life.

It's time to use your journal. Look for 6s in your name. As you work with your name numbers, keep in mind that the letters, F, O, and X are the "6" letters. The average number of 6s in a name is one or two and with one or two 6s you are considered to be willing to take responsibility and are very humanitarian. If you have three or four 6s it indicates fixed ideals and strong opinions, and a strict, dominant, and demanding nature. If you have more than four it indicates a strong sense of responsibility, change is hard to make because of rigid beliefs, there is a significant artistic ability present, and you may struggle with taking on too much responsibility.

If you have no 6s in your name, you're not alone—we see this in many names. It indicates that learning responsibility will play a significant role in your life. If you don't have 6s in your name, look to the Pinnacles, five Core Numbers, and Birthday Number. Generally the number 6 will be found somewhere in your profile and it lessons the severity of the learning curve on responsibility. Go ahead and count the 6s in your birth name and record these in your journal. You'll want to do the same for the 7s, 8s, and 9s in the next chapter.

Easy as 1-2-3

The letters of the 6 are F, O, and X. The letters of the 6 are particularly easy to remember, because they spell out the word "fox."

The Least You Need to Know

- You can depend on the 4.

- The 5 craves change and variety.

- The 6 is dutiful and responsible; spiritually, the 6 is the essence of love.

- You can change the energy of your name if you have too many or too few 4s, 5s, and 6s.

Chapter 6

The Numbers 7, 8, 9: Intuition, Power, and Transforming Compassion

In This Chapter

◆ Number 7 is analytical and spiritual and wants solitude

◆ Number 8 is about power and money and wants to be recognized for achievement

◆ Number 9 is about compassion and intuition and wants to transform

◆ The spiritual essence of the 7, 8, and 9

◆ The energy of numbers 7, 8, and 9

Contemplative and private, the 7 is considered the most mystical of the numbers. The 8 is the number of leadership and leaders, organization and organizations, while the 9 is the number that signifies the end of things but at the same time suggests mastery. Each of these three numbers has clearly identifiable qualities and is unique in its energy.

In this chapter, we examine the numbers 7, 8, and 9 including the energy of each number, a peek at life with each of the numbers (should you be living with one of these three), as well as the spiritual essence, special abilities, and places of growth for each number. We also thought you'd want to know some key words associated with each number, as well as the astrological equivalent, the matching Tarot card, the letters, and the polarity, colors, gems, and flowers, so we've created a chart for each number and its correspondences.

Number 7: Looking to the Inner Self

No other number likes so much time alone, so it should come as no surprise that the 7 is the number of anyone whose work requires solitude and contemplation. Whether a scholar or a computer geek, the 7 will always seek the heart of the matter—and won't be satisfied until he or she knows his or her answer is the perfect one.

Most 7s have a high degree of intellect, and some will demonstrate talent in fields of science, research, or technology. 7s are great with computers or in any field where data needs to be collected and analyzed. You might see a 7 as a forensic specialist, for example, because of the 7's ability to investigate with careful and keen observation.

7s might be found as archaeologists, deep-sea divers, numerologists, or detectives, or involved in spiritual studies—wherever in-depth study or deep analysis is involved. They're dedicated to their study or research, always wanting to uncover the hidden answers. To a 7, knowledge is power, and most 7s are educated in some area where they've been called to investigate in a specialized way.

Easy as 1-2-3

The number 7's astrological equivalent is Pisces and represents the search for spiritual wisdom and mystical meaning.

If technology or science is not the path followed, then you'll often find the 7 doing spiritual, metaphysical, or philosophical work. The 7's unique gift lies in his or her dedication to searching for understanding of human life in relation to a larger universe.

The Number 7: Analytical and Mystical	
Key Words	Intellectual, inner wisdom, scientific-technological minded, metaphysical and occult mysteries, loner, eccentric, intuitive, private, skeptical, reserved
Astrological Equivalent	Pisces

Tarot Card Equivalent	The Hermit (silent, wise, seeks truth. The solitary Hermit is the wise teacher and withdraws to meditate); the 7s of each Minor Arcana suit
Letters	G, P, and Y
Polarity	Yang
Colors	Violet, purple
Gems	Amethyst, alexandrite
Flowers	Lavender for silence, rose-scented geranium for preference and discernment

The Energy of the 7

The energy of the number 7 is withdrawing, concealing, focusing inward, perfecting, and leaving the material world to turn to the world of spiritual understanding, philosophical contemplation, or analytical thought. Its vibration is silent; that is, meditative, contemplative, reflective, and resting.

The 7's energy is spent on inner seeing, whether to examine, analyze, or intuit.

The Timing of the 7

The 7 operates on a different wavelength than others, and comes to his or her own individual solutions, does things his or her own way, and is not particularly adaptable or sociable. The 7 gets lost in time because its focus is inward: into work, play (if there is such a thing as play in the life of a 7), and relationships. The 7's relationships have one thing in common—they must have meaning and depth. The 7's timing is in the abstract and philosophical which is where 7s spend most of their time.

Life with the 7

7s are solitary by nature and love to do things alone, whether it's to think, meditate, contemplate—or just stare at the wall. A 7 is quiet, and likes it that way—the better to think and study. 7s are rejuvenated by the outdoors and by being in nature.

The 7 will choose things that are refined or unusual in some way, and is especially drawn to antiques or things from the past, such as a claw-foot round table or a rolltop desk (but how many antique hand planers does one need?), as well as things that are distinctive, such as Grandma's cameo brooch or volumes of rare books.

Easy as 1-2-3

The **7** is the number of solitude and mysticism; here, you'll find both the philosopher and the analyst.

You'd better love being by yourself if you team up with a 7. Not only will you be alone, but if you're with the 7, he or she will be silent much of the time. Don't expect a "Good morning" from a 7 because morning is an especially quiet time. That's when the 7 is thinking about the day, a dream last night, or that book the 7 is reading.

If spiritually inclined, the 7 finds the "soul" in all things. While the 7 is not necessarily religious, more often than not he or she will seek alternative spiritual avenues. More than anything, the 7 makes holy the experience of life.

Merlin's Notes

Although quite charming and persuasive, the 7 just doesn't do well making small talk and is consequently confused by the social scene. While the 7 may wax poetic on the nuances of thermal dynamics and decoding binary systems, ask the 7 to converse with your guests at a dinner party about the neighbors' affair, and you can forget·it! There will be silence.

The 7 simply does not do the ordinary; the 7 is unusual, even eccentric. Nothing is accepted at face value, and all must be scrutinized, but after all, the 7 is the student of life with a scholarly attitude, never satisfied until he or she has found a way to link the known to the unknown. The 7 is also the number of the skeptic, so the 7 will have to check things out. This number is most often the investigator, scientist, inventor, or occultist.

The 7 is the number of specialization, which is to say that the 7 delves deeply into specific areas of interest and becomes a kind of expert. Eventually, people come to the 7 for wisdom, not only for the specialized field of study, but for the insights and understanding the 7 has about life itself.

The 7 is excellent in jobs that require analysis, factual research, keen observation (a lot of bird watchers are 7s), an inventive approach, or technical data—just so they can do the job alone! 7s are not team players, but rather seek an out-of-the-way location where the job can be executed with slow, methodical precision, careful thought, and, of course, their usual intuitive wisdom. And pul-eeeze! No airheads as job mates!

As a parent, the 7 will often be distant and removed, with more interest in the education of the children than playing with them on a day-to-day basis. When we say "interested in their education," we're talking about both academic education and their philosophical education; after all, thinking about things is the 7's specialty. Teaching kids about nature is a natural for a 7, because the 7 has a spiritual and physical bond with the outdoors and nature.

7s may have very distinct eating habits, choosing particular foods or diets. This is because the 7 has a strong instinct for purification and perfected health.

Remember, the 7 rules the unusual, so don't be surprised to find your 7 choosing clothes, food, and a lifestyle that does not follow the hip trend.

The Blessing of the 7

The 7s are blessed with dedication and a keen sense of observation and insight. The 7 opens the door to higher knowledge and understanding of the mystery of life. The 7 is also blessed with a great reserve of inner wisdom, and, in addition, is gifted with a superb analytical mind. This number is at peace in solitude.

The Challenge for the 7

The challenge for this inward 7 is to have friends, a marriage, or any relationship with another human being. The 7's inward pursuit leaves him or her with viewpoints that may bear no resemblance to those of his or her peers, so not only is the 7 silent and aloof, but now the challenge is to find someone who thinks like the 7 does—in an unorthodox manner, unusually, and with insightful notions. The greatest challenge for the 7 is to learn to deal with aloneness, and to not let the desire for solitude turn into loneliness and isolation. The best match for a 7 would be the supportive, gentle 2, the compassionate 9, or another 7.

The Lesson of the 7

The 7s must learn to not take their search for perfection to the extreme—not be such perfectionists. They also must learn to find love, affection, and tenderness by reaching out into the world.

Relationships with the 7

Introverted, quiet, thinking all the time, the 7 is often distant and removed from normal human relations. The 7 is not the social number—leave that to the 5 or the 3. No, this is the number of the loner, the hermit, the monk, or the one who spends zillions of hours ensconced in a project involving research, analysis, or philosophical pursuit. The 7 actually *prefers* to be alone with his or her books, computer, catalogs, and resource guides. "Private," of course, is the 7's byword, and the 7 can be secretive. Certainly, the 7 tends to be silent, reserved, and introverted. Luckily, a person is not just one number; other numbers in the Numerology Profile help to balance out all of this introversion.

> **Merlin's Notes**
>
> When it comes to money, 7s may have little or no money sense and often live beyond their means—much to the horror of their mates. 7s earn money from specialized fields. They're not the generalists like the 5, but instead know a subject in depth, which brings money and recognition through a specialization.

If you're going to live with a 7, you'll want to know that solitude is very important. The 7 needs a great deal of time alone—to meditate, think, re-examine, or rejuvenate. The 7 isn't comfortable with a lot of people, especially people he or she doesn't know. Actually, the 7 does best in one-to-one situations rather than in groups. The 7 can be depressed, moody, aloof, cynical, and generally hard to get along with. The 7 does, however, possess great depth of feeling (depth is the operative word—the 7 does *all* things in depth). 7s are passionate, sincere, understanding, and wise, but also innately shy and reserved.

7s are very individualistic, maybe even eccentric. The main point is they are unusual. Not particularly domestic and definitely not a caretaker (leave that to the 6), the 7 is the educator. In terms of giving, once the 7 has been convinced, he or she will give generously to a worthy cause.

Quiet and reticent to participate, the 7 finds it difficult to express his or her thoughts and is even less able and willing to express emotions, unless there is a 3, 6, or 9 also in the profile.

If you want a partner who will figure out the system, reroute the wiring, or set up your latest computer program, a 7 is the one to get. If you like mellow, unassuming, spiritual perspectives, you'll love being with a 7! Marriages based on spiritual beliefs and deeper issues will bring happiness.

What's Important to the 7

Here are some of the things that are important to the 7:

- Time alone, privacy
- Solitary retreats: A cabin in the woods, a place on the beach, or a hideaway in the mountains
- A library, work that allows for research or study
- The search for truth and wisdom
- Old gardens, antiques—anything mellowed by time
- To analyze, dissect, examine, and consider

Cosmic Connection

The 7 is often associated with magical powers, perhaps because it's a number that deals with all things deeply, as opposed to the number 5, which deals with things generally. The 7 is the summoning to move inward and discover the universal laws of nature and the connection to the mysteries of life.

Among the concepts associated with the 7, you'll find: seven days of the week, seven days in each Moon phase, seven colors in the spectrum, seven notes on the musical scale, and seven energy centers known as chakras.

There are numerous references to the number 7 in many religious and historical traditions. In the Christian tradition, God rests on the seventh day, there are seven gifts of the Holy Spirit to counterbalance the seven deadly sins, and the Catholic mass is arranged in seven parts.

In the Hebrew tradition, the menorah has seven branches, while the Mayans believed in a seven-layered sky and that the number 7 was the number for orientation in space. In early Egypt it was believed that there were seven paths to heaven and seven heavenly cows, and Osiris, Egyptian god and judge of the dead, leads his father through the seven halls of the netherworld.

Clearly, the 7 has been passed from tradition to tradition, with its many references to the mystical connection to the Divine. The number 7 is indivisible, and it represents the perfection of the God energy. The number 7 has been called the Christ consciousness number as well. No matter what you call it, however, this is the number that represents the movement of spirit over matter.

Spiritual Essence of the 7

The spiritual essence of the 7 is reflection upon the spiritual nature of things, and investigation, analysis, and intuiting of inner wisdom. It's the quest to discover the inner landscape of one's life and place it in relationship to larger, higher truths.

Higher Ground

When the 7 shows up in a person's profile, it calls for retreat and re-evaluation. This number says it is the time to go within, for it's concerned with understanding knowledge on a higher level. This is the stage in the human cycle where it's time for introspection and analysis; it's a call to know oneself and life in the deepest way.

Raising the Vibration for the Number 7

The vibration is the energy a number gives off. The energy of any given number can be expressed positively or as a higher energy. The higher energy of the number 7 is the refined, distinctive thinker. When the 7 is positively expressed it is scholarly, philosophical, and wise, uses dry wit, meditates, and seeks higher understanding.

When the 7 is expressed with a lower vibration it is depressed, cynical, skeptical, withdrawing, unsympathetic, and out of touch with humanity.

A Meditation for the Number 7

Sit quietly in a room where you won't be distracted or disturbed. Close your eyes and take three deep breaths, exhaling slowly. Begin to visualize yourself as a radiant being of light. Your light is becoming brighter and brighter. You are strong, vibrant, perceptive, and aware. Your light is strong.

Imagine you are standing on the edge of a forest and before you lies a path. You are at the gateway to this lovely, lush green forest. Before you enter, see yourself standing there. Listen to the stillness; hear the birds and the gentle wind in the trees. This path is just for you. Ask for a guide or angel to show itself to you and now see this guide standing beside you in glowing white light as you contemplate stepping onto the path which will lead you to your inner sanctuary. Ask this guide for an intuitive message that will help you on your path. Breathe and listen. Now, ask your guide if he or she will be there for you whenever you come back and are ready to begin your journey down the path to you inner sanctuary. Tell your guide your intention for taking this inward journey. You might want to say, "I am ready to move on to explore the inner path. I am ready to connect with my Higher Self. I am open to messages and wisdom from my spiritual teachers." Breathe deeply and feel the serenity of this space. This is the energy you are creating now. Tomorrow you will return and begin your journey down your path with your spirit guide to accompany you. Today your focus is on the solitude and stillness of the forest. At this time you might want to begin to repeat an affirmation to crystallize the vibration of this stillness and serenity. You can create one of your own, or use this one: "I am guided to my inner self. I am divinely protected as I walk the inner path of spiritual wisdom. I am calmed by the stillness." Repeat this affirmation, or your own affirmation, at least three times slowly, breathing deeply with each statement. At this time say goodbye to your guide and assure him or her you will return to take the first steps down the sacred path to discover your own inner sanctuary.

When you are ready, open your eyes, let yourself refocus, and then write in your journal the message you have received from your guide. Now write your statement of intention for this journey in your journal. Stay focused on your intent and know that this connection to an inner world is part of your life purpose.

The Number 7 in Your Numerology Profile

If you vibrate to the 7, whether it's your Birthday Number, Pinnacle, Challenge, Personal Year, Soul, Destiny, Life Path, Personality, or Maturity Number, you must learn through personal experience that, as we have indicated, a 7 has to guard against suspicion, skepticism, and perfectionism. To do this, the 7 has to overcome shyness and isolation to embrace the world of human relationship.

It's time to use your journal. Look for 7s in your name. As you work with your name numbers, keep in mind that the letters, G, P, and Y are the "7" letters. The average number of 7s in a name is one and with one 7 you are considered to have the ability to look beneath the surface with intuitive perception, to have a questioning mind, and a keen sense of perfection. Two 7s indicates a technical, scientific mind, while three or four 7s indicate you are difficult to know and dislike a show of emotion.

If you have no 7s, it indicates you are more open-minded and less inclined to look for hidden meanings or agendas. If you don't like the number of 7s in your name, you might consider changing your name, thereby changing your vibration. Go ahead and count the 7s in your birth name and record these in your journal. You'll want to do the same for the 8s in a minute.

Number 8: Personal Power and Excellence

After the introspection of the 7, the 8 comes on like gangbusters. If it has anything to do with making money, chances are it has something to do with the 8. That's because this is the number of wealth and abundance, as well as excellence and power. Where the 7 works within, the 8 reaches out into the world and expands it. At its best, the 8 is a master of personal power, money, and business. The 8 was born to be the boss.

If there's a military general or C.E.O. in the room, chances are this person has an 8 somewhere in his or her chart. That's because the 8 is the number of natural leadership and power. Where there's an 8, everything will always run shipshape.

The 8 isn't always a fortunate personal number, because of the potential for complete reversals of fortune. However, because of their strength ability to problem-solve, and relentless dedication

Easy as 1-2-3

The number **8** is the number of personal power, materialism, and the boss.

to work, they'll find they have an unusual ability to overcome obstacles. These same qualities often lead to positions of power and authority. Wise, enduring, and exceptionally tough, 8s can go the long haul it often takes to reach the top.

The Number 8: Power, Money, and Success	
Key Words	Authority, achievement, money karma, problem solver, power, expansion, business, mastery
Astrological Equivalent	Capricorn
Tarot Card Equivalent	Strength (strength to harness the elements of power for self-mastery); the 8s of each Minor Arcana suit
Letters	H, Q, and Z
Polarity	Yin
Colors	Rose, pink
Gems	Diamond, rose quartz
Flowers	Hollyhock for ambition, camellia for excellence and mastery

Easy as 1-2-3

The astrological equivalent of the number 8 is Capricorn, which seeks to organize and manage physical reality, and shares the same energy around power. Both the 8 and people with Capricorn prominent in their astrological birth charts must learn to use power wisely and not be dominant or controlling.

The Energy of the 8

The cosmic vibration of the 8 involves the energy of directing, arbitrating, judging, planning, supervising, leading, strenuously driving, being intensely active.

The heart of the 8's energy is strength, power, and vision. However, judicial action is called for in the material world of money, power, and achievement, and higher principles of integrity and authenticity are required. This energy wants to both execute things envisioned in the 7 and lead toward a larger vision in the 9.

The Timing of the 8

The timing of the 8 is similar to the 4: enduring, ordered, and focused. The number 8 is said to be the number of the force that exists between terrestrial order (the square) and external order (the circle). The 8 has a dual nature (one circle on top of another), which represents degeneration and regeneration. Not surprisingly, complete reversals are an ever-present possibility with this number.

8s must have a "shoulder to the wheel" at all times—they have to give everything their all. Shortcuts are not a good idea for this number because 8s resonate to integrity and a job well done.

Life with the 8

An 8 needs a goal and a plan to give direction to this powerful energy. Unlike the 6 or the 9, the 8 isn't motivated by humanitarianism, but rather by the love of work and the thrill of successfully attaining a worthy goal.

Personalities with 8s often have an interest in secret societies where there's structure, organization (especially a hierarchical ladder to climb), and mystical training (Masonic Order, anyone?). They're also interested in the mental sciences (psychology, metaphysics, ancient philosophies), the study of character, vocational analysis, and, of course, business organization. The 8's biggest interest is in money and what it can do—the 8 is the king (or queen) of making money.

The 8 is also proficient at relating feelings and facts, and is a natural as an efficiency expert. Business is the 8's forte, and the 8 has a knack for building up run-down businesses and turning them into successes. The 8 is especially good in fields of industry, commerce, government, politics, real estate, spying, and even literature.

You'll find that 8s have unusual amounts of courage, strength, and self-control. Like the 7, the 8 has keen skills of observation. The 8 is also dependable, trustworthy, of an outstanding character, and is often known locally for his or her good works.

Greed, or abuse of any position of authority will lead to loss, failure, and more karmic debt when you're an 8.

The Blessing of the 8

The 8s are blessed with the ability to size up any situation and create a plan for execution, and it's their ability to organize and see the larger picture, as well as the smaller details, that brings about the achievements and success for which the 8 is known. 8s are blessed with the strength and courage to undertake large projects, financial risks, and the management of large organizations.

Plus, 8s are excellent judges of character and have a unique gift for seeing a person's

Easy as 1-2-3

The 8s have executive abilities that are unique to them—even if they don't know it. Just have an emergency to find the true colors of your 8: He or she will take charge and bring the situation under control.

potential. Even though an 8 may be powerful, the 8 also has the ability to be fair and to see both sides of a situation.

The Challenge for the 8

The challenge is for the 8 to resist the drive to live for money and to be consumed by the acquisition of wealth. The 8 is also challenged to utilize his or her executive abilities without ordering, intimidating, or dominating people.

The Lesson of the 8

Many 8s have come to learn the correct use of power, and so will learn to believe in their own personal power without dominance or intimidation. Many situations will arise to help the 8 learn about becoming his or her own authority. The major lesson is empowerment—claiming and utilizing the 8's own gift of power.

Relationships and the 8

Consider marriage carefully when dealing with an 8—it will pay to give great attention to financial security, because the 8 is money-conscious. The 8 can be generous and understands money as a tool for achieving a dream or a plan, but at the same time, the 8 doesn't like to be subordinate because he or she likes to be the boss.

As a driving force, the 8 may try to be all things to all people. After all, intense action is the daily diet of the 8, and he or she is always doing business, even while in bed. Because the 8 is naturally a doer, others depend on the 8. Who wouldn't? The 8 wants to be the boss, is good at organizing, and knows how the money game works—you just better not want to be the leader, too!

The energy of the 8 is honest and frank, and the 8 lets you know where you stand. When push comes to shove (and you won't be the one doing the pushing), the 8 speaks honestly, bluntly, and—more often than anyone would like—severely. Fortunately, however, the 8's anger blows over quickly.

The 8's driving need for purpose and goals can be overwhelming in a close relationship. With an 8, there will always be rules, a "right" way to do things and a procedure to follow. But the 8 also needs admiration and love for the reward of all his or her efforts and achievements.

The 8 needs to slow down and look at the real value of those dear to him or her. In love, marriage, and romance, this one's loyal but not sentimental—the 8 is too busy for that. The 8 will love deeply (all the while watching the clock to see when his or her next appointment is, or if this display of affection is taking too long). We must remember, to the 8, time is money.

If the 8's lesson is to learn to use its incredible power, then the home front needs to be a place where power is not an issue. Don't expect the 8 to get home for dinner often, for the 8 is a true workaholic. The 8 wants at all costs to accumulate prosperity symbols—they're a sign of 8's success. Still, the 8 will build you a castle and an empire of lasting importance because the 8 builds for permanence. With age, enough symbols of wealth will be acquired and the 8 will be ready to achieve more personal and spiritual goals.

In keeping with new paradigms for the new millennium, the 8 needs to work on achieving more win-win situations and fewer competitive, hard-driven bargains. Most of the other numbers have a hard time living with the 8, and two 8s together can make fireworks with all those power struggles. However, if an 8 has learned to accept his or her own power and feels secure in his or her achievements, and has developed a higher consciousness, the 8 will find that he or she can afford to be more magnanimous in gestures of love, time, and participation at home.

Life becomes happier when the 8 learns to …

- Deal with people patiently.
- Realize he or she can be intimidating.
- Find time to express love, sweetness, and appreciation.
- Share the abundance of the world around him or her.
- Recognize that others know things, too.

Remember, in all relationships, an 8 will have to take responsibility to remain balanced in all that he or she says, does, and doesn't do. Like the 6, for an 8, balance is the key.

What's Important to the 8

The 8 drives and pushes to be the best, to be ahead, and to be on top, because somewhere underneath is a feeling that he or she isn't good enough, won't get there in time, isn't seizing the opportunity, or could be doing more. Often, this demanding 8 is more critical of its own efforts, than anyone from the outside. With all this inner dialogue going on, no wonder the 8 barks out orders.

Most 8s are self-made, and in that arduous pursuit, they often forget that there really is a tender, warm, caring human in there who needs to be reminded that he or she is human and needs to be loved, too. If you're an 8, we'd recommend a 6 to be your partner.

We'll bet you already know what's important to the 8, but we'll make a list here anyway: money, achievement, success, power, competence, toughness, and endurance.

Cosmic Connection

Because the 8 is invested with a natural power that stems from an inherent understanding of universal principles, the 8 is required to participate in the world of form (our material world), honoring what the 8 inherently knows: All power, wealth, success, and achievement come from a power greater than the 8's. When the 8's ego leads, forgetting that he or she is *not the power*, then failure, destruction, and reversal of fortunes often follow. Balance must be restored.

Spiritual Essence of the 8

The spiritual principle that rules the 8 is: You will reap what you sow, the law of karma. The 8 is bound by the law of karma and is challenged spiritually to walk in the realms of power without creating new karma or avoiding previous karmic debts.

The 8's power is not human made, but rather belongs to the higher principle of bringing the infinite into the finite in harmonious balance. Spiritually, the 8 is charged with the responsibility of working with integrity to build a world of the future that is aligned with higher consciousness and serves all of humankind, not just for personal profit or recognition.

The 8's process, at the highest level, may be one of materializing wealth and following a path of power, achievement, and success, but the 8's reward is ultimately the satisfaction of a job well done.

Higher Ground

Until mastery is achieved, much of the energy of the 8 is spent on achieving wealth and grandeur, but mastery comes after the 8 emerges from this long struggle with the material world, through awareness of a higher purpose. Once the 8 is on to the laws of higher consciousness, he or she then truly becomes a powerful being, with his or her own personal power in balance, and can utilize the skills of mastery. This is when the 8 has become adept, drawing successfully upon the laws of manifestation and abundance.

Raising the Vibration for the Number 8

The vibration is the energy a number gives off. The energy of any given number can be expressed positively or as a higher energy. The higher energy of the number 8 cements dreams and visions together. The 8 expands the ideas of the 3, the hard work of the 4, and the re-evaluated theories of the 7. Taking all of these, the 8 creates a larger plan that will serve the greater good. The 8 provides order, knowledge, supervision, stability, and the know-how to expand into the next level to make the dream a reality. The 8's task is great and its burdens are many.

The 8 has the potential to become noble, greatly respected, a fine judge of character and potential, and a master of life's forces. 8s like to theorize (like the 7), and want to discover motive and feelings behind human action (like the 6). Often, the 8's part, and part of its power, is that of the wise counselor and director, without prejudice or illusions. These are hard-won achievements in the life of an 8.

Much of the 8's energy is spent on achieving wealth and grandeur, but the 8 isn't lucky in money like the 3, 6, and the 9. Sure, the 8 loves money, and his or her personal ambition pulsates with the desire to be wealthy, powerful, and recognized for this success, but all of these may fail unless the 8 heeds the higher calling.

8s must work with integrity and must incorporate spiritual wisdom (found in the 7). When this is done, they'll find they have unusual opportunities given to them.

A Meditation for the Number 8

Sit quietly in a room where you won't be distracted or disturbed. Close your eyes and take three deep breaths, exhaling slowly. Begin to visualize yourself as a radiant being of light. Your light is becoming brighter and brighter. You are strong, vibrant, perceptive, and aware. Your light is strong.

Think of a goal you would like to manifest. Let your mind focus on this goal. Bring your focus to your belly button area. Slowly breathe in and out, in and out. See a glowing light pulsating in your belly button area now. Take a deep breath into this area of your body and see the light expanding. On the exhale allow the light to radiate up and down your body and breath again into this area. Now see a light-being moving slowly, lovingly toward you. In his or her hands is a box. The box is placed into your hands. Open it. You notice there is a magic sponge in this box; the light-being whispers that this sponge is for you. It will allow you to soak up all of the negative thoughts that arise when you have doubts about reaching your goal. Take the magic sponge in your hand and place it over one of the limiting thoughts you have about what manifesting your goal. For example, your thought might be, "I can't have (name it) because there isn't enough." Notice how the sponge swells as it soaks up all of the negative thought. Pick up your swollen sponge and wring it out in the golden bucket the light-being is holding out for you. Notice that a sudden stream of radiant light shines into the center of the bucket and in an instant all of the negative energy is dissolved in the light. The bucket is empty, your negative thought exploded into the light. Feel the lightness, of being filled with golden light, as the negative energy leaves. Breathe into this energy.

Now focus on your energy rising as you think about your goal of manifestation. It now seems possible. See yourself as having already achieved this goal. It is now yours. Watch your energy rise. Once you have a strong sense of this golden light of possibility, state your intention for this goal. You might want to say to yourself, "I am ready to allow abundance to flow through my life. It is my intention to bring (name it) into my life now. I create what I have with every thought and action." Or you might want to say to yourself, "My success is assured because I know everything is happening in exactly the right order at exactly at the right time. Prosperity is manifesting in my life now!" Repeat your affirmation to crystallize the vibration of this new energy for your goal. Repeat this phrase, or your own affirmation, at least three times slowly, breathing deeply with each statement.

When you are ready, open your eyes, let yourself refocus, and then write your statement of intention for manifestation of this goal in your journal. Stay focused on your intent and know that it is part of your life path and purpose.

The Number 8 in Your Numerology Profile

If you vibrate to the 8, whether it's your Birthday Number, Pinnacle, Challenge, Personal Year, Soul, Destiny, Life Path, Personality, or Maturity Number, you must learn through personal experience that, as we have indicated, an 8 has to guard against attachment to the material, using its power to control and achieving without integrity. To do this the 8 has to create win-win situations, execute its power in a benevolent way, and be mindful of creating additional karma.

It's time to use your journal. Look for 8s in your name. As you work with your name numbers, keep in mind that the letters, G, Q, and Z are the "8" letters. The average number of 8s in a name is one and with one 8 you are considered competent, business-minded, and able to take charge. If you have two or more 8s it indicates an innate understanding of how money works for profit, and you most likely are overly motivated by power and status.

If you have no 8s it indicates that money and power will be your teachers in this lifetime. If you don't have 8s in your name, look to the Pinnacles, five Core Numbers, and Birthday Number. An 8 in these positions will indicate ability for success. Go ahead and count your 8s in your birth name and record these in your journal. You'll want to do the same for the 9s in a minute.

Number 9: Completion of the Cycle

Now we come to the last and greatest number of the cycle—the number 9. This is a high potency number, with the energy of all the previous numbers infused into it.

The 9 represents the process of understanding the true value of life and the human experience and their subsequent connection to the Divine. Gifted with the intuitive, spiritual, and emotional power to embrace the human condition, the 9 will serve humankind out of a great love for his or her fellows.

Easy as 1-2-3

The number 9's astrological equivalent is Scorpio. It reflects the emotionally intense, deeply transformational nature of the 9 as well as the need for power.

The 9 contains the energy of all the other numbers, and so it represents the eight steps around the cycle of life, plus the motionless center (the 9). It is thought that the 9 symbolizes the height of mental and spiritual attainment.

Some of the 9s in life include …

◆ Nine muses.

◆ Nine months to deliver a full-term baby.

♦ Nine Elected Knights in freemasonry which includes nine roses, nine lights, and nine knocks in their ritual.

♦ Nine steps in the pyramids.

The 9 is also the most important number in Feng Shui, as the number of perfection and the central energy of that system.

The 9 rules the broader issues of life with worldly concerns such as international business. Its energy should be used to educate, comfort, and protect humankind, while working for the betterment of the planet Earth. It's not unusual to find the 9 financially well-off. This is the number of reward, an attraction for money and good fortune. When a 9 is wealthy, no doubt the 9 will be involved with numerous charitable organizations, especially in the arts.

The Number 9: Completion and Compassion	
Key Words	Endings, universal oneness, highly intuitive, fortunate, multitalented, perfection, dramatic, artistic, spiritual, compassion
Astrological Equivalent	Scorpio
Tarot Card Equivalent	The World (completes the journey); The 9s of each Minor Arcana suit
Letters	I and R
Polarity	Yang
Colors	White, pearl, clear
Gems	Opal
Flowers	Magnolia for grief, Michaelmas daisy for farewell, red poppy for consolation, rosemary for remembrance, woodbine for fraternal love.

The Energy of the 9

The energy of the 9 represents completion, conclusion, and ending, and it is here that the energy sphere widens from the local to the global. This number wants to promote improvement for humankind and vibrates to the larger picture.

The 9 is also an emotional energy that moves from one extreme to the other. It is an intense, transformative number.

The Timing of the 9

The 9 is dream time. Procrastination is not uncommon and the strict adherence to timelines is just not part of the 9s timeframe. It dwells in the zone of possibility, therefore, it has to have time to contemplate and dream.

Life with the 9

It's not uncommon to find the 9 marching in civil rights demonstrations, working for the World Hunger Project, or helping with welfare reform. It's their concern for the betterment of all people on this Earth that lives in the soul of the 9. That's because the 9 is the number of compassion, tolerance, and philanthropy. 9s are both inspired and inspiring, and some are exceptionally gifted artistically. They're enterprising, imaginative, and quick thinking.

Easy as 1-2-3

What the 9 learns from the 8 is that reward isn't gained through ambition, recognition, power, or money. There's more to life, the 9 realizes: There's spiritual attainment and inner confidence, both of which have far-reaching benefits. Just look what happened as we moved from the 1980s (the 8 embodies power, money, and ambition) to the 1990s (the 9 manifests the search for spiritual connection, global concern, and unparalleled prosperity).

For the 9, there has to be a soul realization that love equals giving, and through understanding and acceptance of all people without prejudice or thought for oneself, personal love, purposefulness, and abundance will begin to build up in the 9's life. This in turn brings spiritual protection and great reward, both emotionally and materially.

The 9 is the number of reward for all the hard work done in numbers 1 through 8, and the rewards are both material and spiritual. At some point in the life of the 9, he or she realizes that his or her soul's expression is vital to living a whole and balanced life. You could think of the 9 as the 6 grown wiser and much more tolerant—but the 9 is also more emotional. The 9 rules the emotions, which can be experienced in the extreme. You'll find vacillation from intense anger to great tolerance, from passionate outcries to detached observation, from outrageous jealousy to sympathetic understanding.

> **Merlin's Notes**
>
> The 9 has a great passion for wanting to make the world a better place and a deep-seated love for people that kindles the philanthropic, humanitarian outreach characteristic of the 9. Not surprisingly, the 9 is a global thinker and always looking at the bigger picture.

The 9 is learning to surrender. The 9 will be involved in completing unfinished tasks and learning not to take it personally when something is over, but instead understanding how this ending fits into the larger picture, as well as the Divine plan for mankind (this is the number of endings, after all). When the 9 "gets it," the endings begin to look like beginnings.

9s understand that life has been a series of lessons teaching them about the full spectrum of the human drama, so that they can develop a high degree of compassion and tolerance. While a 9 may start out being intolerant, that's not hard to understand because the 9 is an idealist and a perfectionist. Still, the 9's life lesson will be to develop tolerance for all people regardless of race, creed, or color. This number is here to learn and to live selflessly, giving loving service to mankind.

When 9s come of age, they'll be able to acknowledge pain, grief, misery, suffering, and poverty as conditions of this planet. It's then that they'll be able to live in joy, love, beauty, and mystical understanding. 9s want to show everyone a better way, and get involved where they shouldn't. 9s can attract volumes of worries and problems.

9s are unusually artistic or involved with the arts, especially at the philanthropic level (such as being the large donor for the symphony's annual fundraising project, or chair for the statewide Young Writers' Contest).

There's a kind of aristocratic air about the 9: The 9 is stately, worldly, and may well be wealthy.

The Blessing of the 9

The blessing of the 9 is that it has the ability to restore its position, to redeem itself from failure and loss, and to re-establish success. This, of course, is metaphorically the process of death and rebirth, or endings bringing beginnings. It's also related to the astrological sign of Scorpio, who is said to be able to rise from the ashes. As the number of transformation, the 9 has a great deal of power to regenerate.

The 9 has an unusual ability to attract assistance and opportunities for success. This is also known to be the number that attracts money and fortune. Look at the following:

MONEY = 9	FORTUNE = 9
M = 4	F = 6
O = 6	O = 6
N = 5	R = 9
E = 5	T = 2
Y = 7	U = 3
Total = 27	N = 5
(2 + 7 = **9**)	E = 5
	Total = 36
	(3 + 6 = **9**)

9s can make a fortune and lose it more than once in a lifetime.

The Challenge for the 9

The challenge for the 9 is to love unconditionally and to live with tolerance and compassion. Lessons may be learned through tears and pain as well as moments of great joy and ecstasy. Health issues can challenge the 9 because of its highly sensitive and emotional constitution.

9s have to open their hearts to urges to be intolerant, possessive, unsympathetic, selfish, or greedy. To balance this challenge, the 9 needs to turn these lower energies into creating a talent for sympathetic understanding, inclusiveness, compassion, selfless service, and trust in the universe to deliver his or her just reward.

The Lesson of the 9

Lessons for the 9 include: learning to accept, forgive, and let go; learning to detach; to open his or her heart to all, regardless of labels; that its most valuable asset is a heart filled with love big enough to melt resistance; and most of all to love and forgive itself.

More than anything, the 9 must learn that it's been given a generous heart, an array of talents, a belief in the basic goodness of mankind, a deep love of humanity, and a deep understanding of the universal laws of divine order. Along with these priceless gifts, the 9 must realize it's meant to serve and promote universal brotherhood and sisterhood.

Relationships with the 9

The father is often a strong influence in the life of the 9. There can be both misunderstandings and happiness stemming from the father that influence the young 9. Later in the 9's life, the 9 will play father and mother of the world and be a sort of cosmic parent.

> ### Merlin's Notes
>
> For a 9, love must be linked to a higher purpose. Love must come from a place of greater good than personal gain or personal gratification. When the 9 learns to do so, the 9 very well may be a benevolent leader, like Mahatma Gandhi (a 9 Life Path) or Martin Luther King, Jr. (a 9 Soul Number).

Unhappy emotions are not uncommon—remember, the 9 moves to the extremes of emotion. The 9 may fluctuate between ecstasy and depression, and some 9s are manic depressive or bipolar (possibly because they're struggling to reconcile their notions of an idealized vision for the planet with the reality they see all around them).

At the same time, 9s are charming and can show great sympathy, warmth, and understanding. They're usually well-liked and are good companions who love life. Still, the 9's personal charisma and the necessary development of the notion of detachment may make the 9 seem inconsistent and difficult to understand.

9s love with great passion and intensity and experience sorrow and pain with the same intensity. Love fades when the object of the 9's affection fails to live up to his or her idealized version of perfection. Sometimes, too, the 9s will sacrifice those they love until they awaken to higher possibilities.

9s love home, family, and friends. In relationships, happiness will be found when the 9s place all others' needs before their own and remember that giving must be done for the sheer pleasure of giving. The 9 is also romantic and attracted to beauty and lovely surroundings. Creative and sensitive to color, the 9 often has well-developed artistic expression as well.

When you have a relationship with a 9, you'll have to give him or her plenty of space. You may find you share your home with Peace Corp trainees or volunteers for Habitat for Humanity. Generous and loving, the 9 will give time to worthy causes of social concern. The 9's personal life will be mixed with love for humanistic projects, and those at home may find themselves fending for themselves while number 9 is off crusading for whales, the Arctic tundra, or refugees of foreign lands.

The 9 is spiritual, romantic, emotional, magnetic, efficient, responsible, cooperative, and often an independent leader. With the 9's broad outlook on life, the 9 is at his or her best when the 9 has a sense of purpose, balance, and emotional control. As renowned numerologist Juno Jordan says of the 9, "Being the highest number on the scale of human experience, it cannot transgress the principles of inner grace and spiritual living."

Undeveloped 9s appear meek, shy, vacillating, looking upon the dark side of things, fearful, or longing for something but don't know what. When they're like this, they need an understanding guide and a helping hand. At the same time, however, the 9 needs to develop its own individuality.

> **CAUTION**
>
> **Sixes and Sevens**
>
> Because 9 is a high-potency number, it's important that stimulants and habit-forming substances be curtailed. It's very hard for the 9 to break habits or for anyone to reform him or her. Change can come only from transformation and a spiritual alliance with a higher power.

The 9 is the number that learns there's great satisfaction in giving. The healing aspect of the 9's energy is felt when the 9 gives of him- or herself from this loving space and shines his or her considerable warmth and understanding on those seeking assistance. A 9 might be mistaken for a bleeding heart, a pushover, or someone to be taken advantage of, because its loving concern for the good of all can make the 9 overly generous or gullible.

9s need the steady hand of the 4, the nurturing of the 6, and the objective analysis of the 7 to help them through.

What's Important to the 9

Some of the things that are important to the 9 are ...

- Beauty: It balances the ugliness in the world.

- Love and romance: These soothe the intense emotional response to the wrong doings of the world.

- Giving: The compassionate release for all the pent up concern for the world condition.

- Creative and artistic expression: These dramatically express the love that isn't part of the present reality.

You probably won't be surprised to learn that the 9 is offended by lack of compassion, ugliness, and selfishness.

Cosmic Connection

With the number 9, it's a time to finish, draw to a close, complete—and then to let go. The 9 rules the principle of surrender, "letting go and letting God." This is the higher ground of living with faith in a divine plan.

In the Chaldean system of numbers, an older numerology system, the number 9 wasn't used because it was thought to be the number of God. Instead, the Chaldeans based their system on numbers 1 through 8. In modern numerology, the 9 is included in the system of numbers because it is thought to include the energy of all of the numbers 1 through 8, thus giving it great power.

The number 9 is both powerful and potent, and, because it's privy to the wisdom of spiritual law, it's conscious of the needs of humankind and has the talent to bring these two together in a living testimony to the oneness of all life. The 9 also has the power to choose to live with a higher purpose or to suffer the grief and pain of separation from what it intuitively and psychically knows.

The 9 understands that there's only one people, one religion, one race, one nation, and one creed—universal unity. The service of the 9 is to promote, in small and large ways, the unity of humankind.

Spiritual Essence of the 9

The 9 symbolizes spirit as a fully conscious energy, that is, wisdom attained. The power of the 9 is the fusion of a fully conscious spirit with the material world. The 9 is the kundalini force of yoga, symbolizing the surge of energy from the base of the spine to the brain. (If you look at the way the 9 is written, it looks like a spinal cord curving up to a head.) The goal of the 9 is universal love for all, carrying forth its spiritual wisdom into all human experience on Earth.

Higher Ground

The higher vibration of the 9 is …

   ◆ Loving.

   ◆ Caring.

   ◆ Magnetic with money.

   ◆ Completing.

   ◆ Ending.

◆ Releasing.

◆ Transforming.

◆ Forgiving.

Raising the Vibration for the Number 9

The vibration is the energy a number gives off. The energy of any given number can be expressed positively or as a higher energy. The higher energy of the number 9 is always picking up on more than meets the eye, and it's really challenging to have such a keen sense of the beauty of life, and then to see poverty, bombings, and children starving. 9s continuously learn the lesson of surrender—to let go and leave that which cannot be fixed to a higher source or greater plan than can be seen from the vantage point of the emotional 9. Unless you understand compassion, you cannot understand the 9.

Forgiveness is the key for the 9, and this is its life lesson: to forgive all wrongdoing and intolerance and become impartial, impersonal, and detached from its emotions so that it can live with compassion and wisdom.

A Meditation for the Number 9

Sit quietly in a room where you won't be distracted or disturbed. Close your eyes and take three deep breaths, exhaling slowly. Begin to visualize yourself as a radiant being of light. Your light is becoming brighter and brighter. You are strong, vibrant, perceptive, and aware. Your light is strong.

See yourself sitting on a beach. The sun is shining brightly, sparkling on the water. It is peaceful here. Relax and let your mind open. Breathing slowly, begin to focus on ideas coming in on beams of light. Notice that these thoughts are forming a creative idea. It is a dream forming. It is your long-awaited life-dream. Allow the light to continue to stream toward you, filling you with vibrant creative energy. Your life-dream is becoming brighter and brighter. Now you see it bathed in radiant light. What you have always wanted is now clearly seen. What is this dream? What have you always longed for, wanted to be, or wished you could do with your life? See it now; this is the time to allow your life-dream to expand and come into the light.

Deep within this vision of your life-dream you notice something bright purple, off to the right. It is a small book. You see that its title is *Secrets of the Universe*. Go ahead and open this book to any page. What secret is it showing you? This secret is one that will help you bring your life-dream into reality. Without doubt or judgment, allow this secret to guide you. Feel the light all around you, feel your energy rise. Breathe into this light energy and notice it expands, surrounding your body. Taking another deep breath, draw in more light and on the exhale, see the light expanding beyond your body, out over the beach, out over the water. Your life-dream and your secret from the Universe are energized with light. Now, state your intention. You might want to say to yourself, "I am ready to allow my life-dream into my life," or you might say, "I am ready to be shown the steps for bringing my life-dream into reality." You might want to begin to repeat an affirmation to crystallize the vibration of this energized life-dream. You can create one of your own, or use this one: "I move forward in life with joy and ease, knowing I am supported by radiant Universal energy to manifest my cherished life-dream." Or "I am the creative power in my world and all dreams are possible." Repeat this affirmation, or your own affirmation, at least three times slowly, breathing deeply with each statement.

When you are ready, open your eyes, let yourself refocus, and then write into your journal your life-dream vision. What is the secret you have been given from the Universe? Now write your statement of intention in your journal. Throughout the day, stay focused on your intention for your life dream; know that it is part of your life path and purpose.

The Number 9 in Your Numerology Profile

If you vibrate to the 9, whether it's your Birthday Number, Pinnacle, Challenge, Personal Year, Soul, Destiny, Life Path, Personality, or Maturity Number, you must learn through personal experience that, as we have indicated, a 9 has to guard against going to extremes with emotional responses, intolerant judgments born out of idealistic notions, and the hardest of all, to let go. A certain amount of detachment is essential for the 9. To do this the 9 has to contain his or her emotions, idealistic notions, utopian dreams, and intense love for the humane causes, the world's wrongs, and the down and out.

It's time to use your journal. Look for 9s in your name. As you work with your name numbers, keep in mind that the letters, I and R are the "9" letters. The average number of 9s in a name is two or three (after all, 9 is the number of compassion and benevolence and humankind needs more of this energy, not less.) It indicates humanitarian concern and creative ability. If you have one 9 it indicates little awareness of others' feelings and a restricted point of view.

If you have no 9s, it indicates a self-centered focus and in this life you will be learning the lessons of tolerance, compassion, and selfless giving. If you are wishing you had more 9 energy in your name, you might want to consider a name change. Go ahead and count your 9s in your birth name and record these in your journal.

At this time you might also want to be on the look out for Master Numbers in your name. We will be discussing all of the Master Numbers in the next chapter.

The Least You Need to Know

♦ The 7 is the number of inner wisdom.

♦ The 8 is the number of learning to live with power without sowing more karmic debt.

♦ The 9 is the number of returning to one's higher self.

♦ You can change the energy of your name if you have too many or too few 7s, 8s, and 9s.

The Master Numbers 11, 22, 33, and More

In This Chapter

- The Master Numbers reveal increased potential
- The 11: self-illumination through spiritual inspiration
- The 22: self-mastery through self-enterprise
- The 33: self-awareness through selfless service
- The lesser-known Master Numbers

In this chapter, we address Master Numbers, with special focus on 11, 22, and 33. Each of the Master Numbers requires a particular kind of, well, mastery. As you'll learn, each Master Number reveals a particular kind of potential, as well as increased responsibilities.

Do you have Master Numbers in your Numerology Profile? It's time to find out. Master Numbers are double-digit numbers that repeat themselves and at the same time come from a single root number. For example, 11 is a Master Number in which the 1 is repeated. At the same time, the reduced number of the 11 is 2 (1 + 1 = 2). The 2 is the root number and is an equally present vibration in this number.

Three Things You Want to Know About Master Numbers

For all Master Numbers there are three things you should keep in mind. First, each of the *Master Numbers* is called by an esoteric name that gives insight into its purpose and shows how it's meant to serve its time on Earth. For example …

By the Numbers

Master Numbers are considered to have more potential than the other numbers. The 11 is considered the most intuitive of all of the numbers, the 22 is considered the most powerful of all of the numbers, and the 33 is thought to be the most loving of all the numbers.

- The 11 is the Spiritual Messenger.
- The 22 is the Master Builder.
- The 33 is the Master of Healing Energies Through Love.

Second, we write all Master Numbers by representing the double-digit number first and then the reduced base number with it. The following chart shows how to write your Master Numbers.

Master Number	Write As
11	11/2
22	22/4
33	33/6

And third, there are as many Master Numbers as can be configured from repeating the numbers 1 through 9. All of the following are considered Master Numbers: 11, 22, 33, 44, 55, 66, 77, 88, and 99. However, we'll be confining our discussion to the three most commonly found numbers: 11, 22, and 33.

A full list of Master Numbers and their meanings can be found at the end of this chapter.

It's Not Easy Being a Master Number

All of the Master Numbers indicate an opportunity for learning and integrating spiritual information. This learning, however, often comes through trials, tests, or stressful circumstances. The bottom line is, if you're using spiritual, philosophical, universal, or metaphysical principles, you're operating at the Master Number level, which we call working with the higher vibration of the Master Number (11, 22, or 33). If, however, you're focusing yourself on ego, the material world, or lower energies, then you're working within the confines of the base vibration of the Master Number (2, 4, or 6). This is the case only with Master Numbers.

Numerologists believe that (if) you have a Master Number, you've made a kind of contract (back when you were still in spirit form) to come back and help humankind in this lifetime. All of the Master Numbers have volunteered to come back to assist the world in moving to a higher vibration and are doing it because they want to learn more at the soul level.

Spiritual Gifts

Master Numbers indicate spiritual gifts that make them highly sensitive to intuition, extrasensory perception, and the world of higher guidance, including celestial beings, other life realities, and universal spiritual law. Master Numbers have a greater ability to be in touch with their own higher guidance, because they're more fully developed spiritual souls (when they are listening).

The only problem is, a lot of Master Number people don't live up to their spiritual potential. In part, it's because it's so hard to live life as highly sensitive individuals—and they must live in balance. This requirement for balance extends to the physical, emotional, and mental aspects of their lives, and, quite frankly, it's a tall order.

Any Master Number's natural spiritual affinity has to find its place in our world of violence, negativity, materialism, and personal gratification. When it does, it can bring much needed knowledge to a soul-weary world. At the same time, however, for the Master Number to live in our world is very taxing emotionally, mentally, and physically. This means those who carry a Master Number are constantly having to adjust, filter, fine-tune, and remember his or her spiritual origins.

Easy as 1-2-3

Master Number individuals are thought to be old souls who carry much wisdom and spiritual knowledge, which has been learned through many lifetimes. The Master Numbers carry wisdom of the mysteries of life and death.

Sixes and Sevens

The gifts of the spiritually attuned Master Numbers create tension, extreme restlessness, illness, and physical problems if their energies aren't channeled into service to humankind. It doesn't matter what form the service takes; it's just that it must be a service that in some way will help humanity elevate its consciousness toward living with spiritual awareness.

Another reason why it's hard to live as a Master Number is because the ideals and goals of master vibrations are high and the Master Number's inner guidance is developed enough to be a strong presence. This causes the Master Number person to lean toward perfection and to live in a heightened state of awareness, which means that person is not always able to accept what he or she sees.

The Master Numbers have been called "testing" numbers, where life seems to be a series of tests to live up to, so that they can demonstrate all that they know and have the potential to be. Master Numbers have an innate ability to help others overcome their challenges, as well as an extraordinary ability to assist with the challenges of humankind. We like to think of Master Number people as a kind of light, a very bright star shining among all the rest of us stars.

What Master Numbers Share in Common

While each Master Number has unique characteristics (which we'll discuss a few pages ahead), they share the following:

- Vibrations of tremendous power and energy

- The innate ability to achieve fame

- The need to work on a large-scale level to bring about greater good to humanity

- The demand for self-mastery

- The responsibility for the great power Master Numbers possess

- Idealism

- High creativity

- Natural leadership ability

- The frequent need to be alone, to recharge, to find their spiritual center once again, and to detoxify

- The mission to serve in their own way, in their own field

- High introspection and sensitivity

- The need to constantly control their direction

- The expectation that they will do more and set higher standards than the average person

- Extremes in emotions

◆ The need to perform personal tests of mastery, including experiencing both the higher and lower vibrations of their Master Number

For all Master Numbers, the journey in this lifetime is into themselves, seeking the spiritual power that is part of their higher guidance, and learning control over their lesser nature: for the 11, to control the 1 and 2; for the 22, to control the 2 and the 4; for the 33, to control the 3 and 6; and so on. Let's show you the three most common Master Numbers.

The Master Number 11: The Spiritual Messenger

Intuitive, sensitive, and very enthusiastic only touch the surface in describing the Master Number 11. In the ideal, the Master Number 11/2 is on a journey to find its own truth (illumination), using spiritual inspirations as a guiding light, and then bringing these illuminations to others to help raise spiritual awareness on the planet. You might say the 11 is born to bring spiritual insights (messages) to Earth.

Correspondences to describe the 11/2 are as follows:

Master Number 11	
Key Words	Very bright, inspirational, uplifts, humanity, brings light to others, nervous energy, visionary, loves the spotlight, seeks spiritual truth, leader, spiritual teacher, peacemaker, negotiator, highly intuitive
Astrological Equivalent	Sagittarius/Aquarius
Colors	Glossy white, silver, platinum
Gems	Mother of Pearl

Also important to consider is the angel associated with the 11/2 Master Number, the Guardian Angel Uriel. Uplifting and inspirational, Uriel guides 11/2s back to the truth and restores balance.

How these two numbers play out together is the real story of the 11/2 Master Number. You might think of this number as two 1s, which embody individuality, the pioneering spirit,

> **Sixes and Sevens**
>
> Not surprisingly, the demands of the 1 are often at odds with the demands of the 2. No matter what, though, the 11/2 is very sensitive to all within its radar, and, more often than not, is shy and nervous, and lives with intense emotions.

leadership, solitude, and independence; and a 2, which personifies companionship, team spirit, harmony, and peace.

The Master Number 11/2 is sensitive, dreamy, and idealistic, and it will often have revelations born out of its own experiences and search for truth about the mystery of life. 11s love to delve into the hidden mystery behind any of the many challenges they're called to face, whether it's the mystery of relationships, money, or the work world. While 11/2s can participate in the social world (the 2 is good at this), they really live more on the inside than in the external world.

It's the test of the soul of the 11/2 to learn to live honestly and with integrity. This Master Number loves the spotlight and it's not unusual to find people with 11/2s gaining fame. Bill Clinton, for example, carries two 11/2s in his chart—in his Soul Number and his Life Path Number—and we'd say that he, for one, has had more than a few tests in a journey toward living with integrity and honesty.

Merlin's Notes

Even though an 11/2 finds itself in the spotlight, sometimes the fame this number acquires is for the wrong reasons. After all, both Hitler and Mussolini had 11 prominently in their names. Remember, a Master Number is very powerful: How one chooses to use that power is part of what the soul is learning. Even though the 11/2s have come to help the human race, they're faced with choosing how to use their power.

Learning to Surrender to Higher Ideals

With any of the Master Numbers, one is required to *surrender* to higher ideals. The 11/2 must live in truth, which is revealed through life's lessons. Their most rewarding opportunities will come from living and teaching truth as they see it, the truths they've discovered along the road, as well as uplifting others.

The 11/2s are intense, and at times electrifying. They can have trouble with nervousness because the 11 is a highly intense vibration. At the same time, 11/2s have great courage and are highly creative.

The 11/2s are humanitarians to the bone—it arises from their very souls. Perhaps it's the 2 in this number that brings their unique ability to bring peace through negotiations. It's not surprising, then, to find that the 39th president of the United States of America and 2002 Nobel Peace Prize recipient, Jimmy Carter, has an 11/2 last name. He was born to the path of the peacemaker.

The Pathway for the 11/2

The pathway for 11/2s is often hidden, and they must stumble along until their inner worlds are securely established and then they go out into the world to teach the truths they've learned during their stumblings. This number has the capacity to see the broad picture, to see the vision, to hold the dream—but it must find an outlet where it can be an active participant in the vision.

Easy as 1-2-3

Because of its heightened sense of intuition, the 11/2 has excellent insights into personal situations as well as issues of the larger world. This is often the number of someone who's psychic.

The Higher Vibration of the 11/2

The 11/2s are inspirational leaders, but only when they draw on their cosmic or spiritual knowledge through profound intuitive abilities. They're leaders only when their vibrations are raised to the two 1s. If an 11/2 doesn't respond to the higher vibration, the 11/2 will work at the lower vibration of the 2, in a position of supporting others. While this is an excellent outlet for the energy of this number, the 11/2 can't play the supporting role forever: As the master teacher, the 11 is born to lead and to bring spiritual truths to people.

As we've suggested, the 11/2 is a bright light with a spiritual message. The word "light" adds up to 11/2:

L = 3

I = 9

G = 7

H = 8

T = 2

_____

29 = **11/2** (2 + 9 = 11; 1 + 1 = 2)

The Weaker Vibration of the 11/2

The 11/2 walks the fine line between greatness and self-destruction. This number can be given over to fear and phobias or soar to the heights of the enlightened. The 11/2's growth and stability lie in the acceptance of his or her unusual gift for intuitive understanding and spiritual truths. The 11/2 must learn to live with faith: This is where the 11/2's peace is made.

Famous 11/2s

The inspired ones:

♦ Wolfgang Amadeus Mozart, composer

♦ Leonardo da Vinci, inventor, artist, thinker

♦ Jules Verne, author

♦ Antonio Vivaldi, composer

The negotiators for peace:

♦ James Earl Carter, Nobel Peace Prize winner and former U.S. president

♦ Anwar Sadat, Nobel Peace Prize winner

♦ James Schlesinger, secretary of defense under U.S. presidents Nixon and Ford

In the spotlight:

♦ Princess Diana, beloved British royal

♦ Prince William, son of Prince Charles and Diana, heir to British throne

♦ Prince Charles, father of William, heir apparent to British throne

♦ Tony Blair, British prime minister

♦ Bill Clinton, former U.S. president

♦ Rudy Giuliani, former mayor of New York City

♦ Colin Powell, secretary of state under U.S. president George W. Bush

♦ Jacqueline Kennedy Onassis, former U.S. first lady

♦ Katharine Hepburn, Academy Award–winning actress

The Master Number 22: The Master Builder

Master Builder, master planner, and visionary only touch the surface in describing the Master Number 22. The 22/4 has the unique ability to see the large picture, the details, and the spiritual principles needed to execute all of these into concrete form. This number builds things for humanity.

Correspondences to describe the 22 are as follows:

Master Number 22	
Key Words	Master organizer, organizes large undertakings, spiritual, practical idealism, brings dreams into reality, ambitious, intuitive, inspired, methodical, disciplined, natural leader, confident, wise, hard-working, honest, competent, creative
Astrological Equivalent	Capricorn/Leo/Virgo
Colors	Red, gold
Gems	Rose gold

Also important to consider is the angel associated with this Master Number. The 22/4 Guardian Angel is Jamaerah—the angel of manifestation, who opens space for visions to manifest.

This Master Number combines all of the traits of the 2—twice over—and at the same time includes the traits of the 4. As with the 11/2, it is how these two numbers play out together that's the real story of the 22/4. You might think of this number as two 2s, which embody high sensitivity, intuition, harmony, and relationships; and 4, which represents hard work, discipline, practicality, building, organization, and bringing things to form.

For the Master Number 22/4, the demands of the 2 must blend with the 4, and this is its struggle and its glory. Like the other Master Numbers, the 22/4 has a heightened sensitivity that gives it a unique ability to sense things, but also, when out of balance, causes health issues.

Master Organizer for Good of All

The 22/4 has exceptional organizational ability. That's because the 22/4 has the balance of a focused mind and the highest ideals and brings both to any project or undertaking. The 22/4 is a natural leader, and can use spiritual wisdom to

> **Merlin's Notes**
>
> The 22/4 is interested in ideas and fields of work that result in forward movement and the evolution of humankind. These people want to make use of their talents to build something of lasting value that is splendid and uplifting. A 22/4 should choose a field that requires ultra-specialization, for it's in this area that both success and satisfaction will be gained.

achieve tangible results. This Master Number has the desire to build big projects or set big goals—and the lesson is to use these desires to bring greater good to all.

The 22/4 is inspired to apply cosmic principles of metaphysics and spiritual and philosophical teachings to the physical and material world, and in this way invent new ways to apply these age-old principles.

Meet the Master Builder

The 22/4 loves to build systems, programs, projects, and organizations that are useful, practical, and uplifting. Naturally, this Master Builder is highly creative, and is delighted to create something that calls for order, planning, and bringing people to a higher sense of awareness in the process.

Sixes and Sevens

The 22/4 Master Number is an even higher vibration of the 11/2; after all, it's twice the energy. Instead of two 1s, it is two 2s. That means it has greater potential, and a greater struggle to stay in balance.

The 22/4s are intuitive, natural leaders, and they're creative, much like the 11/2, except that they're better adapted to the world and know better how to deliver the same truths in a more acceptable practical language. Life for the 22/4 is more solid than that of the 11/2, partly because the 22/4 is able to bring into tangible form the ideas the 11/2 can only dream of. With its practical know-how and ability to organize and plan, the 22/4 manifests dreams.

It's the mission of the 22/4 to elevate its body and make it conscious of the oneness of mind, body, and spirit. This number carries the root, or reduced, number 4, which governs health. For this reason, it's not uncommon to find 22/4s with weak bodies who have to work on their health, or, at the very least, improve their health using progressive, spirit-honoring methodologies.

It's important to remember that the 2 plays a very important part in Master Number 22/4, because it's the number of the double 2 (as in 22). Therefore, the qualities of the 2 must be honed and perfected with this number, and life will bring the 22/4 many opportunities to be patient, tactful, willing to wait, polish the art of persuasion, be supportive, and become intimate with the perimeters of living a life of balance (physically, emotionally, mentally, and spiritually). Yet most important, the 22/4 learns to become an expert at improving relationships of all kinds. All of this then becomes part of the 22/4's service to humankind.

Sometimes, 22/4s feel as if they live in two worlds or two realities—the slow, everyday world of details and problems; and the inspired world of creativity, where everything and anything is possible. This Master Number is very connected to the earth and loves to work with its hands, yet at the same time is equally connected to the world of universal law, spiritual principles, and other world possibilities.

The Higher Vibration of the 22/4

Like all of the Master Numbers, 22/4s feel things deeply, but don't get caught up in unproductive dreaming. Instead, the dreams of the 22/4 are based on facts and practical usefulness. After all, these are the master doers, and they're willing to work hard to achieve their visions for humankind. The 22/4 is the number of someone who is serious, hardworking, loyal, and supportive.

Interestingly, the root of the 22 is the 4, the number of hard work—and the word "work" adds up to a 22/4:

W = 5

O = 6

R = 9

K = 2

___

22 = **22/4**

The 22/4 can function well in arenas that allow for a broad perspective, encompass national and international interests, and promote universal understanding, peace, and higher consciousness.

> **CAUTION**
>
> **Sixes and Sevens**
>
> If the powerful energies present with 22/4 are abused by indulgence in grandiose dreams of self-glorification, then the 22/4 will lower his or her vibration to the mundane level of the 4 and become the workhorse, bean counter, or laborer, instead of the enterprising spiritual leader this number promises.

The Weaker Vibration of the 22/4

Like all of the Master Numbers, the 22/4 is very sensitive. Because 22/4s have the tendency to be involved in large projects, they can feel overwhelmed when too many obstacles are present, and when this happens, the 22/4 may need to resort to the vibration of the 4 to regain a sense of groundedness.

Remember, Master Numbers are a very high vibration and require balance of the mental, physical, and emotional body. A 22/4 can become a workaholic, so he or she must stay disciplined about achieving balance and then use his or her powerful energy to build wonderful things that contribute to the general welfare of all.

Famous 22/4s

Visionaries and luminaries:

- ◆ Al Gore, former U.S. vice president
- ◆ Demi Moore, actress
- ◆ Woody Allen, writer, comic, film director
- ◆ Alice Munro, author
- ◆ Mike Nichols, film director
- ◆ Isaac Stern, musician
- ◆ Luciano Pavarotti, opera singer

Master Builders:

- ◆ Bill Gates and Paul Allen, businessmen and technology experts
- ◆ J. D. Rockefeller III, entrepreneur and businessman
- ◆ Frank Sinatra, singer
- ◆ Winston Churchill, politician

Leaders of cosmic principles for a material world:

- ◆ Yogi Maharishi, peace advocate and guru
- ◆ Pope Paul I, religious leader
- ◆ Stephen Covey, author and proponent of Principle Centered Leadership

Easy as 1-2-3

The Master Number 33/6 carries two 3s and reduces to a 6. Therefore it carries all of the qualities of the 3 and the 6.

The Master Number 33: The Master of Healing Energies Through Love

Intuitive, altruistic, and selfless only touch the surface in describing the Master Number 33. This number is on the journey of discovering its powerful healing energy through an open heart and unconditional love. Through love and example, the 33/6 awakens others to its depth and understanding of how to make spiritual truths work in the material world.

The correspondences to describe the 33 are as follows:

Master Number 33	
Key Words	Visionary, sensitive, selfless service, ministering, avatar, altruistic, caring, nurturing of the spirit, mystical, sympathetic, tenderhearted, emotional, protective, forgiving
Astrological Equivalent	Cancer/Pisces
Color	Deep sky blue
Gems	Lapis lazuli

Also important to consider is the angelic association of the 33, the Guardian Angel Michael—the angel of protection, who is dedicated to the preservation of the spiritual destiny of each soul.

Mystic or Martyr?

For a long time, the 33/6 was thought to be the highest Master Number, signifying the highest human consciousness possible. Because of this, the number 33 has been given nearly divine status, and called the number of the *avatar*. However, with the expansion of human consciousness, we now allow for other Master Numbers beyond the 33.

In daily life the 33/6 is a champion of the underdog, and exudes compassion, love, and empathy. This Master Number willingly gives of itself, lending encouragement and heartfelt understanding to all who need help. It's thought that the 33/6 has Christlike qualities of sacrificing itself for the sake of others. However, because of their tenderheartedness and sensitivity, 33/6s can easily be swept into the despair of others, feeling the deep pain of the world.

By the Numbers

Avatar is a Sanskrit term meaning "descent." In Hinduism, an avatar is thought to be a human incarnation of the Divine who mediates between people and God. Krishna, an East Indian deity, is considered the most perfect expression of the Divine, and so an avatar. In popular usage, this word is used to indicate a person or program of superior spiritual achievement in consciousness development.

The 33/6s are highly emotional and can find themselves in emotional distress from their heartfelt identification with those in need. It is not unusual for those with this number to find themselves locked into codependent situations. Like all Master Numbers, the 33/6 will need to master balance and detachment (but with a caring attitude). These are not easy lessons for this number. Because it's made up of two 3s, this number experiences a double dose of emotional expression. Plus, with the number 6 (3 + 3) as its root number, it carries the weight of self-imposed responsibility for the welfare of others.

The Prime Directive of the 33/6

The prime directive of the 33/6 is to benefit, serve, and administer to as many people as possible. The 33/6 would like to heal all with its love. Because of the strong presence of the need to right injustice and human rights, those with this number are often found caring for the elderly or the handicapped, or in some form of service which benefits humanity. This number is exemplified by Elisabeth Kübler-Ross, whose life work is devoted to teaching and helping others understand the process of death and dying.

The Higher Vibration of the 33/6

This Master Number has a special gift of working with humility and is unaffected by the power it possesses. If you're a 33/6, and you're living the higher energy of this number, many will perceive the light that glows from you and will gladly follow you: Your faith and love show them the way. You see beyond the situation to the good in all people, regardless of color, race, or creed. You're Love personified.

Both the 3 and the 6 of this Master Number carry the creative, artistic energy. With a double dose of 3s (33) it is not unusual to find entertainers with the 33/6 number. They can be highly expressive and dramatic.

Sixes and Sevens

Because the number 6 is carried within this Master Number 33/6, there will be a tendency to become burdened and overly responsible. This is where the 33/6 gets out of balance.

The Weaker Vibration of the 33/6

The greatest challenge for the 33/6 is to focus his or her emotions on higher goals in tune with spiritual laws, rather than staying on the superficial level with distracted 3 energy, or by trying to solve each and every problem of humanity. This Master Number is here to learn detachment, to express love and kindness, and to willingly respond to the needs of others. If the 33/6 remembers the universal principle, "everything happens for a reason, and there is a divine plan for all of life," then the 33/6 will lessen his or her stress and restore balance. In this way, the 33/6 will find direction for his or her own spiritual growth.

The 33/6s may have trouble distinguishing where their service is truly needed due to their confusion over hearing someone's story and deciphering fact from fiction. They will learn that they can't be all things to all people. Remember, 33/6s have come to learn mastery for themselves through loving service, and they must always strive for balance, emotionally and spiritually.

Clear expression of the 33/6's own needs and a willingness to let others be responsible for their own "stuff" is part of what the 33/6 is here to learn. Sacrifice is valuable only as long as there is still a "self" left to do the sacrificing. The 33/6 may be the "Cosmic Parent," and the Master of Healing Energy, but, like all parents and healers, the 33/6 must hold some back for him- or herself.

The lesson of healing with love is to love yourself first and to heal yourself first, so that you may truly be of service to mankind.

Famous 33/6s

The expressive ones:

- ◆ Meryl Streep, actress

- ◆ Ben Affleck, actor and screenwriter

- ◆ Britney Spears, singer

- ◆ Francis Ford Coppola, film director, producer, and screenwriter

- ◆ Fred Astaire, dancer

- ◆ Reba McEntire, singer and songwriter

- ◆ Mikhail Baryshnikov, ballet dancer and actor

- ◆ Bonnie Raitt, singer and songwriter

Leaders of compassion:

- ◆ Christopher Reeve, actor and activist for spinal cord injury research

- ◆ Steven Spielberg, visionary filmmaker

- ◆ Dr. Elisabeth Kübler-Ross, psychiatrist and author

- ◆ Rev. Jesse L. Jackson Sr., civil rights leader

A Final Note on Master Numbers

With all of the Master Numbers, it's important to remember that these are not indications of perfection, nor do they have greater significance than the other numbers. All Master Number people have come here to learn mastery and at the same time to fulfill an agreement to help the human race.

All of the Master Numbers are challenged to live according to spiritual principles and higher consciousness. Most will have numerous tests and challenges to overcome in an effort to develop their mastery. With each Master Number, there is also a calling to become a leader, or a model of living awareness and reconciliation of the spiritual world with the material world.

Not all those with Master Numbers are sterling folk. Some have taken the path of least resistance, showing disregard for the humanistic and spiritual principles. It's not uncommon to find alcoholics, drug addicts, or vagrants among those who share Master Numbers. For some, the higher vibration is too much of a challenge, and, having free will, they'll choose not to rise to the challenge. Others choose to disregard their original contract to help advance the race this time around. These choices create karmic debt, which is no escape but merely a postponement. We devote an entire chapter to discussing karma and karmic debt next.

The Not-So-Common Master Numbers

The Master Numbers 11/2, 22/4, and 33/6 are the most common. Less frequently we see other influential doubles. We thought you might be curious about the other Master Numbers as well, so here is a summary of the other Master Numbers and their meanings.

44/8 Master of Material and Spiritual Power

The challenge for this Master Number is to develop self-control and perseverance through hard work while organizing time and talents. The test is to make the best spiritual use of the material abundance that comes naturally to this number.

55/1 Master of New Thought Forms

As nonconformists, people with this Master Number's challenge and test is to expand spiritual consciousness into new spiritual insights that come from new patterns of thought. These thought patterns include mental activities such as healing, astral projection, mental telepathy, clairvoyance, and prophecy.

66/3 Master of Cosmic Love

The challenge and test of this Master Number is for personal transformation through suffering and sacrifice so that one's energy and love can be available to all nations and all people for teaching and sharing of wisdom.

77/5 Master of Spiritual Energies

The challenge for this Master Number is to make soul contact through silence and to achieve inner wisdom and transmute it into cosmic love through personal application. The test may take them to the ends of the Earth, but understanding the mysteries is the goal. This number is required to make continual analysis and choice with full knowledge of living according to spiritual principles.

88/7 Master of Material Reform

This Master Number is a karmic vibration that brings the opportunity and challenge for a new awakening that aligns the use of power and authority with the spiritual universe to link and reform the affairs of the material world. The demand here is for self-mastery for control of the power of thought and emotion. This number is learning about the right use of material resources.

99/9 Master of Universal Compassion and Love

This Master Number assumes great burdens for humanity. With the ability to motivate others, this number is the leader of leaders and teacher of teachers. The challenge is to sacrifice itself and personal love, for the greater, altruistic form of universal love. It must serve with compassion and tolerance and bring the light of love to all relations. This number is a powerful vibration for transformation of itself and others. The challenge and achievement inherent in this number is for health and purity of mind and body so that he or she may give love purely as the most potent healing force of the universe.

Don't Miss Your Master Number

Any time you see a 1, 2, 3, 4, 5, 6, 7, 8, or 9 as one of your numbers, check to see if you have mistakenly reduced a Master Number. For all of you with Master Numbers, doing your work out there helping all of us move forward in the universal scheme of things, we say thank you.

The Least You Need to Know

◆ The Master Numbers are the numbers of those who have come to this life with special purposes.

◆ The 11/2 is the spiritual messenger.

◆ The 22/4 is the Master Builder.

◆ The 33/6 is the healer through love.

◆ Numbers 44/8, 55/1, 66/3, 77/5, 88/7, and 99/9 are also Master Numbers, but aren't seen very often.

Chapter **8**

The Karmic Numbers 10, 13, 14, 16, and 19

In This Chapter

- ◆ Karmic lessons and karmic debts
- ◆ The 10 represents rebirth and completion
- ◆ The 13 represents work to do
- ◆ The 14 represents temptation
- ◆ The 16 represents the abuse of love
- ◆ The 19 represents the abuse of power

Do you seem to pick the same kind of guy or girl over and over? Or do you never seem to learn to save money even though you're often on the brink of bankruptcy?

The last of the numbers we'll be defining for you are the Karmic Numbers. These numbers represent life lessons you haven't yet learned, and which you are destined to repeat over and over until you do learn them. Knowing what your Karmic Numbers are can help you understand why you have the patterns you do—and then help you break them as well.

What Is Karma?

Karma is the belief that one reaps what one sows. In esoteric literature, karma is thought of as the universal law of cause and effect, which is played out over many cycles of rebirth, and so the playing out of karma can take place over many lifetimes. Obviously, this belief system subscribes to the notion of reincarnation: The soul of an individual is reborn again and again into different physical bodies, and karma is worked out through each incarnation. There is both good karma and bad karma.

By the Numbers

Karma, whether good or bad, is a playing out of the universal cause and effect, which takes place over many lifetimes of the reincarnated soul.

Karma is a term used to designate thoughts or actions of the past which show up in the present and require retribution, or, to put it colloquially, "pay-back time." The idea is that all life is connected, and so what you do, say, and think will eventually come home to roost.

While the word karma comes from Eastern philosophy, we have a similar saying from Western culture: "What goes around, comes around" (which originates from the Christian teaching, "You reap what you sow"). Basically, both mean the same thing: That there is some labor of the soul that has to be righted. Karma is a belief that says, quite simply, each of us is responsible for our actions and thoughts.

Karmic Debt

First, we want to introduce you to the idea of karmic debt (not to be confused with karmic lessons). Karmic debt is a kind of a debt people accumulate, whether it's a debt of abuse of love or of power. Similarly, numbers 13, 14, 16, and 19 (*Karmic Debt Numbers*) are about selfishness in love, power, work, or freedom in past lives, and indicate a total disregard for others, for consequences, or moral concern. The idea is that if you were self-serving, lazy, cruel, irresponsible, or greedy in the past life, now, in this lifetime, is your chance to set the record straight.

By the Numbers

The **Karmic Debt Numbers**—13, 14, 16, and 19—represent past life abuses which must be addressed in this lifetime.

The number 10 is a different story. It is not a Karmic Debt Number, but it is a Karmic Number. We will explain the number 10 in a minute.

Each of the metaphysical sciences have a unique way of identifying your karmic responsibility. In the Tarot, for example, we see the karma story played out in the cards from the Major Arcana: Card numbers 10 through 19 are considered to be karmic cards. Note that the Karmic Debt Numbers are 13 (the Death card), 14 (the Temperance card), 16 (the Tower card), and 19 (the Sun card). The number 10 (the Wheel of Fortune card) is a good karma number. In astrology, your karmic pattern is told in the South and North Nodes.

While there are several kinds of karmic indicators in numerology, in this chapter we're concentrating on only two of them: karmic lessons and Karmic Debt Numbers.

Karmic Lessons

Karmic lessons are indicated by the numbers missing in your birth name. When a number and its vibration are absent from your birth name, it's an indication of an energy that you haven't experienced in a previous life, and so is a vibration missing in your energy field at birth. In this life, you are given the opportunity to experience this energy.

Whether the missing energy was purposely avoided in past lives, or whether circumstances prevented you from including this in your field of experience is open for debate among numerologists. Nonetheless, the missing number(s) will make a significant mark on your life this time. The experience of the missing number or vibration will show up in your life over and over again, until you finally master the energy of that number.

> **By the Numbers**
> **Karmic lessons** are things you must learn in this life because you haven't experienced or addressed them in past lives.

Your Karmic Lessons by the Numbers

Your Karmic Lesson Number or numbers identify the specific action, thought, or understanding you want to pay attention to in this lifetime. You can think of karmic lessons as a way to learn what's out of balance in your vibrational pattern or your makeup: Once you know what number or numbers are missing from your name, you'll know what to work on. It's kind of a neat system for bringing balance to your life. Of course, while you're doing the work, it won't seem so spiffy!

But just think, you might get it together this time! When we make the effort, life flows. And what if you have no missing numbers? Lucky you! This means you have all of the challenges—or none. You have complete free will in this lifetime. Bill Clinton has no missing numbers; you might say he has created new karma for himself. It's a lot of responsibility to have 0 karmic lessons.

Meeting Your Lessons—Not Again!

To find your Karmic Lesson Numbers, find the missing numbers in your birth name. Note that you can have more than one number missing, and in some cases, there might be as many as five numbers missing. The fact that you're missing numbers in your name means it will be necessary to use these numbers' specific energies to deal with the situations life brings you this time.

> **Numerology Rule:** To find your karmic lessons, look for the missing numbers in your birth name.

The important thing to remember is that missing numbers represent vibrations missing in your overall essence, a part of yourself you would want to reclaim so that you might be whole.

Finding the missing numbers in your birth name requires that you lay out your birth name, assign the appropriate numbers to the letters in your name, and then determine which numbers are missing. You're looking, of course, for numbers 1 through 9 only—no letter will have a number higher than that.

Merlin's Notes

Whether you have to start from scratch and develop the missing qualities indicated by the missing numbers in your name depends on whether any of these Karmic Lesson Numbers show up in your five Core Numbers. If you do have any of your Karmic Lesson Numbers in your Core Numbers, then the overall effect of the karmic lesson is lessened. This means that you have an innate ability to handle these karmic situations as they arise—unless, of course, you're expressing the negative qualities of the number. Then the karmic lessons will prove to be obstacles.

A Karmic Lesson for George W. Bush

First, let's write out George W. Bush's full birth name and each letter's number:

```
G e o r g e   W a l k e r   B u s h
7 5 6 9 7 5   5 1 3 2 5 9   2 3 1 8
```

In George W. Bush's case, we find one missing number: the 4. This means that in this lifetime, George W. is working on the lessons of the 4: learning to be practical, reliable, and disciplined without becoming controlling, rigid, or stubborn. Since issues of security are indicative of the karmic 4 lesson, setting boundaries and fear-based thinking will also be lessons for Mr. Bush in this lifetime. In addition, the missing 4 will bring lessons around money: practicality, careful planning, frugality, and accountability.

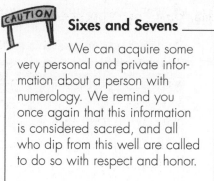

Sixes and Sevens

We can acquire some very personal and private information about a person with numerology. We remind you once again that this information is considered sacred, and all who dip from this well are called to do so with respect and honor.

How do you think he's doing? Of course, we can't know George W. Bush's personal, inner work, only what the media shows us—but we'd say he's working on these lessons every day, just as we're all addressing our own karmic issues.

Getting It Right This Time

Remember, these are karmic lessons, so it's implied that you'll be working on your karma with other people in the picture, very likely karmic souls from another life. There's speculation in metaphysical circles that 2000 presidential candidates Al Gore and George W. Bush were doing some kind of a karmic dance. Were they possibly opponents in a past life who betrayed each other? Or, perhaps, competitive warriors?

Karmic Debt Numbers

The second karmic aspect we look for in numerology is the presence of Karmic Debt Numbers in a Numerology Profile. These numbers will show up as your Birthday Number or one of your five Core Numbers. No matter where they show up, however, it's a signal that you're working with issues from the past. The number itself will tell the nature of the issue you are facing.

Finding Karmic Debt Numbers

As we described in Chapter 3, when you're figuring your birth name or birth date, you reduce first and then add across. It's precisely this process you'll want to check again to see if that final total included any Karmic Debt Numbers (13, 14, 16, or 19) before you reduced them to 4, 5, 7, or 1. Got it? Look to see if you have Karmic Debt Numbers hidden in your name or birth date, or if you have a karmic Birthday Number.

Remember, a karmic debt is owed because of something that occurred in a past life where there was misuse of power or love—and now it's payback time. In other words, some action you took in a past life is now requiring you to set matters right.

Merlin's Notes

Karmic Lesson Numbers and Karmic Debt Numbers are not the same thing! The numbers missing from your birth name represent the karmic lessons—experiences you didn't have or master previously. Karmic Debt Numbers, however, are found in your five Core Numbers, or your Birthday Number: Look for numbers 13, 14, 16, or 19. In both cases, you'll be called to consciously address them or unconsciously encounter them. When working with Karmic Debt Numbers remember that it is the double-digit number that tells if it is a Karmic Number or not.

Payback Time

Chances are you're already familiar with this concept, whether because the same people keep showing up, or the same situations keep repeating themselves. Either way, it's clear you're meant to be learning something.

The Karmic Debt Numbers 13, 14, 16, and 19, are defined like this: The number 1 in each number signifies selfish abuse of the number that follows. The number following the 1 indicates the arena in which the debt was created:

- The number 3 in 13: creativity energy and joyfulness turn into frivolity, superficiality, and using words to hurt others—that old sharp tongue routine.

- The number 4 in 14: discipline, hard work, accountability, and stability turn into rebelliousness, irresponsibility, and indulgence, all in an effort to escape what's required.

- The number 6 in 16: love, commitment, and responsibility have been forsaken.

- The number 9 in 19: wisdom, spiritual knowledge, and power have been used for personal gain.

Numerologists write these numbers as 13/4, 14/5, 16/7, and 19/1, because the reduced number or the root number tells where the debt lies and what the remedy is for releasing the debt. But we'll discuss each of these in depth in a few pages.

Easy as 1-2-3

As you reduce any number, watch for Karmic Numbers. By the same token, when you find the final reduced number is 1, 4, 5, or 7, look at its double-digit origin, which may reveal a Karmic Debt Number. When a 4 is a reduction of 13, a 5 of 14, a 7 of 16, and a 1 of 19, a Karmic Debt Number is present.

The Burdens of Karma

One thing to keep in mind with these Karmic Debt Numbers is that it's believed that anyone with one of these numbers has taken on an additional burden in order to learn the necessary lesson. This burden will offer opportunity to repay the karmic debt. These four Karmic Debt Numbers take on great significance if found in the numbers of the …

♦ Life Path.

♦ Destiny.

♦ Soul.

♦ Birthday.

Number 10: The Wheel of Fortune

Let's take a look at a Karmic Number that's not often listed with the Karmic Debt Numbers because it has a different sort of karma—good karma—and is not really about a debt yet to be paid.

The number 10 means karmic completion, and is the number of rebirth. It suggests that the karmic debt has been paid and now the person is free to begin again, free from past debt. Look to see if this number shows up in your Numerology Profile. Remember, a 10 might be reduced to a 1 (1 + 0), so be sure to look at your 1s to see if any of them might actually be a 10/1.

No matter where the 10 is found in a profile, it refers to a kind of destiny. This means you'll encounter situations and people in this lifetime that will allow you to complete the karma present in those situations. The 10 gives you the opportunity to stand on your own and to use all of the positive traits of numbers 1 through 9.

Merlin's Notes
In the Tarot deck, the number 10 is the Major Arcana's Wheel of Fortune, which signifies a new cycle of luck is about to begin. In numerology, the 10 signifies all of the energy of the number 1—a new beginning, a time of planting seeds and starting again. But it also carries the energy of the 0, which suggests there's something unknown about the new beginning, which promises potential. As you can see, the Karmic Number 10 identifies a period of new growth—debt free!

In addition, the 10 indicates that you're now called to use courage, independence, and leadership to bring about the destined rebirth. It's a time when your life needs to link up with the universal.

The 10 is considered a fortunate number and holds the promise of victory in difficult situations. This rebirth has been a long time coming. Go forth with courage!

Number 13: All Work and No Play

While the number 13 is usually associated with bad luck, when it appears as a Karmic Debt Number, it's not about luck. Instead, expect hard work in all areas of your life. In fact, the 13 is one of the most misunderstood numbers of all.

The purpose and goal of this vibration is to bring a spiritual consciousness into matters of how you express yourself (read this as: not being critical) and to develop discipline. For example, when you "tell it like it is," you will have to learn how to do it without being abusive or hurtful in your presentation. The other part of the 13/4 debt is to be disciplined in practical matters, such as not waffling on your commitment to lower your cholesterol. It's not just a matter of you being "good" this time, it's about understanding that what you abuse now will eventually require retribution, either in this lifetime or the next.

The 13 indicates that you are developing a spiritual conscience and beginning to see that all things are linked. With a 13/4 in your Core Numbers or as your Birthday Number, you'll have obstacles that have to be overcome again and again until the lesson is fully learned and the debt completed.

Merlin's Notes

In numerology, the 13 is written 13/4 because if you add the 1 to 3 you get the reduced number 4. It's the number 4 that tells of the hard work, and a person with this number will face tests of discipline, integrity, and hard work. The debt that's been incurred from the past is that of possible laziness, allowing others to carry your share of the work, choosing frivolousness and superficiality as opposed to serious endeavors, and abusing the power you have with words (as in being a gossip, manipulating others with words, or negativity).

At some point in their lives people with 13/4 will exhibit the negative side of the energy of the 4, which is …

◆ Being rigid.

◆ Needing to control.

- Being dogmatic.

- Blaming others for limitations they feel.

Living with a 13/4

In this lifetime, the 13/4 will need to accept limitations and restrictions and learn to work constructively through the hard work. If the 13/4 should resort to laziness or negativity (just as the last life), then the problems only magnify. The lesson is to just hang in there, gut it out, and do the hard work.

However, even if you were been born on the 13th of the month or have a 13/4 Life Path, do not despair. Many famous people (and companies, too) carry karmic 13 birthdays:

- Thomas Jefferson (born April 13)

- Paul Simon (born October 13)

- Whoopi Goldberg (born November 13)

- Harrison Ford (born July 13)

- Microsoft (March 13)

Even the queen mother of England (born 8-4-1900) has a 13/4 Life Path.

Wherever the 13 shows up, you'll be given the opportunity to succeed by focusing your energy. Usually there will be temptations in this life to take the shortcut or to go for the quick way out. But because this is the number of discipline and hard work, shortcuts are not recommended.

To have success with this number, you must maintain order in your life (the 4 rules order). This means you'll have to keep your appointments, follow through on commitments (yes, you'll have to be the chairman for next year's auction—you promised!), keep your house neat and tidy, and never procrastinate.

With a 13/4 in your profile, you're here to learn this lesson of focus and discipline. But there's good news, too: If you make a steady and consistent effort, you will find reward and success. The key is to concentrate and direct your energies.

What if you don't do it? What if you say, "Forget it, it's too much work"? Well, that's how you got into debt last time! If you choose (and we do mean choose, because we all have free will) to blow off the required focus or discipline, then know that you'll be doing this routine over and over again, in this life or in the next. Remember, this is karma: Debts have to be paid!

Number 14/5: The Temptations

The Karmic Number 14/5 involves past lifetimes where freedom was abused. The debt is to relearn the value of freedom and the discipline required to earn this freedom. In a past life, those with this number will have found freedom for themselves at the expense of others, and that's where the debt comes in: There was some kind of irresponsibility and lack of accountability in the past.

Now it's your time to set things right. The 14/5 is the number of the rebellious free spirit who knows no limits to his or her desire for adventure, risk, and escape.

As you may remember from our discussion in Chapter 5, the number 5 is also the number of sex and sensuality. So it follows that someone with the Karmic Number 14/5 will take huge risks in the name of sexual or lustful pursuits. At the end of this chapter, we'll let you in on someone with a 14 in her profile who's had her 15—make that 14—minutes of fame.

Sixes and Sevens

In numerology, 14/5 is written as such because it reduces to a 5 (1 + 4 = 5). It's that 5 that calls for change in behavior. Those with a 14 karmic debt (whether as your Life Path, Birthday, Soul, or Destiny Number) will have to spend this lifetime adjusting to ever-changing circumstances and unexpected events.

The number 14/5 in one of the five Core Numbers indicates that you'll tend to exhibit the negative traits of the number 5—jumping from relationship to relationship or job to job, for example—with no sense of accomplishment or goal firmly in mind. There's also a tendency to pleasure oneself through physical sensations, be it food, sugar, sex, drugs, or anything else that meets your fancy.

The 14/5 represents the craving for something new and exciting rather than doing the boring, hard work of discipline or building something by sticking to it and seeing it through (all traits of the 4). Eventually, once you see that this is not the road to freedom, you'll take a more constructive path.

Getting to the Root of the 14/5

Let's look more closely at the root of this number, the 5. The 5, remember, is the number of change and freedom. That means that when the 5 shows up as the Karmic Debt Number 14, the issues will be about having to rein in any escape mechanism tendencies such as drug abuse, alcohol or food addictions, or overindulgence in sensual pleasures. We're talking about past uses of these addictive behaviors as ways to escape (because you crave freedom) from the task at hand.

Now, in this life, you're required to become moderate—not with disregard for tomorrow, but using temperance today. It should come as no surprise that the number 14 card in the Tarot deck is the Major Arcana's Temperance.

The key to this Karmic Debt Number is commitment, something that a person with this number will have found hard to do in previous lives. This means commitments will be hard to make until you've learned the lessons of the 4 in the 14, which says, "You've got to have order to your life to maintain clarity and focus."

Sixes and Sevens

No matter how bad it gets, you can't succeed with 14/5 if you try to gain freedom using destructive methods. This will bring loss, sickness, and, in extreme cases, even death.

The 4 also suggests that mental and emotional stability are called for in order to hold a steady course as your life presents you with endless changes. You must commit to order and structure in your life, and being flexible and adaptable are at the very core of this struggle.

What else can you expect when the 14/5 is one of your Core Numbers?

◆ If you have 14 as your Soul Number, you might expect emotional upsets and delays.

◆ If 14 is your Destiny Number, then you'll possibly learn these lessons through setbacks, disappointments, and reversal of fortune, or, at the very least, be presented with life circumstances where you have to make commitments, stick to your goals, and weather the many ups and downs that come with this number.

◆ If 14 is the number of your Life Path, you are here to learn to let go, resist the temptations of indulgence, allow things to change, and steer a steady course.

Success lies in being able to establish a belief system for yourself that allows you to magnetically draw what you need to maintain order to your life and do all things in moderation. You cannot become fixed, rigid, or controlling under this number, for the law of change will demand that you roll with the punches.

These Karmic Debt Numbers require that we go back and do it over. This time, however, it helps if you know what the lesson is you're trying to learn and be aware of the name of the challenge you're facing. You can do it—just remember this universal law.

Sixes and Sevens

Remember, the number 14/5 suggests that in some way the person with this number has misused, avoided, or misunderstood freedom in past lives, and now in this life he or she is meant to bring the freedom issue into balance. The 14/5 is basically going to have to learn to love the Universal Law of Change, because it will be a constant in his or her life.

> **Universal Law:** You're never given more than you can handle.

The thing to remember with the number 14/5 is *temperance* in all things.

Number 16/7: The Abuse of Love

The karmic debt of the 16/7 arises from past involvement in illicit love affairs that caused suffering to others: In some manner, love was abused. Quite simply, the 16/7 indicates a failure in the past to act responsibly in matters of love, or to act responsibly where you had made a commitment.

As with all Karmic Debt Numbers, the 1 in this number indicates self-centeredness. The 6 in 16 suggests a lack of responsibility and distortion of loving feelings. Past abuses might have stemmed from a lack of integrity with regard to the feelings of others, including the notorious "love affair."

CAUTION

Sixes and Sevens

Permanent relations are hard to maintain with the 16/7. Remember, the 7 doesn't like to bother with having to relate to others if it appears difficult. People with this number meet with substantial difficulties until they can devote themselves to selfless, loving ways. With this number, it's not unusual (the 7 *is* unusual) to find that sudden, strange circumstances bring loss of friends and relationship.

We write this Karmic Debt Number as 16/7, for it's the reduced number 7 where the remedy is for releasing the debt. Until they learn to act otherwise, people with a 16/7 number usually exhibit the of negative traits of the number 7:

- Indifference
- Analytical aloofness
- Withdrawal
- Difficult to approach
- More concern for his or her own needs of privacy than for the feelings of others
- Intellectualizing emotions

The influence of the number 7 is that it's the number of the mystic—one who goes within and relies on his or her higher guidance. The 7 requires that a person look to the source of all things as the guiding inspiration. It's only then that a 16/7 person is no longer torn by the outer world. Similarly, the goal with the 16/7 is to link the personal spirit with the universal spirit. Only then does the person's path become tranquil and the repetitive cycle of destruction and re-birth stop.

The Karmic Debt Number 16/7 is also the Major Arcana Tower card in the Tarot deck, which symbolizes destruction of the old and a rebirth of the new. When unforeseen and sudden events tear down what was established, this card-carrying 16/7 is forced to rebuild yet again. The Tower indicates an awakening to the spiritual truths that lie deep within, and the essence of the number 16/7 carries the same message: A spiritual rebirth is required to release the karmic debt. What happens is that there's usually some kind of fall from the "tower" in one's life.

Destruction and rebirth are two interwoven themes of the number 16/7. Life presents the 16/7 with challenges that will humble the individual, and it's precisely this humility that's the key to future success. An individual with this number will learn to follow a course of higher consciousness that will come from the continual cycle of destruction and rebirth that dominates the 16/7's life.

The number 16/7 indicates that the person with this number has a tendency to use his or her highly intuitive and refined intellect to look down on others. The 16/7 won't be a stranger to alienation and loneliness in this lifetime.

You Can Run, but You Can't Hide

The number 16/7 is the path of personal development and spiritual growth. It presents the opportunity to transform, but it demands a kind of tearing down and rebuilding of one's life to do so. The key word for the number 16/7 is "awaken": The person must awaken to the higher principles of living life on Earth. This number will take you down the path that "rises out of the ashes," reconstructing your life on higher ground.

Remember, this number has great significance if you have a 16/7 Life Path, Soul, Destiny, or Birthday Number. If that's the case, your life will be a series of events that bring you to the bottom, only to rise up again, to fall again, and so on. The pattern will continue until you finally grasp the notion that you must honor the spiritual, higher nature of all things, and that now you must rebuild your life on those principles. That's the debt, the story, and the release of the number 16/7.

Number 19/1: Abuse of Power—and You Knew Better

The last of the Karmic Debt Numbers is 19/1. With this number, you might think that the gods are not happy, because the 19/1 is a travesty against all that is sacred, compassionate, and spiritually correct. You can be sure there's been some kind of abuse of power when the 19/1 is present: The karmic debt of this number stems from past abuses of acting in a completely self-centered manner, blind to everything except self-fulfillment of one's own desires. The basis of this number is learning to stand on your own and the proper use of power.

The reduced number 1 of this number indicates that a 19/1 person will often exhibit the negative traits of this number, until the lessons have been understood. The negative traits are …

Easy as 1-2-3

The central lesson of the 19/1 is that while learning to stand on your own, you must also learn to seek support, assistance, and understanding from others. Of all the Karmic Debt Numbers, this one will learn in spades that "no man is an island."

- Selfishness.
- Intimidation.
- Dependence.
- Failing to stand up for oneself.
- Stubbornly resisting help from others.
- Egotism.
- Laziness.
- Aggression.

Merlin's Notes

The 19 is made up of the numbers 1 and 9 and when reduced is written as 19/1. The 1 here indicates past life selfishness, and the 9 represents attainment, particularly of spiritual knowledge. In the old days, 9 was considered the number of God, and in current times, it's still thought to be the number of high cosmic consciousness. The point is, in a past life this person has had the power of the universe at hand. Even with this knowledge and power, the person chose to pursue selfish ends, disregarding the rights of individuals or cosmic consequences.

When you have this number, don't be surprised to find that throughout your life you're forced to stand up for yourself or, worse, are left to stand alone. Difficulties faced in this life will teach independence, consideration of others, and having to assert yourself rather than hang back and appear weak. Because of a tendency to stubbornly resist help from others, you may find yourself in a self-imposed prison.

Paying a Little Karmic Debt

It is thought that the karmic debt of the 19/1 developed from the abuse of power in the past. In some manner, there was a life of selfishness—disregard of anyone else. The 19/1 indicates a past life where you had a position of power in some way, and in that position you chose to live life for yourself instead of for the good of all. In some way, you used your power to gain favors and status or satisfy personal desires.

In this life, 19/1s repeat these patterns until situation after situation arise that call for them to rectify these past abuses. Usually, the 19/1 person will be immersed in his or her own concerns and have difficulty becoming aware of the needs of others. The 19/1s are often surprised by others' negative reactions because they're so used to thinking of themselves that when they finally do see themselves through the eyes of others, they're surprised and often confused. The 19/1s just can't seem to see themselves realistically in relation to others.

Easy as 1-2-3

As with all the Karmic Debt Numbers, if the 19/1 shows up as your Destiny, Soul, Life Path, or Birthday Number, you're dealing with a karmic debt.

Sometimes 19/1s may appear unable to act on their own. Unhappy with their dependence, yearning to be independent, but unable to take action, they find solace in blaming others or the environment for their own inability to stand on their own two feet.

Success comes from looking past your own needs to the needs of others. When you work toward independence, resisting the urge to be dependent or feel weak, you'll begin to pay off this karmic debt. Of course, just being aware that you have a karmic debt will help you see a path for changing your life and changing your ways. After all, the 1 always promises a new beginning.

A Little Karma in Real Life

One of the most famous and prominent figures in the free world has a 19/1 Karmic Debt Number. Former President William Jefferson Clinton was born August 19, 1946, so his Birthday Number is the Karmic Debt Number 19. His fame, aside from having been president of the United States, we think in part originates from this Karmic Debt Number.

There is more to this karmic story. Bill Clinton was named William Jefferson Blythe at birth, and with this original name his Numerology Profile shows he has no Karmic Debt Numbers and 0 karmic lessons. However, he changed his name to William Jefferson Clinton and with this name he brought the energy of a Karmic Debt Soul Number 14/5 and gained a karmic lesson of 6.

So we begin to question, "Was Clinton's infamous affair with Monica Lewinsky (who happens to have a 14/5 Life Path) a karmic drama played out on the world stage so that Mr. Clinton might begin to pay off his karmic debt?" Were these self-serving interludes and Clinton's seeming inability to ask for help a repeat of a very old pattern?

One wonders, with the intensity of this story, if in fact Lewinsky, possibly independent counsel Kenneth Starr, and of course, Hillary Clinton, might also be karmic figures reappearing to help Mr. Clinton face his karmic lessons. You don't have to have a Karmic Debt Number to play a role in someone else's karmic story. Perhaps, as might be the case with Hillary who has no Karmic Debt Numbers, you are here to help someone else make right karmic wrongs from previous lifetimes.

Looking at his current name energy, William Jefferson Clinton, we note that he has the missing number 6. So part of his karmic journey involves the lessons of the 6: commitment, love, marriage (and divorce), responsibility, and duty. Of course, Hillary Clinton plays a role in Bill's karmic life. She just happens to have a 2 karmic lesson because there is no 2 in her birth name, Hillary Diane Rodham. The 2 karmic lesson is about reversing past life patterns of criticism, sensitivity to others, and cooperation within partnerships. With Bill's 6 and Hillary's 2 karmic lesson there is no doubt their karma, and the roles they play for each other in working out their karma, will be around issues of marriage and relationship. Metaphysically speaking, we might say that Monica was helping both Bill and Hillary work out their karmic lessons.

Let's take a look at this karmic play and see what comes up.

In this remarkable story of sex, scandal, abuse of power, and search-and-destroy mentality, we find it an equally remarkable coincidence that each of these players has a Karmic Debt Number influencing his or her life. Or is it a coincidence?

Let's start with Monica Lewinsky. She has a 14/5 Life Path Number, which indicates indulgences of the flesh and a karmic debt to be repaid.

Next, there's Kenneth Starr. He has a 16/7 Life Path Number, which represents an abuse of love stemming from an illicit love affair in a past life, and now, in this life, the karmic debt is to be paid (by having to wade through someone else's affair?).

Last, there's former president Bill Clinton. He has a 19/1 Birthday Number, among others, which indicates an abuse of power for personal gain. He, too, is required to pay his karmic debt.

It's believed that those with Karmic Debt Numbers have taken on an additional burden in order to learn their lessons and pay off their debts. We'd say some kind of extra burden is at work in the lives of Monica Lewinsky, Ken Starr, and Bill Clinton.

When a karmic opera such as this one is played out on a world stage, there is a resonant note for all of us. Because the story is played out in a public forum, we are allowed to see the lessons and mistakes of these people and recognize them in ourselves as well. This in turn calls forth our higher consciousness and reminds us to live with honesty and integrity in all of our dealings and decisions—avoiding further karmic debt.

The Least You Need to Know

◆ Karmic lessons and karmic debts are not the same thing.

◆ Karmic lessons are numbers missing in your name.

◆ Karmic debts are past abuses of love, power, work, or freedom.

◆ The Karmic Debt Numbers are 13, 14, 16, and 19. The Karmic Number 10 gives you added resources to address your karmic debts.

◆ Karmic debts mean extra burdens, but also profound opportunities to grow and evolve in this lifetime.

Part 3

Your Five Core Numbers: Life Path, Destiny, Soul, Personality, and Maturity

You've learned the meaning of each number. Now it's time to learn how to calculate your own numbers and take a closer look at what each of your special Core Numbers means. We'll begin, simply, with your Life Path Number, which is calculated from the numbers of your birth date, then we'll move on to your Destiny, Soul, and Personality Numbers to examine what your name reveals about you. Finally we'll look at the Maturity Number, which is calculated from both your birth date and your birth name—it reveals the true essence of who you are.

Chapter 9

Your Life Path Number

In This Chapter

- Your Life Path Number shows you which road to follow
- Your birth date reveals your Life Path Number
- Your Life Path Number is the first of your five Core Numbers
- Finding your own special opportunities

While you can change your name, your birth date will never change (unless your parents got it wrong in the first place). Your birth date is all yours, so it has a tale to tell about you alone. Your birth date—that is, the month, day, and year you were born—is very important in numerology. It's called your Life Path.

Here's one place to look for your career and vocational options—because your Life Path Number shows your inherent talents and abilities. If you feel as if you're on the wrong path, you'll want to read what your Life Path Number has to say—it's part of your Numerology Profile. Even if you know you're on the right path, your Life Path Number can help you understand why.

Learning to Read Your Life Path Map

Some numerologists consider the *Life Path Number* to be the most important number in your Numerology Profile. That's because it tells of the road you'll follow throughout your life, and it's the number that indicates your talents and abilities that will help you along that road. These very skills are the ones that will help you reach your destiny—but we'll get to that in Chapter 10, where we explore your Destiny Number and discuss your overall purpose in life.

By the Numbers

Your **Life Path Number** reveals your inherent talents and abilities and shows the best career path for you to follow to use those skills. It's calculated by adding together all the numbers of your birth date.

Finding Your Life Path Number

You find your Life Path Number by adding together the month, day, and year you were born. To illustrate, let's look at how to figure this number for one of the legendary golf pros of all time, Eldrick "Tiger" Woods.

Tiger Woods's birth date is December 30, 1975, so we lay it out like this:

Tiger Woods's Life Path Number Calculation: December 30, 1975

Month of birth = December = 12 (1 + 2 = 3), so December = 3.

Day of birth = 30 (3 + 0 = 3), so the birthday is reduced to the number 3.

Year of birth = 1975 (1 + 9 + 7 + 5) = 22/4.

Life Path Number (add the reduced month, day, and year) = 3 (month) + 3 (day) + 4 (year: reduce 22 here to its root number) = 10; = 1 + 0 = **1.**

Tiger Woods's Life Path = A number **1** Life Path.

We reduce the 10 by adding the two digits together to get one number, which in this case, is a 1. This means that Tiger Woods has a Life Path of 1, and his path is one of independence, excellence in his field, and leadership. To find out more about the meaning of a 1 Life Path Number, read the definition for the number 1 Life Path that follows in this chapter.

Finding Your Life Path

Now, it's your turn. Let's review the steps for calculating the Life Path Number. Let's use the birth date July 22, 1985:

1. Find the number of the month. July, for example, is a 7 month. We've provided a chart for you to find the number for your birth month.

Months and Their Numbers

Month	Number	Month	Number
January	1	July	7
February	2	August	8
March	3	September	9
April	4	October	(10) or 1
May	5	November	(11) or 2
June	6	December	(12) or 3

2. If your birth day is a double-digit number, reduce it to a single number. If it's 22, for example, 22 is reduced to 2 + 2 = 4. (As you learned in looking at Tiger Woods's Life Path calculation, this is one time you reduce your Master Numbers.) Once you've reduced the day to a single number, add that number to the birth month number. So, for our example of July 22, we add 7 + 4, for the month and day.

3. Now, add the year numbers together to get a single number. For our example, we need to reduce the year 1985:

   1985 = 1 + 9 + 8 + 5 = 23

   Then, add 23 together: 2 + 3 = 5

Easy as 1-2-3

Calculate your Life Path Number by adding together all the digits of your birth date, including the month, day, and year.

4. Next, add all three reduced numbers for the month, day, and year, together.

   7 + 4 + 5 = 16

5. Last, reduce the final double-digit numbers. The final single-digit number is the Life Path Number.

   16 = 1 + 6 = a **7** Life Path

   (In this case, because the final double-digit sum is 16, a Karmic Number, this 16/7 represents a karmic Life Path.)

Easy as 1-2-3

You must always include all four digits for calculating the birth year. For example, some people refer to their year of birth as '42 or '59. You have to use all of the digits of a birth year. Don't just add 5 + 9 for the year 1959. Add 1 + 9 + 5 + 9.

At the end of this book we have a Numerology Profile for you to calculate all of your five Core Numbers, or those of your friends, family, and co-workers. Who knows what insights you'll find?

> **Numerology Rule:** To find your Life Path Number, use this formula, adding the reduced, or root, numbers for each: *Birth month + day of birth + year of birth = Life Path Number.*

Following Your Own Life Path

Are you ready to calculate your own Life Path Number? We've provided spaces below for you to do just that.

1. Birth month number (reduce to a single digit, if necessary): __2__

2. Birth day number (reduce to a single digit, if necessary): __6__

3. Add birth year numbers together and reduce their double-digit sum to a single-digit result: __7__

4. Add together your results for the birth month, day, and year reduced numbers (you may get a double-digit result): __15__

5. Reduce the final double-digit sum of your calculation (if the double digit is a Master Number, write down both numbers with a slash between) to get your Life Path Number (don't forget to look for Karmic Debt Numbers, too): __15/6__

What's your Life Path Number? Write it in the star!

What Your Life Path Number Reveals About You

As one of the major tools for navigating the road of life, your Life Path Number tells what you can depend upon to find success in the world. This is your own unique path in life. While others may share the same number, it's the combination of all of your numbers that will help to clarify how to proceed down this path of life. Yours can be a path of thorns and roses, or even the Yellow Brick Road, but this road, with all its bends and turns, will present you with opportunities to use your innate talents. Your single-digit Life Path Number shows the spiritual demand that is made upon you as you explore the road, one foot in front of the other!

The Life Path Number can be used to indicate positive vocational/career options. It tells of areas in which you will excel, even without training. You may draw upon this energy as a source of power all throughout your life because it's what you have—inherent skills and talents. Your Life Path Number works hand in glove with your Destiny Number, which we'll be discussing in Chapter 10. Your Life Path Number sets the tone for your life experience!

Sixes and Sevens

If you get a Master Number as the double-digit sum of your Life Path calculation, write the number as 11/2, 22/4, or 33/6. A Master Number Life Path has special significance! Also, be on the lookout for the Karmic Number 10 and Karmic Debt Numbers 13, 14, 16, and 19.

Life Path Number 1

Your path will take you down the road to independence, and you'll learn the benefits of independence, standing on your own two feet, standing alone when necessary, and becoming a strong individual. Once these traits have been honed, you move to the next level of the 1 Life Path—leadership.

Sixes and Sevens

People with 1 Life Path Numbers sometimes work for a variety of companies in different positions, all the while feeling vaguely unsatisfied but not quite knowing why. When these same people strike out on their own, however, they suddenly come into their own. That's because a 1 Life Path likes to lead, and taking orders from anyone else just won't work for them. Bruce Springsteen has a Life Path of 19/1, which as a karmic Life Path adds further energy to his challenge and opportunity to seek leadership through the support of others.

You're a born leader and your path in life will present you with many opportunities to demonstrate your ability. You have executive and administrative capability, although it may be latent in developing. Your strong pioneering spirit, courage, and determination will serve you well along this road.

What are your career/vocation options if you've got a 1 Life Path? Any situation that allows you to utilize your unique ideas and pioneer spirit will be a career bonanza. Look for a field where you can use your quick mental agility, such as business, health, the entertainment industry, government, or even a bookstore.

For an in-depth discussion of the number 1, the number of independence, be sure to review Chapter 4, which is all about the numbers 1, 2, and 3. Remember to double-check your number 1 Life Path Number; is it possibly a 10/1 or 19/1? If so, you will want to turn to Chapter 8 on the Karmic Numbers for a look at this Karmic Debt Number.

Life Path Number 2

Your path will lead you to seek balance and harmony in all that you do, and you'll learn the benefits of cooperation and compromise, as well as patience and peacekeeping. Once you've incorporated these traits, you'll move on to the next phase of the 2 Life Path Number—drawing others together.

You were born to relate to others—and to make certain that others relate well to each other as well. If there's a fight brewing, a 2 Life Path person will do everything in his or her power to head it off at the pass. If you have a 2 Life Path, you'll need to remember not to ignore yourself and your own needs while you're making sure everyone else is cooperating.

People with 2 Life Paths are extremely sensitive—so sensitive, they need to be careful not to become the doormats of the world. Still, these born peacemakers work best behind the scenes and can do much for the rest of the world in the process.

What are the career/vocation options for a 2 Life Path? You're best at jobs that allow you to mediate, negotiate, take care of details, be in a supportive role, or gather facts. If you find a job that will allow you to utilize your sensitivity, you'll be using one of your greatest assets, and will naturally thrive.

For an in-depth discussion of the number 2, the number of balance and harmony, be sure to review Chapter 4.

Life Path Number 3

Your path will entice you to be both creative and spontaneous, to live your life with joy and imagination. You'll learn the benefits of optimism and enthusiasm, and how to express your emotions and your exuberance. Once you've mastered these concepts, you'll move on to the next phase of the 3 Life Path—inspiring others.

You're a born communicator, and your wit and lightheartedness will help others see the joy in any situation. People with 3 Life Path Numbers are artistic, creative, and articulate, painting pictures with their words that spark the imagination and understanding of those lucky enough to hear them. With a 3 Life Path, your inspiration to others lies in the way you speak and frame things, as well as your creative approach to life, because bringing a creative flair to each task is your trademark.

Easy as 1-2-3

Your 3 Life Path means you'll walk a path of using your creative gifts (especially the gift of words) to say your truth, which is a compilation of your creative ideas, optimistic view of the world, and unique ability to articulate your own discoveries. Having learned to speak from your heart (a hard-won lesson), as a 3 Life Path person, you'll inspire everyone around you.

What are your career/vocation options? With your 3 Life Path Number, you'll do well in anything artistic, be it writing, speaking, designing, illustrating, dancing, or acting. You'd make an excellent cheerleading coach (or any kind of a coach), where you can encourage and motivate. You'll also do well in any job where feeling and emotions are valued financially, such as public relations or customer service.

For an in-depth discussion of the number 3, the number of joyous self-expression, be sure to review Chapter 4.

Life Path Number 4

Your path will lead you to work hard and systematically. You'll learn the benefits of loyalty and following the rules, all the while remaining loyal and steadfast. With a 4 Life Path Number, reliability is the name of the game, and once you've learned this lesson, you'll move on to the next phase—building for the long term.

You're a born builder because security is a big deal to you. Others look to people with 4 Life Path Numbers to manage, control, and make sure that everything falls into place. If you've got a 4 Life Path, you know how important it is to not rock the boat, to move slowly and steadily, and to make sure everything is nailed down and in the right place.

Merlin's Notes

Stick in the mud. All work and no play. The aphorisms that come to mind for a 4 Life Path aren't always the fun ones—especially if a 3 or 5 is the one talking. It's important to remember, however, that someone's got to make sure the road is paved smoothly so those who aren't paying much attention won't encounter unexpected speed bumps. People with 4 Life Path Numbers may be conservative, yes, but they're also the ones who plan ahead—so the rest of us can have a good time.

Here are your career/vocation options: With your 4 Life Path Number, you'd be a natural as a systems or construction manager, or as a bookkeeper or accountant. You'll also do well at any work where organization is valued, be it administration, education, or business, or where documents or a product requires careful management. Your success will be found in work where systems need to be established and maintained, or where you're working to build things of lasting value.

For an in-depth discussion of the number 4, the number of stability, be sure to review Chapter 5 on the numbers 4, 5, and 6. Remember to check carefully to see if your 4 is really a 13/4, as is that of Martin Luther King, Jr., a karmic Life Path. In that case, you'll want to review Chapter 8 for a more detailed look at the number 13/4.

Life Path Number 5

You'll have many forks along your path, and you'll welcome each change as a new opportunity with unknown results. With a 5 Life Path Number change is the name of the game, and once you've learned this lesson, you'll move on to the next phase—championing freedom.

You're a born progressive—forward thinking, liberal, super-resourceful—and because of those things, you're also a dilettante, equally good at many different trades. If you've got a 5 Life Path Number, you're probably good at sales, marketing, or promotion of any kind, and believe in freedom in all things—whether it's of speech, movement, or moving to the beat of different drummer.

The career/vocation options best for you are working with the public, new-trend companies, communications, advertising, publicity, or sales—any kind of

CAUTION

Sixes and Sevens

Other numbers may find those with 5 Life Path Numbers hard to pin down, or worse, unreliable. It's important to remember that 5 Life Path people aren't really unreliable—they just have short attention spans. As soon as something new catches their interest, they'll forget all about what they were interested in a moment before and rush off to explore the new.

work, in other words, that calls for energizing power rather than routine. You'll also do well as a detective—or as a writer of mysteries! Travel is well suited to you.

For an in-depth discussion of the number 5, the number of adaptation and travel, be sure to review Chapter 5. You will want to double-check for the possible Karmic Number 14/5. If you discover your 5 Life Path Number is really a 14/5, turn to Chapter 8 for a more detailed look at this karmic Life Path.

Life Path Number 6

Your path will lead you to live responsibly at home and at work, to achieve balance between giving and receiving. The path of those with a 6 Life Path Number is one of service and aid, and once you've learned this lesson, you'll move on to the next phase—achieving balance between giving and receiving.

You're a born counselor—sympathetic and caring—and you love everyone from the smallest child to the oldest, scroungiest mutt. Others seek out those with 6 Life Path Numbers for advice and wise counsel, and you may well do these things professionally, as a counselor, advisor, teacher, or therapist. With a 6 Life Path, you'll learn to achieve balance between your domestic life and work life, and will seek to beautify the world all around you.

Easy as 1-2-3

Look for the teacher who helps as much as he or she teaches to embody the meaning of a 6 Life Path. Who is the teacher who made a difference in *your* life?

What are your career/vocation options with a 6 Life Path Number? You'll love any job in the service industry, where you can make life more comfortable, easy, and luxurious for others. Medicine, retail sales in furniture, remodeling, decorating, beauty products, family-run or home-based business, training animals, teaching, and counseling are all naturals for you. Of course, it goes without saying, gardening and any related businesses are your path, too—the garden path!

For an in-depth discussion of the number 6, the number of nurturing and family, be sure to review Chapter 5.

Life Path Number 7

Your path will lead you to study, test, and analyze everything, because with a 7 Life Path Number, you can't be satisfied with anything at face value. You'll seek the meaning of existence, and will always be exploring mysteries and the unexplainable to find meaning for your life. Once you've learned this lesson, you'll move on to the next phase—sharing your wisdom of the spirit with others.

You're a born seeker—spiritual, philosophical, scientific, or technological—and, because of your solitary exploration of the unknown, others will seek you out for your wisdom. People with 7 Life Path Numbers are often teachers or professors, or ones who specialize, and this specialization makes them the obvious source others turn to for answers.

Easy as 1-2-3

The 7 is both private and secretive, which can have a higher or lower vibrational expression as a Life Path. Saddam Hussein (4-28-1937) and Slobodan Milosevic (8-20-1941) both have a 7 Life Path, as do two heads of state, Vladimir Putin (10-7-1952) and Queen Elizabeth II (4-21-1926).

With your 7 Life Path Number your career/vocation options could include computer programmer, technological specialist, or working at any job that calls for analysis, deductive reasoning, scientific knowledge, or technical ability. Bookkeeping and accounting may hold interest as well, although we traditionally would find the 4 or the 2 doing these jobs. Any field where you'll be allowed to study, contemplate, or commune with the higher forces, such as law or teaching, or being a spiritual leader, monk, or nun, will also suit a 7 Life Path well.

For an in-depth discussion of the number 7, the number of research, wisdom, and solitude, be sure to review Chapter 6 on the numbers 7, 8, and 9. Remember to double-check to see if your 7 Life Path Number is really a 16/7. If so, you will want to turn to Chapter 8 for a more detailed look at this Karmic Number.

Life Path Number 8

Your path will lead you to work out the difference between money and the real value of life. It's a path of mastery, where you must learn what to do with your natural power and authority. This is not an easy path (it's not considered a lucky one), but once you've learned its lesson, you'll move on to the next phase—being in charge.

You're a born boss, born to be involved in business or a large organization. People with 8 Life Path Numbers know that it's lonely at the top, but their power and authority come naturally to them, so others naturally look to them when a decision needs to be made. The reward for you, if you've got an 8 Life Path Number, won't necessarily be financial but may come in terms of accomplishment and yes, legacy.

What are your career/vocation options? Any field where you can be in charge, be it C.E.O., C.F.O., chief administrator, financial advisor, real estate broker, or even athletic director, is perfect for the 8 Life Path—the person with authority. You'd make an excellent choice for a judge, head of hospital, president of the bank—or any job where you can utilize your superior skill of good judgment. In addition, all business-related work is ideal for this number, because the business environment is a place where you can organize and run things with authority.

For an in-depth discussion of the number 8, the number of materialism and achievement, be sure to review Chapter 6.

Life Path Number 9

Your path will lead you to understand the interconnectedness of all things. It's a path of universal love that learns compassion and tolerance. Once you've learned this lesson, you'll move on to the next phase—tolerance for all, and the importance of caring for each other.

You're a born healer, and your healing may take the form of writing, composing, painting, or sculpting—reaching others by truly connecting to them, in other words. With a 9 Life Path Number, you'll also be learning how to let go, to surrender the self for the greater good. People with 9 Life Path Numbers truly understand the Golden Rule—and don't understand why others don't.

> **Merlin's Notes**
>
> She was born powerful. Martha Stewart is clearly a take-charge person, and organization, business skill, and achievement are her signatures. Martha is the undisputed boss of her multiple enterprises so it should come as no surprise to find she has an 8 Life Path. We'd say power has been her strength and her potential downfall. Is Martha learning the part about good judgment on this 8 Life Path?

> **Easy as 1-2-3**
>
> Former U.S. presidents Jimmy Carter and Abraham Lincoln, Shirley MacLaine, Mohandas Gandhi, and Cher all share a 9 Life Path. A mix of the arts and humanitarian service, all these people have all been concerned with the broader view of life.

The career/vocation options suited to the 9 Life Path include international business, the arts (including the stage, literature, filmmaking, dance, sculpting, pottery, painting, writing, and arts administration), education, and health. In addition, any line of work that is designed to help, heal, or humanize belongs to this humanitarian number.

For an in-depth discussion of the number 9, the number of completion, be sure to review Chapter 6.

Master Life Paths

People with Master Number Life Path Numbers have unique and special paths to follow. When we get to these numbers, remember, we've moved to a higher plane (the one envisioned by the 9), that inspires, manifests, and truly gives. For an in-depth discussion of the potent potential of Master Numbers be sure to review Chapter 7.

Master Life Path Number 11/2

With this Life Path, much is expected of you. Your special path will lead you to illuminate humankind spiritually and inspirationally. You'll sometimes operate at the level of the 2 to attract meaningful associations so that others will find you accessible. Once you've mastered your lessons, you'll move on to the next phase—becoming an inspirational leader.

You're a born charismatic leader, magnetic and electric. The platform is meant for you, and you'll find yourself in the spotlight. Your mission is to be someone others look to for truth and illumination (sometimes spiritual in nature), and the truer you are to universal principles, the happier and more successful you will be on your path.

> **Merlin's Notes**
>
> Interestingly, both Bill Clinton and Al Gore share an 11/2 Life Path, along with Colin Powell. These magnetic leaders have spent a good deal of their lives involved with conflict resolution in one form or another, often playing the role of peacemaker.

The career/vocation options for 11/2 include any field that allows you to be the teacher, diplomat, or speaker, because these will utilize your considerable talents at uplifting and inspiring others. This is also the number of the airplane pilot, film director, television personality, charismatic spiritual leader, or philosopher, and you'll do well in any venue that puts you in the spotlight, deals with media or aviation, or allows you to work with large groups.

> **Easy as 1-2-3**
>
> While not saints, it is undisputed that both Bill Gates and Paul Allen built their dream and brought cyberspace into our homes, making the Age of Information a reality. Both have a 22/4 Life Path, as do the 14th Dalai Lama, Barnes & Noble.com, Garrison Keillor, and Oprah Winfrey. Master Builders they are indeed.

Master Life Path Number 22/4

Your special path will lead you to turn dreams into reality. The 22/4 Life Path Number, like the 4, is seen as one who builds and manifests—but with a larger purpose. Once you've mastered this lesson, you'll move on to the next phase—becoming a Master Builder.

You're a born creator of activities that benefit all of humanity, and you're viewed by others as extraordinary. You back up your word with deeds, again and again, and others know that your word is as good as gold—or even better. With a 22/4 Life Path Number, good management principles are behind what you do—and what you do is for the lasting good of humankind. Lucky us!

With a 22/4 your career/vocation options could include a planner, organizer, statesman, diplomat, ambassador, president, business executive for a large organization (national or international), or promoter, because you'll thrive in any line of work that allows you to utilize your considerable talent for organizing, being efficient, and applying your practical know-how to build a dream. You command respect and are seen as an expert in your field. You're destined to be a leader who is both practical and inspirational and who understands that success comes not only from cooperation, but from being of service to humankind.

Master Life Path Number 33/6

Using our reduce-first method for calculating your Life Path number, the 33/6 Master Number is not possible. The highest calculation for a Life Path Number would be $9 + 9 + 9 = 27$.

A Few Pointers for the Road

You're bound to have the same Life Path Number as someone else, but that doesn't mean you'll have the same experience. The difference will be found in the month, day, or year each of you were born. For example, if you have an 8 Life Path Number and your birth date is January 5, 1964, you'll be influenced on your path by a 1 (January), a 5 (birth day), and a 2 ($1 + 9 + 6 + 4 = 20 = 2$). Your friend (also with an 8 Life Path Number) may have been born February 27, 1959. He or she will be influenced by a 2 (February), a 9 (birth day is 27, which is $2 + 7 = 9$), and a 6 ($1 + 9 + 5 + 9 = 24 = 6$). That's just one example of how two people with the same Life Path Number will nonetheless have quite different journeys.

You will have lessons along your path, which are spelled out in the month, day, and year you were born. The lessons of the first 28 years of your life are found in the month you were born. For example, for the person born 1-5-1964, the first set of lessons will be about the number 1—learning to become independent. The second set of lessons for age 28 until age 56 are found in the day you were born. So, using our example, the lesson is in the 5, meaning that this person will be learning the lessons of the 5—to accept change. The last set of lessons from age 56 on—that is, for the rest of your life—are found in the year you were born. Once again using our example of 1964 ($1 + 9 + 6 + 4$), the number 2 tells us that he or she will be learning about the number 2—how to live in relationship with others. To sum it up …

- The first 28 years resonate to the energy of your birth month number.

- From age 28 to 56, your lessons resonate to the energy of your Birthday Number.

- After age 56, you learn the lessons that resonate to the energy of your birth year number.

Our 8 Life Path person with a birth date of January 5, 1964, will find his or her path influenced by the lessons of the 1, 5, and 2—just to spice things up!

The Life Path Number works with the Destiny Number, or, to put it another way, the date of your birth works with the name you were born with. We'll be discussing your Destiny Number, the second of the five Core Numbers, in the next chapter.

The Least You Need to Know

- Your Life Path Number is calculated from the month, day, and year of your birth.

- Your Life Path Number shows you your potential paths.

- Knowing your Life Path Number helps you live your life to your fullest potential.

- It's easy to calculate your Life Path Number and find your own special path.

- You may have a Master Life Path or a karmic Life Path.

Your Destiny Number

In This Chapter

◆ Your birth name spells your destiny

◆ Your Destiny Number reveals your purpose

◆ Use the full name as it appears on your birth certificate

◆ Your Destiny Number tells what you must live up to

Your name has meaning—it tells what you'll be most successful doing in this lifetime. Your name tells of the your best direction and major accomplishment, and points the way to living a fulfilled life. In other words, your name is your destiny.

The second of the five Core Numbers, your Destiny Number describes your purpose in life—your mission—and indicates what you must do, for it's your destined direction. Both opportunities and inner resources will come from this Core Number, and describes the area of your life that must be explored, developed, and embraced for your soul to grow to its full potential in this lifetime, and for you to be whole.

Are you ready to meet your destiny? If so, prepare to meet your Destiny Number.

What's Destined for You?

If someone told you that by living a particular way, success was all but guaranteed, wouldn't you want to know how to do it? Now you can, because it's as simple as knowing your *Destiny Number*. Your name is a vibrational energy pattern that spells out the direction for your life, and from your birth name, we can find your Destiny Number. In this way, the numbers of your birth name will give you your own personal cosmic code for success.

By the Numbers

Another of the five Core Numbers, your **Destiny Number** is calculated from the letters in your name—your birth name.

Not only does each letter of your name have meaning, each part of your name does as well, and a numerologist will see the individual talents and unique characteristics present in the name you were given at birth. Your name reveals a picture of the real you. Much in the same way you view an astrology birth chart, you could think of your birth name number as a blueprint and a cosmic code of your potential.

There's a wealth of information in your birth name:

Sixes and Sevens

Numerologists debate whether our names are accidental, or if our parents subconsciously chose our names from an urge born out of a divine plan for our lives. We believe you were not given your name by mistake. Misspellings and last-minute changes of your name are merely part of the fine-tuning process that takes place to give us the vibration that is truly us.

- ◆ Your first name gives you the most personal lessons.

- ◆ Your middle name reveals hidden abilities that you don't necessarily like.

- ◆ Your last name tells of the characteristics you've inherited from your family.

What the Destiny Number Reveals About You

As one of your five Core Numbers, the Destiny Number is one of the most important numbers in your Numerology Profile. Your Destiny Number reveals ...

- ◆ Your life's purpose.

- ◆ What you must live up to in this lifetime.

- ◆ Your opportunities for success.

- ◆ Your spiritual mission.

- ◆ The qualities and manner of living you must develop.

♦ What you are destined for.

♦ The target you are aiming for in life.

♦ The kind of work that would be a natural expression for your Life Path. (For an in-depth discussion of the Life Path Number, see Chapter 9.)

Finding Your Destiny Number

The Destiny Number is calculated from the name you were given at birth. Traditionally, whatever name appears on your birth certificate is the name that's used to figure the Destiny Number (as well as the Soul Number, which we'll be discussing in Chapter 11 and the Personality Number, which we'll be discussing in Chapter 12). That's your *full* name—even if you never use it, hate it, or have spent years hiding this name from everyone!

Let's go over the most often-asked questions about finding the Destiny Number.

What Name Should I Use?

The name on your birth certificate is generally considered the name to use when figuring your Numerology Profile and specifically in calculating your Destiny Number. If you don't have a copy of your birth certificate, you may need to contact the office of vital statistics in the county where you were born. Records are also kept in hospitals, although these do not always contain your name as it appears on your birth certificate. Once you've gotten your birth certificate in front of you, keep a few of these tips and warnings in mind!

♦ **Clerical errors.** Yep, mistakes are made on birth certificates. There are a lot of stories about somebody goofing up the name on the birth certificate. What to do? Here's the key: If your parents accepted the name goof or allowed the misspelling of the name (or wrong name!) to remain on your birth certificate, then the name on the birth certificate, *with errors*, is used to find your Destiny Number.

♦ **Spelling errors.** It's always fun to check your birth certificate when you do this calculation because you may find out that the way *you* spell your name is not what's actually on your birth certificate. You may be someone other than who you thought you were!

Merlin's Notes

Here's an example of a spelling error on a birth certificate. Kay has a client who for 50 years spelled her name Carol. Then one fall, when she went to visit her elderly mother, she happened to mention that she was doing her Numerology Profile. When she showed her mother the calculations for her name, her mother said, "That's not how you spell your name. It's spelled with an 'e.'" When Carol went to the county courthouse and got a copy of her birth certificate, sure enough, there was her name in bold print: **Carole.**

The spelling of your name does make a difference when figuring the numbers for your Numerology Profile (especially the Destiny Number, Soul Number, and Personality Number), so check carefully before you calculate your name numbers.

Adopted Names

If you were adopted and given a new name, and you know your original birth name, use the original name to figure your profile. You will, however, also want to figure a second profile for your adopted name. In this type of situation, no doubt you will have grown up living out the adopted name, and therefore you'll want to figure a Numerology Profile for your adopted name to see what energy has been influencing your life with this name. Then, with the two profiles, you can piece together the story of who you really are.

If you have an adopted name and a different one on your birth certificate, consider the original name the true essence of who you are, and the adopted name the energy you drew to you to work within this lifetime. Give the most credence to the original birth name profile as your true essence, but consider the impact your adopted name has had on your life and all of your decisions. Think of it this way: You've been given multiple opportunities to achieve your destiny.

If you don't know your original name and have only the adopted name to work with, you won't be working with your true essence, but rather with the influences of your adopted name. If this is the case, your Destiny Number will indicate the type of energy and influence your adopted name has brought you in this life.

It's not unusual for adopted children (as well as adults) to feel unclear about who they are. Numerologists would argue that without knowledge of their original names (which also include the inherited traits of the family name) these individuals may be experiencing a "lost self." If at all possible, learn your original name and integrate it into your current life. In that way, you'll reclaim yourself and your original energy pattern.

I Never Use That Name

Even if you've never used your original name (everyone's always called you "Kathy" instead of "Kathryn," or "Ted" instead of "Edward," for example), it's still the essential data that holds your cosmic code and blueprint for life. When figuring your Numerology Profile, it's best to use your original name.

I Had That Name for Only a Few Days

Some babies were given a name at birth and then their parents had a revelation and changed the baby's name within a day or two after their birth. If this is the case, the change must have been made official, that is, the birth certificate must have been changed shortly after birth. This new name is then considered your original name. You will, however, find it interesting to work out the "would-be" name and see what energy that name would have carried for you.

Sacred Names

Many people have been given a name at confirmation. Or perhaps a spiritual teacher or guru gave you a sacred name. Such names are not used to figure your Numerology Profile and your Destiny Number. Like the earlier example, however, it will be valuable for you to figure this sacred name to see what new energy you've brought into your life. Figure this type of name separately from your original birth name. It represents a new influence in your life.

More Than Three Names

If you were given more than one middle name or last name, use all of the names you were given at birth. Some people from other cultures and many modern American families use a series of hyphenated or family names, and an individual may end up with up to six names. Whatever is on your birth certificate is the name to use. Remember to check the spelling—every letter counts!

Junior, Senior, or The Third

If you have a name that has Jr. or Sr., or uses Roman numerals after your name, disregard all of these addenda. For example, if your name is William Gates III we figure your numbers only on William Gates. We drop the "III" when figuring the Numerology Profile. And yes, this means you will have the same name (and numbers) as your father or mother, or grandmother or grandfather. You will walk a different path however, as indicated by your birth date.

Easy as 1-2-3

Did you know that Bill Gates has three names, William Henry Gates? More important, all three names are 7s, which could also be read as an abundance of nerdiness, or as a truly analytical, private guy.

Married Names

Married names are not figured in the Destiny Number or the basic Numerology Profile. Note that we will discuss married names and their significance in Chapter 20.

In case we haven't made it clear, you will use only your original birth name to do these Destiny Number calculations!

Calculating the Destiny Number

To figure your Destiny Number, you will lay out your full name and assign the appropriate number to each letter. We've included a handy little number and letter chart here for your use.

Letters and Their Numbers

1	2	3	4	5	6	7	8	9
A	B	C	D	E	F	G	H	I
J	K	L	M	N	O	P	Q	R
S	T	U	V	W	X	Y	Z	

To illustrate how to figure the Destiny Number, former U. S. president Bill Clinton once again offers a unique example. First, he was born with another name: Clinton's birth name was William Jefferson Blythe, and the name we know him by—William Jefferson Clinton—is his adopted name. In keeping with what we've said about figuring the Destiny Number, we must use Clinton's original birth name.

First, figure each name separately, assigning a number to each letter.

```
W I L L I A M        J E F F E R S O N        B L Y T H E
5 9 3 3 9 1 4        1 5 6 6 5 9 1 6 5        2 3 7 2 8 5
34 (3 + 4) = 7       44 (4 + 4) = 8           27 (2 + 7) = 9
```

Next, add the reduced total of each name, first, middle, and last. In this case, we'll add:

7 + 8 + 9 = **24**

Because 24 isn't a Master Number, we reduce it to a single root number:

2 + 4 = **6**

So, when we look at Bill Clinton's original birth name, we see he has a 6 Destiny Number. This is the destiny of one who's to be an advisor, such as a lawyer or counselor of some type, who's sympathetic and understanding, and a hard worker who consciously wants to please and avoid conflict. Sound like anyone we all know? Perhaps more than we realize … Hillary Clinton's Destiny Number also is 6.

Now, even though President Clinton doesn't use this name, it is his original energy pattern that is present throughout his life. Just for fun, however, let's see what Destiny Number his adopted and current name gives him.

W I L L I A M	J E F F E R S O N	C L I N T O N
5 9 3 3 9 1 4	1 5 6 6 5 9 1 6 5	3 3 9 5 2 6 5
34 (3 + 4) = 7	44 (4 + 4) = 8	33 (3 + 3) = 6
7 + 8 + 6 = 21; 2 + 1 = **3**		

When we add together the reduced number for each name (7 + 8 + 6), we find that Bill Clinton has a 21 total, which is reduced to a 3. This means that Clinton's new Destiny Number is a 3, the number of the optimist who has a gift with words. (And that's an understatement!) With a 3 Destiny Number, success will be found whenever he can use his words to influence people: public speaking and appearances, writing, or just communicating with folks. You can read more about the number 3 Destiny Number later in this chapter.

Easy as 1-2-3

Remember to match your letters (and numbers) carefully. One letter left out or assigned the incorrect number will make a big difference in your final result.

Because Bill Clinton's adopted name brings him a 3 Destiny, it's considered to be additional energy that's added to the original Destiny Number 6. Since both of these numbers are emotional numbers, we can expect that an additional element of feeling is added to the way Clinton responds to situations and people.

As you looked at our calculations for Bill Clinton, you might have noticed that the name "Jefferson" is a 44, a Master Number, and that "Clinton" is a 33, another Master Number. This means that by changing his last name to William Jefferson Clinton, he has brought a second Master Number onboard. This name is a more powerful energy than his original name, and the vibration of this new name will bring more demands and challenges, and of course, more potential.

Another interesting element for President Clinton comes from the current name he is called by the public, Bill Clinton. When we look at the name "Bill," it equals an 8 and "Clinton" equals a 6, and together we have 14/5, a Karmic Number! Read Chapter 8 for a full discussion of the 14/5.

A 6 Destiny Number means service to the world will direct both personal and career choices. This is the number of the humanitarian and since is both Hillary and Bill's destiny, it tells that they have a similar mission in life that significantly bonds them as they address the concerns of humanity, especially care of the elderly, the welfare of children, and the nurturing of community and environment. With the same 6 Destiny Number, you can trust that family will rate high on their list of priorities. It's just that Bill has that 14/5 energy to work around. Issues of truth, justice, idealism, and responsibility are the lessons of this pair's destiny path.

When we consider Bill's Destiny pattern 6 along with Clinton's 11/2 Life Path (Remember? We figured it in the previous chapter.), it becomes apparent that this is a person with a very powerful and challenging energy. He will be constantly called on to be responsible, to rise to the higher vibration, to change addictive patterns, and will be required to follow the dictates of spiritual principles that are inherent in his Master Numbers. Hillary's Life Path happens to be a 3, so her life journey will be to express her truth and learn to play, while moving toward her 6 Destiny of responsibility to family, home, and service to humanity.

As you can see, using the system of numerology to uncover the mysteries in a name reveals fascinating and useful information about a person. Who would you like to know more about? You can figure anybody's numbers if you know his or her full name at birth.

Numerology Rule: Use the following formula to find your Destiny Number, using your original name at birth: *First name + second name + third name = Destiny Number.*

Some of us have only two names at birth, some have as many as six. The number of names doesn't matter, only that all of the names you use to find your Destiny are the ones (with the correct spelling) that were given to you at birth.

Reviewing the Steps for Finding Your Destiny Number

Let's review the steps for finding your Destiny Number:

1. Write out your birth name and assign the appropriate numbers to each letter.

2. Add each name separately; you may get a double-digit sum.

3. Reduce any double-digit sums you get for each name to its single-digit root number, but take note of any double-digit sums that equal a Master Number or Karmic Number.

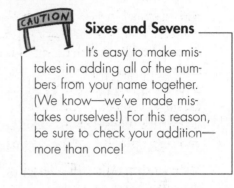

Sixes and Sevens

It's easy to make mistakes in adding all of the numbers from your name together. (We know—we've made mistakes ourselves!) For this reason, be sure to check your addition—more than once!

4. Add the reduced numbers for your first, second, and third names together.

5. Reduce the double-digit sum to a single root number—unless your result is a Master Number (11, 22, or 33).

You can read the meaning of your Destiny Number in the section that follows. You might also want to look to see if your Destiny Number is a Karmic Number: 10, 13, 14, 16, or 19. (See Chapter 8 for an in-depth discussion of Karmic Numbers.)

Easy as 1-2-3

Watch for Master Numbers when figuring the Destiny Number!

Here are the two main things to remember when calculating your Destiny Number:

◆ Add each name separately. Each name in your original birth name has meaning, and it's important to preserve the number of each name.

◆ Once you know each name's number, reduce each name to a single-digit number. Then, when adding these single numbers across your name, you will get a clear idea whether a Master Number is present or not.

At the back of this book, we've provided a form for you to figure your whole Numerology Profile, but here's a space for you to figure your Destiny Number. Be sure to take your time—and figure each of your names separately before adding them together.

1. Write out your birth name and assign the appropriate numbers to each letter.

   First name: _Kent_

   Numbers: _2 5 5 2_

   Second name: _Joseph_

   Numbers: _1 6 1 5 7 8_

   Third name: _Campazzie_

   Numbers: _3 1 4 7 1 8 8 9 5_

2. Add each name separately and enter the sum in the correct space. In this calculation, reduce any Master Number sum to its single root number.

   First name: _14_ **Second name:** _28_ **Third name:** _46_ = 88

3. Reduce the total of each name to a single-digit base number.

   First name: _5_ **Second Name:** _1_ **Third name:** _1_

4. Add the single-digit root numbers from each name together and reduce the double-digit total to a single number. If your double-digit result is a Master Number, record its full energy (11/2, 22/4, or 33/6).

   First name _5_ + **Second Name** _1_ + **Third name** _1_ = _7_ Destiny Number

What's your Destiny Number? Write it in the star!

A Walk Through the Destiny Numbers

As we told you at the beginning of this chapter, your Destiny Number uses your birth name to find the vibrational energy pattern that spells out the direction for your life.

You can think of your Destiny Number as your own personal cosmic code for success. Have you calculated your Destiny Number? If so, then you're ready to find out what your Destiny Number reveals about you.

Number 1 Destiny

With a number 1 Destiny Number, your mission in life is to develop the self and to become a leader. Your purpose in life is to be courageous, take the initiative, be independent, original, innovative, and take charge—all to develop your sense of self, your will, and your determination.

The field of opportunity is where you learn to stand alone, think for yourself, and individualize your character. New ideas, new things, and unique activities give great opportunity for you to move toward your destiny. Even if you lack confidence or are holding back, you are still called to embrace your destiny.

You are destined for leadership. Be it and teach it.

Number 2 Destiny

With a number 2 Destiny Number, your mission in life is to create harmony. Your purpose is to find balance, seek cooperation, and be the patient team player—all to develop your sense of relationship.

The field of opportunity is where you learn gentleness and to be emotionally receptive, and being both adaptable and persuasive will give you greater opportunity to move toward your destiny. Even if you are passive or indecisive, you are still called to embrace your destiny.

You're destined for peacemaking. Go forth and share it.

Number 3 Destiny

With a number 3 Destiny Number, your mission in life is to energize and inspire. Your purpose is to encourage others through your optimism and enthusiasm, using your inspirational creativity to make certain that joy is spread to others.

The field of opportunity is where you learn to express your emotions through your gift of words, and being both lighthearted and witty will give you greater opportunity to move toward your destiny. Even if you are moody or critical, you are still called to embrace your destiny.

You're destined for expressing yourself. Speak up, be positive, and encourage.

Number 4 Destiny

With a number 4 Destiny Number, your mission in life is to build something of lasting value. Your purpose is to be practical and do the hard work, all the while keeping order and convention so that security is assured.

The field of opportunity is where you learn to express traditional values, and being steadfast and stable will give you great opportunity to move toward your destiny. Even if you are stubborn or suspicious, you are still called to embrace your destiny.

You're destined for managing and organizing. Create the foundation and build on it.

Number 5 Destiny

With a number 5 Destiny Number, your mission in life is to adapt, change, and progress. Your purpose is to embrace freedom and follow your curiosity wherever it leads you, all the while using your resources and magnetism to keep you moving.

The field of opportunity is where you learn to express your resourcefulness, and being a free spirit will give you great opportunity to move toward your destiny. Even if you are restless or discontented, you are still called to embrace your destiny.

You're destined for liberation and freedom. Move forward and embrace change.

Number 6 Destiny

With a number 6 Destiny Number, your mission in life is to serve. Your purpose is to nurture family and loved ones, all the while using your love of beauty and community to create harmony in life around you.

The field of opportunity is where you learn to express generosity, and giving comfort to others will give you great opportunity to move toward your destiny. Even if you are codependent or tend to martyr yourself, you are still called to embrace your destiny.

You're destined for nurturing and beautifying. Love with balance.

Number 7 Destiny

With a number 7 Destiny Number, your mission in life is to analyze and seek out. Your purpose is to dig deeply and contemplate all you encounter, using your skill at research and your perfectionist ways to find inner wisdom.

The field of opportunity is where you learn to express your keen observation, and being thoughtful and discerning will give you great opportunity to move toward your destiny. Even if you are cynical or skeptical, you are still called to embrace your destiny.

You're destined for educating the world. Specialize and teach your wisdom.

Number 8 Destiny

With a number 8 Destiny Number, your mission in life is to gain mastery of self. Your purpose is to achieve and succeed, using your skill at business and organization.

The field of opportunity is where you learn to express your authenticity and discover your own power, and being visionary will give you great opportunity to move toward your destiny. Even if you are ruthless or overbearing, you are still called to embrace your destiny.

You're destined for material success. Get out there and be the masterful leader you were born to be.

Number 9 Destiny

With a number 9 Destiny Number, your mission in life is to perfect and love unconditionally. Your purpose is to strive for universal brotherhood (and sisterhood), using your selflessness, sensitivity, and healing art.

The field of opportunity is where you learn to transform and heal, and being tolerant and forgiving will give you great opportunity to move toward your destiny. Even if you are gullible or intolerant, you are still called to embrace your destiny.

You're destined for broad horizons. Reach out and help someone.

Master Number 11/2 Destiny

With a Master Number 11/2 Destiny Number, your special mission in life is to inspire and uplift. As an old soul, your purpose is to live up to and accept your destiny and to recognize that your creativity and intuitive skills are to be used for the good of humanity. Your job is to reform, elevate, and transform others' lives.

The field of opportunity is where you learn to express your teaching ability and rise to the challenge, even though it feels like a test. Stepping into the spotlight will give you great opportunity to move toward your destiny. Even if you are impatient, critical, or high-strung, you are still called to embrace your destiny.

You're destined for inspired leadership. Live up to the demands of spiritual living and you shall be the leader you were born to be.

Master Number 22/4 Destiny

With a Master Number 22/4 Destiny Number, your mission in life is to build the dream and execute plans and projects that will benefit humankind. Your purpose is to make things happen by working in a practical way in the material world using spiritual principles.

The field of opportunity is where you learn to express your efficiency and competence, and being grounded and true to your nature, which is to never give up, will give you great opportunity to move toward your destiny. Even if you are stubborn— or unable to accept the faults of others, you are still called to embrace your destiny.

You're destined to be a Master Builder. Bring spiritual law into the material world.

Master Number 33/6 Destiny

With a Master Number 33/6 Destiny Number, your mission in life is to joyfully bring forth the higher consciousness of love. Your purpose is to serve with a loving heart and to teach that life can be fun and full of love.

The field of opportunity is where you learn to accentuate what the 3 represents—joy, light, and creativity—and being a leader in the arena of loving service will give you great opportunity to move toward your destiny. Even if you are overly emotional or demoralized by the poverty you see, you are still called to embrace your destiny.

You are destined to be a master healer. Love and teach love to heal us all.

A Final Note About the Destiny Number

There is no such thing as a bad number. All of the numbers will lead to success and point the way to your purpose in life. So don't be wishing you had somebody else's number—yours is perfect for you.

It takes many years and many cycles for us to become aware of how this Destiny Number fits us. When we don't like a number, it's often because we're working on the negative aspects of the number and don't like that part of ourselves. Hang in there—there's great learning to be realized from these numbers.

The Least You Need to Know

♦ Your Destiny Number shows unique abilities for your life, and reveals what you are destined for.

♦ Your Destiny Number is determined using your full original name as it appears on your birth certificate.

♦ Your first name tells what your personal lessons are, your second name reveal hidden abilities, and your third name gives insights in inherited traits.

♦ Your destiny is what you are aiming for, and only *you* can determine how your Destiny Number informs your course in life.

Chapter 11

Your Soul Number

In This Chapter

- ◆ Finding your heart's desire
- ◆ Add up the vowels
- ◆ A word about the "y"
- ◆ Finding your inner vibration

Hermann Hesse once said, "Each man's life represents a road toward himself … and we can understand one another; but each of us is able to interpret himself to himself alone." Not only is this our challenge, it's at the very heart of what the Soul Number is all about.

As the third of your five Core Numbers, your Soul Number is placed at the center—nestled between your Life Path, Destiny, Personality, and Maturity Core Numbers—and is one of the most important numbers to be figured and analyzed in a Numerology Profile. The Soul Number is the number of your heart's desire.

The Heart of the Matter

Your secret thoughts and wishes are told in the *Soul Number* in numerology. This is the number that says, in your heart of hearts, what you long for, and what is your dearest desire.

Advancing the Soul

In spiritual numerology, it's believed that in each lifetime, your soul has needs and is here to learn and grow. The thinking goes something like this: As an incoming soul, you determined what it is that you need to advance up the spiral path of soul evolution; so you chose a name that would give you the correct energy pattern that would attract certain opportunities to you so you could learn and grow.

By the Numbers

Your **Soul Number** tells what you long for and what your soul wants to express in this lifetime.

It's not uncommon for people to learn of their Soul Number and find that it reveals their heart's desire, because the Soul Number merely confirms what you already know—deep inside. You know what's in your heart; your Soul Number will give you a framework and language for understanding more about yourself at the very core.

What Your Soul Number Tells You

Among the things your Soul Number can help you discover are …

- ◆ Your heart's desire.
- ◆ Your true motivation.
- ◆ What you long for.
- ◆ What you love best.
- ◆ What you need to feed your soul.
- ◆ What you value most.

The Song of the Soul

There are times when the Soul Number will dominate your energy, subordinating all other traits and characteristics, even those of the Life Path and Destiny Numbers. When this happens, your Soul Number will call you to people and places that resonate with your own energy. For example, it will cause you to feel you must travel to a certain spot or be with certain people, or it may cause you to call out in anguish. These times are asking you to hear the song of the soul, and are times to nurture and feed the very core of your being.

Merlin's Notes

Each of us is born a free soul, and the times we live in seem to require that we own up to what pulses at the very core of our being. It seems we're being asked to live honestly, both with consciousness and intention, which require that we know our inner selves. As we each come to understand that inner peace, living without stress, and living healthily, demand that we know who we are, knowing our Soul Numbers is enormously useful in helping us to achieve these goals.

There will be other times when this soul energy will lie dormant, possibly repressed by the current situation. This, then, is the soul energy suppressed. Eventually, however, the energy of the soul will awaken and become active with a startling force, changing the direction of your life. The energy of the Soul Number tells of an inner longing, a yearning for expression. You have a choice, as we all do, to begin to listen to the song of your soul.

Sixes and Sevens

It should come as no surprise that those times when your soul seems to call out to you in anguish have been referred to as the "dark night of the soul."

Your soul may long to be happy, to live in the energy of enthusiasm and optimism, or it may long to be away from everyone, to experience silence, and to read and study mystical teachings. Or your soul may long to travel, to be thrilled with the newness of the unfamiliar, or to heal people. Whatever your soul desires, you have a tool at your fingertips for finding out what it is that speaks to your heart. All you need is your name at birth.

Using Soul Number Information

People use what their Soul Number reveals in a variety of areas, including …

◆ Career decisions.

◆ Love relationships.

◆ Family relations.

◆ Any time they want to understand why they feel a certain way.

In business partnerships, understanding the Soul Numbers of your partners (as well as their Destiny Numbers) can help you understand what will motivate them and be the driving force behind all of their actions. That's because the Soul Number gives you insight into the inner nature of the person you're dealing with, regardless of how he or she appears on the outside. The Soul Number gives a more complete picture of who a person is, so it rounds out your perceptions.

Easy as 1-2-3

If you think about it, the vowel sound of any name or word is the soft inner vibration, and the same can be said of the Soul Number—it's the soft inner vibration of our being.

Even though a person may change with the times, the person will never change his or her heart's desire or Soul Number, because somewhere in the background, a person's soul is quietly participating (or not participating, as the case may be) in the affairs of the day. A soul doesn't change—it merely expresses its energy over and over through a multitude of experiences to make itself known to us. Understanding your Soul Number can bring deep insight and greater happiness.

Finding Your Soul Number

Just like the Destiny Number, the Soul Number is calculated from your full name at birth—the original name on your birth certificate. Unlike the Destiny Number, the Soul Number is found from the vowels of your name, which are the letters a, e, i, o, u, and sometimes y. We'll be taking a close look at that "sometimes y" in the following section.

> **Numerology Rule:** To find your Soul Number, all you have to do is add together the vowels in your full name.

The Y as a Vowel

When figuring the Soul Number, eventually you'll run into a name with a "y" in it, or sometimes more than one "y." What to do? Here's the trick: The "y" is considered a vowel (not a consonant) when it's the only vowel sound in the syllable. Sound complicated? It's not really.

In the name "Lynn" it's easy to see that the only vowel sound is the "y," making the sound "*ih*," as in "sit." Similarly, in the name "Yvonne," the "y" sound is "*ee*" as in "ether," so this "y" is counted as a vowel, too. To figure the Soul Number for Yvonne, you write it like this:

```
   7      6         5
Y  V  O  N  N  E
```

When we add Yvonne's vowel numbers, 7 + 6 + 5, together, we get a total of 18, which reduced becomes a 9. This means that the name Yvonne has a Soul Number 9.

Let's look at the name "Pythagoras" for another example:

```
     7    1  8  1
P  YTH AG OR AS
```

Add the vowel numbers together:

7 + 1 + 8 + 1 = 17; (1 + 7) = **8**

Then reduce the final number. When we add 1 + 7 together, we get an 8. So, Pythagoras, the father of the science of names and numbers (and supposedly the father of mathematics), has a Soul Number 8, which is the number of self-mastery, leadership, and achievement.

Now let's look at an example where the "y" is not figured as a vowel sound:

| **Vowel numbers** | | | | | 9 | | 5 | |
| B | R | I | T | N | E | Y |

Why didn't we figure in the "y" in the name "Britney"? Because the "y" in this case is silent—the "e" produces the vowel sound. Because of this, we don't use the "y" to figure the Soul Number for Britney.

Here's a list of names in which the "y" is considered a vowel. Use this list when in doubt about how to calculate a Soul Number when a name includes a "y":

Names with "Y" as a Vowel		
Amy	Lucy	Sissy
Betsy	Lynda	Stacy
Bobby	Lynn	Sybil
Dusty	Nysa	Tammy
Elly	Patty	Tansy
Henry	Ruby	Toby
Jaclyn	Rusty	Tybalt
Judy	Ryan	Welby

continues

continued

Names with "Y" as a Vowel		
Kyla	Sally	Wyatt
Lily	Sandy	Wyn

Easy as 1-2-3

Use the "y" to figure the Soul Number in names in which the "y" is the only vowel sound in the syllable.

When Not to Use the Y as a Vowel

The "y" isn't always used as a vowel in calculating the Soul Number. For instance, in the name "May," the vowel sound is "*a*"—the "y" doesn't have a sound itself; it is silent, unpronounced. We figure May like this:

Vowel numbers   1

                        M   **A**   Y

Because the "a" is the only vowel pronounced, the "y" will be figured as a consonant. We'll be discussing consonants in Chapter 12, when we figure the Personality Number.

Here's a list of names for which you shouldn't use the "y" as a vowel:

Names with "Y" as a Consonant			
Bentley	Jayme	Maya	Sayer
Chearneyi	Jayne	Ramsey	Tanya
Day	Kay	Ray	Yale
Jay	May	Ridley	Yates

The "y" is not the only vowel sound in the syllable (or it's used as a consonant) in all of the above names and should *not* be used as a vowel to calculate the Soul Number.

Calculating the Soul Number

To illustrate the calculation of the Soul Number, let's look at the Soul Number of J. K. Rowling, author of the *Harry Potter* books. Remember, you must use your full, original birth name to find your Soul Number, so we're using Joanne Kathleen Rowling here.

Vowel numbers

```
      6 1      5          1       5 5          6     9
    J O A N N E      K A T H L E E N      R O W L I N G
```

Add the vowel numbers for the names Joanne Kathleen Rowling separately, and reduce to a single-digit root number:

First name vowels   6 1   5 = 12; (1 + 2) = 3

```
    J O A N N E
```

Second name vowels   1   5 5 = 11; (1 + 1) = 2

```
    K A T H L E E N
```

Third name vowels   6   9 = 15; (1 + 5) = 6

```
    R O W L I N G
```

The vowels in "Joanne" equal 12 or 3; the vowels in "Kathleen" equal 11 reduced to 2 (Note, in her middle name, the Master Number isn't a final total, so we reduce it to the 2); and the vowels in "Rowling" equal 15 or 6.

Last, add these three reduced numbers together. When we add 3 + 2 + 6, we find the Soul Number 11/2, a Master Number. This means that, according to her Soul Number, J. K. Rowling (as she is called) is the creative, insightful soul who uses the mystical, magical, or spiritual to uplift and inspire others. If the sum of the vowels of any of *your* names produces a Master Number, reduce the number within the name (as we did for J. K.'s middle name) but not at the end of your calculation as a final total.

Easy as 1-2-3

When figuring a name, the numbers for the vowels go *above* the name and the numbers for the consonants go *below* the name.

Sixes and Sevens

The Soul Number and the Destiny Number work together for wholeness so that you can achieve success and happiness in this lifetime. Neither of these two Core Numbers can ignore the other, for you may succeed in the outer world and still feel unfulfilled if you haven't honored what it is that you truly long for.

Synchronizing the Soul Number and the Destiny Number

Where your Destiny Number is outer, your Soul Number is inner. This means that your Soul Number works with your Destiny Number: It tells of the inner path to follow, while the Destiny Number tells of the outer direction to pursue.

Your Soul Number and You

At the back of the book we've provided a complete Numerology Profile form for you to figure your five Core Numbers and more. But here's a space for you to calculate your Soul Number:

1. Write out your full birth name. Next, above your name, write down the number equivalent for each vowel. (Be sure to determine if any "y"s in your name are vowels or consonants.)

   Vowel numbers: _Kent Joseph Campazzu_

   Birth name: _____

2. Add the numbers of the vowels for each name; reduce each to a single digit.

   Total first name vowel numbers: _5_____

   Total second name vowel numbers: _2_____

   Total third name vowel numbers: _7_____

3. Add together the numbers for your names and reduce them to one single-digit root number (unless your result is a Master Number). If your result is a Master Number, write the Master Number and its root number, separated by a slash (as we did for J. K. Rowling).

   _____

So what's your Soul Number?

Once you've found your Soul Number, write it in this star!

What Your Soul Number Reveals About You

Just as you have a responsibility to others, you have a responsibility to yourself to pursue your calling and the inner promptings that come from your very soul. To that end, it's time to examine the meaning of each Soul Number to gain insight about following the road to ourselves.

Soul Number 1

A Soul Number 1 wants to lead most of all, and may want control over others as well. People with 1 Soul Numbers don't like taking orders or being subordinate, and they're often headstrong, willful, ambitious, and independent. Not surprisingly, the number 1 Soul Number stays away from teams, committees—and mediocrity.

In matters of the heart, romance is the name of the game—when the object of the 1 Soul Number lives up to his or her expectations. These people expect their partners to be as charming, clever, and independent as they are, so they won't always want to own up to their romantic sides. They may sometimes seem cold and distant—but it's only because they're protecting themselves. It is not unusual to find 1 souls seeking singular pursuits; the 1 often prefers to be or work alone rather than suffer "fools."

Soul Number 2

In its heart of hearts, the 2 Soul Number wants harmony at all costs. People with 2 Soul Numbers can't stand conflict, and so don't want to lead—they want peace, and to be supportive. The 2 Soul Number has the unique ability to see both sides of a situation. So we should not be surprised to find them as negotiators and arbitrators. After all, they are sensitive to others and can make them feel good about themselves. They are tactful and can speak the truth in such a way that one feels supported instead of demoralized. The 2 Soul Number is a warm and loving soul who can bring support when paired with any other number.

In matters of the heart, giving is what a 2 Soul Number does best, and these people can sometimes give so much they forget all about Number 2—that is, themselves. The appreciation of others is paramount to a 2 Soul Number, and criticism can hurt him or her to the very core. Always happier paired than alone, no one makes a more devoted companion than a 2 Soul Number.

Soul Number 3

The heart's desire of the 3 is to make people happy, to laugh, to create enthusiasm, and to encourage all to reach for their best. The 3 soul loves life! People with 3 Soul

Easy as 1-2-3

The 3 Soul Number has all the creativity to be spontaneously romantic—from balloon bouquets, to monogrammed pajamas, to hand-painted invitations—and will arrive at the party dressed in sparkling colors. That's the 3 Soul Number: fun, expressive, and, oh, such a joy.

Numbers love to use their creative talents, whether to write, design, dance, decorate, or sing their hearts out.

In matters of the heart, a 3 Soul Number can be a flirt. This person may change his or her mind often, but let's not call it fickle—3 Soul Number just wants to have fun. You may find the 3 Soul Number tripping over his or her enthusiasm. Trust us, the 3 Soul Number will romance your socks off.

Soul Number 4

In the heart of every 4 Soul Number is the desire to have a plan, to meet life in an organized way, and to be practical about all that it does. A 4 Soul Number loves his or her appointment book, an agenda, setting clear boundaries, and knowing the expectations of all concerned. A 4 Soul Number likes to know the plan and be in control, with no surprises along the way. That said, the 4 can be a great facilitator who brings out the best in each individual, building a synergy between people that can create miracles.

In matters of the heart, the 4 Soul Number is practical in emotional attachments, and here, too, likes to keep things under control. The 4 may not seem romantic, instead preferring to give and receive practical gifts, or to have a well-planned dinner engagement executed in an efficient manner—but the result is often romantic indeed, designed to thrill and delight.

Sixes and Sevens

What's more challenging than trying to have a relationship with a wanderlust, free-spirited 5 Soul Number? How about a 55 Soul Number, a double dose of the 5 energy? That'd be the notoriously elusive actor George Timothy Clooney—good luck trying to tie him down!

Soul Number 5

First and foremost in the heart of a 5 Soul Number is the desire to be free from restrictions, followed closely by a passion for change and travel. People with 5 Soul Numbers can't stand to feel trapped—or lulled by routine. They love to experience the variety and stimulation life has to offer.

In matters of the heart, the 5 Soul Number is ruled by three letters—S-E-X—and is s-ensual, e-xquisite, and x-traordinary. Rebellious and sensual by nature, the 5 Soul Number is ruled by the sexual drive in matters of the heart (if this energy isn't repressed by other numbers or outside circumstances). The 5 is adventurous and ready to risk—unless repressed. (Tantra, anyone?) Most of all, the 5 craves variety.

Soul Number 6

The three things most dear to the heart of the 6 Soul Number are beauty, harmony, and home. Understanding, loyal, devoted, affectionate, and heavy on commitment, you won't find any 5s here. People with 6 Soul Numbers want to protect, nurture, and love their families and homes.

In matters of the heart, these are the idealistic romantics—you'll definitely want to get out the roses and candles. With a 6 Soul Number the love is deep, as in "committed" and "the marrying kind." This Soul Number wants to be married and to have a family and a home to beautify. Don't even think about just hanging out with this one—it's marriage or forget it.

Soul Number 7

These emotional hermits rarely show their feelings. Many never even marry but prefer their own thoughts and company to those of another. This Soul Number could easily be a priest, a nun, or a wilderness guide, because he or she prefers solitude. It's the lure of silence, quiet, and peace that's seductive and intimate to the 7 soul. People with 7 Soul Numbers really do prefer to be left alone—and read!

In matters of the heart, if a 7 soul should team up with a partner, expect it to be a private affair. You can bet that the partner is probably a 7 Soul Number, too. The thoughts of people with 7 Soul Numbers will be kept secret, as will their beliefs and their unusual (shall we say eccentric?) lifestyles. These are highly sensitive souls who, with their need to think and analyze, often possess psychic powers and highly developed skills of perception. Don't try to fool a 7 about how you feel—he or she can sense it a mile away.

Soul Number 8

This Soul Number wants to be the boss, or at the least to have power of some kind in the world. It's hard for people with 8 Soul Numbers to understand the emotions of others, and they prefer to stick to business rather than messy emotional affairs. In their heart of hearts, 8 Soul Numbers want to feel important—not just at home, but more important, in what they perceive to be the real world.

In matters of the heart, don't go getting fancy notions in your head of a romantic little dinner for two in some cozy corner of the restaurant if you're dealing with an 8 Soul Number. More often than not, such a dinner would be interrupted with a business call, which the 8 *will* take, and the closest to intimacy you'll get is to have a detailed conversation about the latest transaction. This Soul Number will look for a strong, capable (and yes, you'd better be organized) mate who's equal to his or her ambitions. In a rare moment, you may enjoy the warm, loving nature 8 Soul Numbers possess—when they can let their guards down—but for the most part, they're just too busy for romance.

Soul Number 9

This is the very soul of compassion. In its heart of hearts, the 9 Soul Number wants to love the world and all that's in it, and, with its high ideals and power to influence others, it strives for universal perfection and universal love. Deeply intuitive and charitable, people with 9 Soul Numbers are often torn by their own emotional needs and the greater needs of others.

In matters of the heart, the 9 Soul Number is loving, idealistic, and romantic. We'd bet that this is probably the Soul Number that first started the search for a soul mate. The intensity of a 9 Soul Number's love seems boundless—because it is.

Master Soul Number 11

The Master Number 11 soul is extremely sensitive, bordering on psychic. People with 11 Soul Numbers have more emotional ups and downs than the other numbers (no wonder—they're trying to balance all of that incoming psychic information). In addition, they're wise beyond their years, understanding and seeing more than most. In their heart of hearts they want to bring peace to all relations—whether it's partnerships, loved ones, families, neighboring countries, or ethnically diverse groups. People with 11 Soul Numbers have strong hunches and most often these hunches prove to be correct. This is the number of an old soul, one who brings ancient knowledge and spiritual wisdom to all of its undertakings. You may know someone like this—that person seems wise beyond his or her years.

In matters of the heart, like the 2, the 11 can be sweet and gentle, and these people want to please. But watch out for those 1s—two of them to be exact. This Soul Number wants to be the leader and won't settle for playing second, even if its greatest desire is

Easy as 1-2-3

Don't be surprised to hear talk of angels, fairy-folk, legends of wizards, or that magic is real as part of the unusual lifestyle of an 11 Soul Number.

for harmony. This Master Number will bring a spiritual quality to any relationship, for it knows things—of other worlds and things beyond our realm of imagination.

Master Soul Number 22

At the heart and soul of all Master Number 22 Soul Numbers is the desire to build something tangible that will benefit humanity and will live on after them. These souls are capable of bringing about magnificent reforms while at the same time bringing spiritual understanding through their leadership. This is the Master Number of the futurist who will leave this Earth having achieved substantial material security.

In matters of the heart, this soul is cautious like the 4, looking for a partner who's practical, has clear goals, and has achieved security. The 22 Soul Number will want to find a love with whom he or she can build his or her dreams.

Sixes and Sevens

There will be self-sacrifice with a 33, but there's also a strong healing energy with this number. If you're lucky enough to share a relationship with a 33, know that after the emotional drama, you will be showered with love that heals the heart—that's the 33's heart's desire.

Master Soul Number 33

The Master Number 33 Soul Number longs to give freely to all who are in need. Joyful, loving, and energetic, this one touches the hearts of those who ask for its protection, care, and assistance, and this is the Soul Number of one who raises the love vibration to its highest level—compassion for all.

In matters of the heart, with double 3s, this Soul Number will need to master its emotions. Those with this Master Number have volunteered to come back as returning souls to elevate the race to a higher understanding of the meaning of love. Note that we do not see this number very often.

Other Master Soul Numbers

We so seldom see other Master Numbers (44, 55, 66, 77, 88, 99) in Soul Numbers that numerologists address them only when they appear. In our culture birth names are traditionally two to three names long, so the consonant number count just doesn't get that high. In other cultures where there are four to six birth names, it is possible to see higher Master Numbers. Chapter 7 includes summaries of the meanings of the other Master Numbers.

Putting Your Heart and Soul into It

Now that you've read what we have to say about your Soul Number, consider these questions as well:

- How does your Soul Number fit with your Life Path Number and your Destiny Number?

- How might you integrate these numbers and allow for them to work harmoniously and supportively together?

The point to remember is that your Soul Number works together with all of the five Core Numbers. For balance and wholeness, it's important to incorporate your Soul Number into the other aspects of your overall energy pattern.

We thought it would be fun to show you one way of understanding how each Soul Number contributes to the whole. What part of a project might each of these Soul Numbers love to do? We're going to take a look at how each would get a job done working from the heart.

Twelve Ways to Get a Project Done

How do you put your heart into a project? Find your Soul Number in the following list:

- Number 1 wants to think it up and begin the project.

- Number 2 wants to gather things together for the project.

- Number 3 wants to design it and talk about it.

- Number 4 wants to plan it, facilitate, and manage it.

- Number 5 wants to network it—and sell it, of course.

- Number 6 wants to help nurture it.

- Number 7 wants to analyze it some more.

- Number 8 wants to be the boss.

- Number 9 wants to finish it, and then give it to everyone.

- Number 11 wants to improve it.

- Number 22 wants to make a monument of it so it will last forever.

- Number 33 wants to love it to death—and teach it to everyone.

Now you know three of your five Core Numbers. In the next two chapters, we'll be looking at the other two Core Numbers—your Personality Number (see Chapter 12) and your Maturity Number (see Chapter 13).

The Least You Need to Know

♦ Your Soul Number reveals what you desire in your heart of hearts.

♦ The vowels of your full name add up to your Soul Number.

♦ Your Soul Number helps you find the road to yourself.

♦ Your Soul Number is one of your five Core Numbers.

Path - 6   service, teaching,
Destiny - 7   research, observe (educate the world)
Soul - 5 . variety freedom

Chapter 12

Your Personality Number

In This Chapter

- Finding your Personality Number
- Adding together the consonants
- How, what, "y," when, again …
- The outer you: how others see you

Your personality is what others remember after a first encounter, and your Personality Number, the fourth of the five Core Numbers, not only helps you make the best possible impression, it invites you to see *yourself* as others see *you*.

Finding your Personality Number is as simple as adding together the consonants of your name. Are you surprised others think you come on strong? Could it be you've got a 1 Personality Number? Or do others find you shy and reserved? You could well be a 7 Personality.

Of course, what others see may not really be a true reflection of who you are, of your inner self, which is why we leave that to the Soul Number. But, in this chapter, Personality is what we're after.

The Outer You

The *Personality Number* is one more of the five Core Numbers of your Numerology Profile. Sometimes called the "outer you" or the "external image" by other numerologists, the Personality Number is what's most obvious to others about you; in other words, it's how others view you.

By the Numbers

The **Personality Number** offers clues to habits, mannerisms, and behaviors of the people you know in your life, as well as for your own self discovery. It's found by adding together the consonants of your birth name.

Figuring the Personality Number

As you may recall from the previous chapter, we used the vowels of your birth name to find your Soul Number. Now we'll use the consonants of your birth name to find your Personality Number.

Calculating the Personality Number

To calculate your Personality Number, you'll once again lay out your birth name (all of your names), just as you did for the Destiny and Soul Numbers. To illustrate how this works, we're going to use the example of Oprah Winfrey, whose original birth name is Oprah Gail Winfrey.

First, we write out the name and then we assign the appropriate numbers to each of the consonants in the name. (Remember to write the consonant numbers *below* the name.) Because the "y" in "Winfrey" is silent, we consider it a consonant and count it as such. (See Chapter 11 for more on how to determine if a "y" is a vowel or consonant.)

	O P R A H	G A I L	W I N F R E Y
Consonant numbers	7 9 8 7	3	5 5 6 9 7

Next, add together all of the consonant numbers for each name—first, second, and third—separately:

	O p r a h
First name consonants	7 9 8 = 24; (2+1) = 6

	G a i l
Second name consonants	7 3 = 10; (1 + 0) = 1

	W i n f r e y
Third name consonants	5 5 6 9 7 = 32; (3 + 2) = 5

Last, add the final reduced number for each name together to find the Personality Number. In our example, we add 6 + 1 + 5 to get a total of 12 and then reduce it to a single digit of 3, the number of the enthusiastic, optimist entertainer and actor:

$$6 + 1 + 5 = 12; 1 + 2 = \mathbf{3}$$

Remember, if your final double-digit total is one of the Master Numbers 11 or 22, do not reduce it further.

Easy as 1-2-3

You will find your Personality Number in the consonants of your name—your birth name, that is. Like the Destiny and Soul Numbers, the Personality Number is calculated from your original name at birth—the one on your birth certificate.

We're not writing in this chapter about further Master Numbers as Personality Numbers because, while these Master Numbers do show up for the 33, 44, 55, 66, 77, 88, or 99 Personality, the body of knowledge is limited at this time. The reason we don't see these higher Master Numbers often is because in our culture birth names are traditionally two to three names long, so the consonant number count just doesn't get that high. Of course, there are exceptions, but not enough so that we have a clear idea of the true characteristics of these Master Numbers as personalities. However, in other cultures where there are four to six birth names, it is possible to see higher Master Numbers.

As well, numerologists do not consider Karmic Numbers when figuring Personality Numbers. So except for the Master Numbers 11/2 and 22/4, all numbers are reduced to their single-digit root numbers for figuring the Personality Number.

What Your Personality Number Reveals About You

At the back of this book, we've provided a form for you to figure your complete Numerology Profile, including the five Core Numbers and more, but here's a space for you to calculate your own Personality Number.

1. Write out your full birth name. Next, below your name, write down the number equivalent for each consonant. (Be sure to determine if any "y"s in your name are vowels or consonants. See Chapter 11 for help in deciding how to classify the "y.")

   Birth name: _____Kent____Joseph___Campazzie____

   Consonant numbers: _____9_____8_____30____

2. Add each name together separately and reduce each to a single digit.

   Total first name consonant numbers: ___9___

   Total second name consonant numbers: ___8___

   Total third name consonant numbers: ___3___

3. Add together the consonant numbers for your names and reduce them to one single-digit root number. If your double-digit result is a Master Number, record it as (11/2, 22/4, or 33/6).

   ___9   2___

What's your Personality Number?

So what's your Personality Number? Write it in the star!

Okay. Ready? Personality Number in hand? It's time to look at the typical traits for each number. Just by becoming aware of all of your personality traits as indicated by the Personality Number—the things about you that other people see and that you (consciously or unconsciously) present to the world—you can make better decisions about how you respond, act, and behave as you travel your Life Path to meet your Soulful Destiny.

> **Merlin's Notes**
>
> As you do for the Soul Number, when figuring the Personality Number, you need to determine whether to count "y" as a vowel or as a consonant. The "y" is counted as a vowel when it is the only pronounced vowel sound in a syllable; "y" is counted as a consonant when it is not producing a syllable's vowel sound and is considered silent.

Personality Number 1

Here are some of the traits of Personality Number 1:

- Appears to be dominant, forceful
- Creative
- Appears confident and self-reliant

- ◆ Courageous
- ◆ Comfortable standing out in a crowd
- ◆ Projects a stylish, professional image
- ◆ Loves to wear designer clothes but prefers to create his or her own fashion statement
- ◆ Tends to wear bright colors, even loud, bold patterns

Do you want to change? If you're too impeccably dressed, your 1 Personality may be seen as unapproachable and might put others off. Or you can be perceived as too aggressive and dominant in social situations. If you've got a 1 Personality, you will tend to favor straight lines and well-fitted clothing.

Personality Number 2

Here are some of the traits of Personality Number 2:

- ◆ Can appear reserved and shy
- ◆ Careful to keep in the background
- ◆ Appears clean and neat
- ◆ Cooperative, tries to please
- ◆ Is quiet, peaceful, and diplomatic
- ◆ Modest
- ◆ Appears artistic
- ◆ Can be critical over details
- ◆ Considered a good companion by the opposite sex
- ◆ Charming
- ◆ Will look and be uncomfortable when in the limelight
- ◆ Can have a fussy appearance, with not a hair out of place
- ◆ Prefers classic styles that don't draw attention to themselves
- ◆ Good listener
- ◆ Does not tend to argue (can't stand conflict or discord)
- ◆ May look as if he or she needs protection

Do you want to change? With a 2 Personality Number, you may risk appearing *too* colorless to others, and so should cultivate a visible flair by wearing clothing with soft flowing materials and colors that are personally significant to you. There's also a danger of seeming too inconspicuous or willing to become a "doormat" for others—but if you're aware of this you can overcome it.

Personality Number 3

Here are some of the traits of Personality Number 3:

- Looks like fun—and he or she is
- Magnetic personality
- Friendly and animated
- Life of the party—sometimes too much so!
- Great talker—usually has something interesting to say—unless it's gossip
- Entertaining and charming
- Extroverted and sociable, sometimes hogs the spotlight
- Attractive physical appearance
- Optimistic outlook
- Contagiously enthusiastic
- Witty and excellent with words
- Has a great sense of humor
- Looks great in most colors and styles

> **Easy as 1-2-3**
>
> With a 3 Personality Number, you'll be gifted at choosing unique accessories to add sparkle to an otherwise ordinary-looking outfit.

Do you want to change? If you've got a 3 Personality Number, you can tend toward exaggeration (as we've told you a million times already!), so others may not take you as seriously as you'd like, and may even distrust your judgment at times. It's also possible that your jealousy will get you into a lot of trouble, so it will be a good idea to get a grip on these feelings.

Personality Number 4

Here are some of the traits of Personality Number 4:

- Likes the country-outdoor look
- Looks like a sober, solid, honest citizen

- Does things to the letter of the law

- Doesn't takes shortcuts for fear of ruining the end result

- Prefers sensible shoes

- Chooses clothing that's practical, economical, and lasts

- Conservative in most matters and trends

- Can be frugal

- Hardworking and industrious

- Reliable, trustworthy, and responsible

- Shy and reserved

- Finds it sometimes difficult to enjoy luxurious and frivolous things

Do you want to change? Because the 4 Personality can sometimes be perceived as boring and dull to an outsider, you may want to be more flexible in your life, your wardrobe, or your outlook. Stubbornness and rigidity are two traits that may be contributing to any sense of restriction you might feel. Loosen up and find a new way to do things—it can bring a whole new dimension to your Master Builder reputation.

Personality Number 5

Here are some of the traits of Personality Number 5:

- Sexually attractive

- Sparkling, witty

- Likes change and variety

- Freedom of choice is the number-one priority

- Dresses fashionably, in touch with the latest trend

- Can wear bright, flashy colors

- Outgoing and exuberant

- Magnetic personality

- Youthful in appearance

- Can live completely in the moment

- Sensual, enjoys all of the five senses

◆ Likes movement—dance, aerobics, travel, and changing jobs, home, and partners

◆ The consummate networker, likes to talk

◆ Progressive thinker

Sixes and Sevens

With their innate understanding for promoting, advertising, and selling ideas or products, people with 5 Personalities can sell you everything from cars to vitamins to the Brooklyn Bridge—even if you didn't realize you needed it.

Do you want to change? Because you live only for today if you've got a 5 Personality, as you age, you might want to consider the value of planning for the future. Curb those urges to throw in the towel and get on the road—travel is an elixir to a 5 Personality, but others may see it as merely another way you escape responsibilities. Try to project a little stability; it does wonders for having a life to come back to after the journey.

Personality Number 6

Here are some of the traits of Personality Number 6:

◆ Gracious host or hostess

◆ A perfectionist and idealist

◆ Protective and reliable

◆ Accepts more than his or her share of responsibility

◆ A great problem solver

◆ Counsels and advises others

◆ Domestic, has a motherly or fatherly approach to situations

◆ Has an artistic flair and loves to make things pretty

◆ Has an excellent eye for color

◆ Prefers comfortable clothes that are pleasing to the eye

◆ Needs to be appreciated

◆ A natural-born teacher—every opportunity is a chance to teach a lesson

◆ Sympathetic and inspires confidence

Do you want to change? Some people with 6 Personalities may be perceived as careless with their appearance or live in an untidy, disorganized home. If you're a 6

Personality, in your need to be the center of the family, with all of your nurturing, caring, and problem-solving ability, you might want to be careful not to be viewed as interfering in family matters. Also, you can have idealized notions of romance and marriage, which can make it a challenge for you to find a "perfect" mate.

Personality Number 7

Here are some of the traits of Personality Number 7:

- Has an air of mystery and secrecy
- Seems absorbed in thought
- Perceptive and observant
- Intelligent
- Dignified and reserved
- Aloof
- Dresses with refined taste
- Well-dressed, well-groomed
- Loves antiques—anything from the past, including old movies, old tools, old books
- Introspective and introverted
- Has unusual, even eccentric, tastes
- Difficult to get close to at first
- Mystical and philosophical
- Can be good conversationalist—when you can get him or her to talk
- Good style is important
- Very private

Do you want to change? If you've got a 7 Personality, you can appear to other people as sometimes negative, skeptical, and cynical—and so some might believe you are hard to live with. You withdraw easily, and this can be misunderstood by others as emotional unavailability (and they may be right on occasion!). A 7 Personality may risk loneliness by seeming too aloof and quiet, because people will mistake your withdrawal for a lack of interest.

Personality Number 8

Here are some of the traits of Personality Number 8:

◆ Dresses for success—power suits

◆ Appears influential and powerful

◆ Ambitious

◆ Emanates strength

◆ Can appear larger than life

◆ Appears to be an authority

◆ Wears expensive clothes and accessories—loves that Rolex!

◆ Can be controlling

◆ Business-minded

◆ Organized

◆ Visionary

◆ Knows how to delegate

◆ Confident, assertive, and competent

◆ Intelligent

◆ Has natural maturity

◆ Well-balanced

◆ Traditional

◆ Good judge of character

> **CAUTION**
>
> **Sixes and Sevens**
>
> Kay's students sometimes say, "Hey—that's not me!" Don't look to any one number to fully describe you—you are, after all, a composite of five Core Numbers plus a myriad of smaller numbers. You're not ever just one number, but a cluster of energies—just like the Pleiades or any cluster of stars.

Do you want to change? With your 8 Personality's natural air of authority, you may come across as cold, formal, tactless, and authoritarian—as someone who wants to control others. These traits need to be softened so people will trust you to lead them and to show them the way to success.

Personality Number 9

Here are some of the traits of Personality Number 9:

- Generous and often gullible
- Tolerant and compassionate
- Philosophical
- Warm, kind, and caring
- Idealistic and romantic
- Emotional and intuitive
- Fortunate
- Vibrant
- Accomplished
- Unable to make quick decisions
- Vulnerable
- Abstract and distant
- Very wise in the ways of the world
- Doesn't judge others on material accomplishments
- Sympathetic
- Greatly loved and respected by others
- Clothes are striking, with a flair for the dramatic
- No tolerance for injustice
- Looks young for a long time

Do you want to change? If you've got a 9 Personality, you may find yourself too involved in other peoples' problems and can become unbalanced by the emotional strain. You may tend to wear black, but it's not recommended for the 9—lighter colors will bring lighter moods.

Master Personality Number 11

Here are some of the traits of Master Personality Number 11:

- Visionary
- Inspirational
- May have genius intelligence
- Seems to be more spiritual than others
- Dresses in an original, artistic, inventive way
- Individualistic
- Idealistic
- Has a real zest for life
- Creative and innovative
- Has a kind of special aura
- Intense
- Creates own reality
- Has the ability to handle details
- Super-sensitive
- Intuitive, psychic, or even telepathic

Do you want to change? If you're an 11 Personality, you may seem overly dependent on your mate in an unhealthy way. You can also be seen by others as tense, depressed, or high-strung. Through refinement of your creative expression and leadership skills, you will reach the limelight—something that's dearly sought by an 11 personality.

Master Personality Number 22

Here are some of the traits of Master Personality Number 22:

- Has an aura of competence, gives the impression of being superwoman or superman
- Purposeful
- Determined
- Solid and stable

- Practical and creative, brings material success

- Uses a common-sense approach to problems

- Problem solver

- Builder

- Looks as if he or she could control the world

- Appears masterful, efficient, diplomatic

- Dresses conservatively in tailor-made clothes

- Honest

- Productive

- Serious

- Responsible

- Likes to plan things, make lists, and have an agenda

Do you want to change? The word "workaholic" may have been invented to describe how other people see the 22 Personality. Need we remind you that there's more to living than just work—even if you're a master at it? Let people see you relax and enjoy life.

Inner You, Outer You

Now that you've read what we have to say about your Personality Number, consider these questions as well:

- How does your Personality Number fit with your Life Path Number, Destiny Number, and Soul Number?

- How might you integrate these numbers and allow for them to work harmoniously and supportively together?

The point to remember is that your Personality Number works together with all of the five Core Numbers. For balance and wholeness, it's important to incorporate your Personality into the other aspects of your overall energy pattern. Thinking about how other people see you can be informative regarding how you choose to follow your Life Path, direct your Destiny, and nurture your Soul.

The Least You Need to Know

◆ Your Personality Number reveals the outer you that others see.

◆ Your Personality Number is calculated by adding together the consonants of your name.

◆ Knowing your Personality Number can help you see what you might want to change about the way others perceive you.

◆ There's more to you than your personality; it's time to start putting all the Core Number influences together.

Your Maturity Number

In This Chapter

- Finding your true self
- Your birth name + your birth date = your Maturity Number
- A midlife message
- Living to your best potential
- Finding the number that governs the second half of your life

Novelist and poet Hermann Hesse once said he wanted to live only in accordance with his own true self. If we, like Hesse, wish to do that, we first need to know who our true self really is.

The Maturity Number, also called the reality number, realization number, power number, ultimate goal, or true self number, attempts to tell of the nature and function of this final of the five Core Numbers—the nature of your own true self.

The Maturity Number is a compilation of your name and birthday vibrations. This number gives insight into what you can expect in the second half of your life and indicates how you might interpret the combined energies of the Destiny Number and the Life Path Number. Introduced to the field of numerology by Dr. Juno Jordan (and very likely a result of her work with the California Institute of Numerical Research), the Maturity Number completes the core energies of your Numerology Profile.

Your Mature Self Is Your Own True Self

Your *Maturity Number* is the number of the true you. Because it shows how your Soul Number, Destiny Number, and Personality Number work in concert with your Life Path Number, it reveals the true essence of who you are.

By the Numbers

You can think of your **Maturity Number,** the fifth of the five Core Numbers, as the ultimate harmonic vibration of you. It's found by adding together your birth date and your birth name.

Your Maturity Number becomes fully functional as you approach midlife, so as you age and mature, the energy of this number will become the dominant force in your life. The influence of your Maturity Number increases as you grow older.

The underlying force of this number begins to surface at around age 35 to 40, and emerges as you gain a better understanding of yourself. By age 50, you have entered the full vibrational impact of the Maturity Number. The gift of maturity is that you no longer waste time and energy on things that aren't moving you toward your ultimate goal in life.

It follows that, when we're younger, we're not conscious of the influence or energy of this number. However, it is present and informs many of your decisions and actions unconsciously. So, whether conscious or unconscious, your life is always affected by your Maturity Number.

Merlin's Notes

As you age and as you move through the midlife passage, you'll begin to truly sense the pathway of your Maturity Number. You may not have known what to call this sensing, or perhaps you call it something else, but careful study and knowledge of this particular number will point the way to success—the rest, of course, is up to you. Your Maturity Number reveals the ultimate goal of your life.

What the Maturity Number Offers

The success of your Maturity Number must be lived up to and earned. This is the number that tells of …

- The ultimate goal of your life.

- The essence of all your experiences—what they add up to, what they were for.

- What's waiting for you when you've reached your peak.

- What you should and can develop.

- The true you.

- Where your destiny is leading you.

The Maturity Number Is Not Active in Early Ages

Even though this number isn't at full throttle until after age 50 or so, its characteristics *are* felt at an early age. That's because there's always going to be some kind of realization about your true inner nature, what we like to think of as an understanding of your soul energy.

The Maturity Number always shows itself in the most important experiences of our lives. Another way to say it is that your Maturity Number will show its influence in the most important moments of your life, even before you have reached the midlife point. Because this number is the symbol of the compilation of your birth name and your birth date, it shows your true power, your highest development, and your real goal in life.

> **Numerology Rule:** Your Maturity Number is found by adding together the energies of all that you are: *birth name + birth date = Maturity Number.*

Finding the Maturity Number

Your Maturity Number is the sum total of the vibrational pattern that is you. By adding together your birth name number (Destiny Number) and birth date number (Life Path Number), you'll find your Maturity Number, which equals your final, ultimate goal.

Calculating the Maturity Number

A simple way to remember the formula for the Maturity Number is …

Destiny Number + Life Path Number = Maturity Number

Refer to Chapter 9 for how to calculate your Life Path Number and Chapter 10 for your Destiny Number. It's that simple! The final number is called your Maturity Number and tells of the true goal of your life.

Juno Jordan, the "grandmother" of modern numerology, called this number the lighthouse at the end of the road. The idea goes something like this: We'll all travel our own unique path in life (the Life Path) and as each of us works our way down the path (following our Destiny), there's at first, in the early years, a faint calling of a foghorn somewhere in the distance. As we advance farther and farther down the path (as we age), the sound becomes more and more clear, beckoning to us, "This way, over here." Finally, when we've been on our path for more than half of our lives, and the sound of the foghorn is no longer deniable, we begin to see that there *is* something out there—a *lighthouse*, beaming down on our path, clearly showing us the way. Thus, we find the reality of who we truly are and begin to live upon our path in full awareness of who we are and all that we can be.

This is essentially the journey to the Maturity Number. It's your final attainment—although it just may take you 50 years or more to get there. In the future, this number may prove even more telling for those who will be focusing on the second half of life, or in some cases, a second childhood. Since the human lifespan has added about 30 years over the last century, the Maturity Number may be an indicator of what one might expect and the type of planning that would be helpful to allow one to live a fully authentic life.

A Sample Maturity Number

Let's look at an example of how to calculate the Maturity Number. Oprah Winfrey has an interesting Maturity Number. Here's how we calculate it. We do it in two parts, birth name total (Destiny) and birth date (Life Path) total:

Oprah's Destiny Number:

O P R A H	G A I L	W I N F R E Y
6 7 9 1 8	7 1 9 3	5 9 5 6 9 5 7
31/4	20/2	46/1

4 + 2 + 1 = **7** Destiny for Oprah

Oprah's Life Path Number:

Birth date: 1-29-1954

1 + 11 + 19 = 1 + 2 + 1 = **4** Life Path for Oprah

Applying the formula for Oprah's Maturity Number:

7 Destiny + 4 Life Path = **11/2** Maturity Number for Oprah

Oprah has an 11/2 Maturity Number—a Master Number signifying that from here on out, she will be living more and more a life of the 11/2. We can expect that Oprah's second half of life will find her in the spotlight (still), being an inspiration to a great number of people, a leader, bringing about reforms, uplifting humanity, and possibly being a mediator or peacemaker. Her intuition will play an important role at this time. In light of her intention to retire from the *Oprah* show in 2006, we can rest assured that we won't lose sight of her; instead, we can expect she will be out there in some capacity still functioning for the public as "Our Lady of Perpetual Help and Hope."

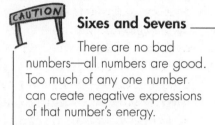

Sixes and Sevens

There are no bad numbers—all numbers are good. Too much of any one number can create negative expressions of that number's energy.

Sometimes, a number feels negative or too hard to deal with. If that's the case, check to see if you might have too many of this same number surrounding you—in your name (see Chapter 20), your house number (see Chapter 21), or just in the numbers that "come up" over and over in your life. An overabundance of any one number will be too much of that energy for anyone. While you can't change your birth date, you can change your name, house number, and even your phone number as a way to redirect the energy of your future.

You cannot, however, change your original Maturity Number because it's part of your original blueprint for life. If you change your name, you can add or subtract the intensity of energy from your original Core Numbers, but, your "real" code for life remains operational all throughout your life and your Core Numbers are the formative influences of your life. Like each of your five Core Numbers, the Maturity Number is part of your cosmic code, which is perfect in its design.

If an imbalance seems to be present, it's best to examine the full meaning of each Core Number, both the negative and positive attributes, and see if you're exhibiting any of these attributes to an extreme. Remember that this particular Core Number is about maturity—something we all strive for!

Finding Your Maturity Number: Living Your Life to the Fullest

Finding your Maturity Number is simple now that you know your Life Path Number and Destiny Number. Just add them together:

Life Path Number 6 + Destiny Number 7 = Maturity Number 4.

What's your Maturity Number? Write it in the star!

So what's your Maturity Number? Is it the same as any of your other Core Numbers or your Birthday Number? You'll want to go through this chapter carefully to find out what your Maturity Number says about you—and your relationships.

Interpreting the Maturity Number

Remember, your Maturity Number will resonate more and more strongly as you mature, finally reaching its apex in your elder years. Now that you know what your Maturity Number is, it's time to find out what your Maturity Number reveals about you.

Maturity Number 1

With a 1 Maturity Number, you can expect to learn leadership early in life. Your best results will come from beginning new things, and your strong opinions and ambition will lead you to positions of authority, although you should be careful to temper your tendency to be bossy and domineering. With your good memory and excellent power of concentration, you're a natural for taking over what needs to be done, and doing it.

Your true self naturally attracts unusual people and experiences that are different in some way. You have a broad vision and do things in a big way, and, because you like to do what you're thinking, you're seldom without something to do.

The 1 Maturity Number can be set in his or her ways—and we mean that just as we wrote it. That's because the 1 Maturity Numbers are usually a stickler about one thing. Be it their taste in paintings or their approach to raising children, there's usually a good deal of discipline and order evident, because while the 1 Maturity Numbers are not necessarily conventional, they will think that their ways are the best ways—and will expect all others to follow suit.

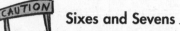

Sixes and Sevens

With a 1 Maturity Number, you're so single-minded once you're focused that, if you haven't got a plan, you may feel uncertain about how to proceed. As long as you've got a plan, though, you'll forge ahead—often in your own unique way.

Maturity Number 1s are not always as strong as they think when it comes to their health, but they do recover quickly, because being active is what they live for. Anywhere originality and dynamism are required are places you'll find 1 Maturity Number people living up to their potential.

These years of ripe potential will give you an opportunity to be truly independent, self-reliant, and you may possibly find that you're in business for yourself.

Maturity Number 2

With a 2 Maturity Number, you can expect to get others to help you, because you'll naturally attract those who will want to support you. You may have trouble with relationships early in life until you learn that helpfulness is the name of the game, both in giving and receiving.

Your true self is a peacemaker to the core, and you will do whatever is necessary to ensure harmony in both your surroundings and relationships, although you will fight for your peace if you're pushed too far. Naturally sensitive, you have inherent artistic ability, be it in music, painting, writing, or dancing, which, if ignored, may cause you regret as you grow older.

Easy as 1-2-3

The Number 2 Maturity Number will excel anywhere diplomacy is required, and will also shine in groups and organizations where cooperation is key.

Maturity Number 2s find happiness through ensuring harmony all around them, which they accomplish by expressing the beauty, tenderness, sincerity, and spirituality of their nature. Often psychic, always intuitive, Maturity Number 2s must guard against self-consciousness, which comes as a result of intuiting (sometimes incorrectly) the opinions of others. Cooperation is the byword of the 2 Maturity Numbers, and they long for the same sincerity and sympathy of others that they give to them.

The second half of your life will find you in a relationship, not alone, and very possibly living from a place of true inner peace.

Maturity Number 3

With a 3 Maturity Number, you can expect a vibrant imagination and a notable artistic talent to be yours, although this may be repressed early in your life. Because a 3 Maturity Number means your creativity comes naturally, the more you use it, the happier you'll be.

Easy as 1-2-3

A 3 Maturity Number signals that the second half of your life will be filled with friends, creative urges, and opportunities, and life will become easier with each passing year. Remember, the 3 is the number of luck.

Your true self is both sensitive and expressive, and if either of these is not allowed to flourish, you can become depressed, touchy, or even childishly insolent. At the same time, you have a true gift for words (among your many other talents), you're fun and humorous, and you're a master of the quick retort. Most notable is your zest and enthusiasm for life.

The Maturity Number 3 does best when allowed to create and accomplish great things. As Juno Jordan said, "It is the 3s who give color to life, who amuse, thrill, and inspire." Friendship is of utmost importance, and the 3 Maturity Number's ability to enjoy everything draws others to them. People with 3 Maturity Numbers can do very well financially when they're working in harmony with their world.

The years ahead of you should be filled with the joy of friends and time for creative pursuits.

Maturity Number 4

With a 4 Maturity Number, you can expect the desire to make dreams practical, and in your younger years, you'll learn the value of discipline and hard work. As you mature, you'll make sure to create opportunities for yourself to contribute to something lasting. Your 4 Maturity Number indicates that you're a natural organizer, able to build, plan, and order things, and bring ideas into form—always with a backup plan, of course.

Your true self has a talent for organizing, and you're steadfast, honorable, straight, and true (just like a Boy Scout!). Permanency is your byword, and you have both high standards and expectations, as well as the responsibility and fortitude to see things through to their conclusion.

In addition, there can be a tendency toward self-righteousness, or worse, to not take responsibility for your mistakes; but if a 4 Maturity Number holds true to his or her strong principles, he or she is bound to succeed. Hard working, never idle, and never one to waste time or money, a 4 Maturity Number person is reliable and down-to-earth.

Sixes and Sevens

Maturity Number 4s are often certain their ways are the best ways (and they often are). Because being "right" is very important, they can become domineering or dogged in their efforts to get things done their way. Management is their forte, micro management their downfall.

You can expect to build something of lasting value in the manifestation of coming years. Your health will be of great interest, and you will find practical, economical ways to organize around your health needs as you age.

Maturity Number 5

With a 5 Maturity Number, you can expect your life to be exciting and full of changes—because if it's not, you'll see to making a change. Interested in many things and curious about everything, you may have the tendency early in your life to be confused about what direction your life should take.

Your true self is resourceful, many talented, and independent, and you may truly believe that "freedom" is what it's all about. People with 5 Maturity Numbers thrive on the new and consider life to be full of opportunities for stimulation and adventure. You are attractive to the opposite sex, a quick thinker, bold, and probably unconventional.

Sixes and Sevens

There is a destructive side to the 5 Maturity Number— a desire to tear things down or just plain cause trouble brought about by this number's inner restlessness, rebellious nature, and sense of invincibility. Usually money is good with this Maturity Number—you just have to like living with uncertainty!

Maturity Number 5s understand the value of change and new opportunities, but also have learned to get everything they can from each experience before moving on. People with 5 Maturity Numbers can be great leaders because they make working with them fun and exciting mainly because they want to try new, progressive ways, and are willing to take risks. Your biggest life-long struggle is to find stability, stick-with-it-ness, and commitment.

You can expect to travel the world over—*again* (world travel was no doubt a pursuit of your youth as well)—meet people from a variety of cultures and backgrounds, and be on the go, taking risks and exploring new things. This is the number of someone who is said to be "forever young."

Maturity Number 6

With a 6 Maturity Number, you can expect the welfare of others—all others—to be of utmost importance. This is the number of the humanitarian and the giver, and with your strong principles about fairness, goodness, and family values, you'll shine when you learn the balance between giving and receiving.

Your true self loves both things of beauty and the home, so your home is quite literally your haven, your nest. You're a nurturer and a giver, and your kitchen is often the center of activity. You need to beware of giving too much, as well of as clinging to your ideals, especially when it comes to your idea of the perfect mate. Generous and helpful, though, you'll never stop giving no matter how many problems are put on your plate.

Easy as 1-2-3

With a Maturity Number 6, you can expect to have a good earning capacity because you have a natural financial attraction.

Maturity Number 6s are often wealthy through marriage or inheritance and love to surround themselves with beautiful and comfortable things. Often devotees, they must take care to not become zealots; but at the same time they are unhappy if they're not serving others. At their best, they'll share what they have with the world, because when they're helping humanity, they're truly happy.

With a 6 Maturity Number, in the latter part of your life you'll find yourself surrounded by your family, children, grandchildren, and great-grandchildren. Contentment and harmony should be yours all the days of your life. You may teach, counsel, or be highly involved with community projects.

Maturity Number 7

With a 7 Maturity Number, you can expect to live your life in your own unique way. Solitary and analytical, you truly do travel to the beat of a different drummer and are at your best when left to your own devices.

Your true self values solitude and specialization, and if you're left to your own devices, you'll find an area in which you can shine. Getting to the truth of a matter is what excites you—although you won't seem excited to others. Wasting time is a waste of time to you, and you won't be caught doing anything frivolous or—God forbid—fun. Seeking the truth, be it spiritual, scientific, or philosophical, is what suits you best.

Maturity Number 7s are often solitary and may seem aloof or reserved to others. Sometimes unmarried, because expressing love isn't what they're good at, people with 7 Maturity Numbers nonetheless demand and appreciate the best life has to offer. These people enjoy the finer things in life, often preferring antiques (things from the past) and quality. At the same time, when working at their best, 7 Maturity Number people may become well-known for their discovery of something new, because following their hunches is what this number's all about.

Easy as 1-2-3

If you've got a 7 Maturity Number, while you're young you may have trouble understanding why others need other people so much; but as you mature, you'll learn that they're not like you—the person who understands the value of introspection and silence.

Ready now to pursue the path of wisdom, you can expect to follow spiritual and philosophical interests, moving farther into the interior landscape of your own world and imagination. Long hours of contemplation, writing, and reading will be the normal lifestyle for the 7 Maturity Number. Solitary, though not alone, 7 Maturity Numbers will find people seeking them out for their insightful wisdom. You've become an ageless guru!

Maturity Number 8

With an 8 Maturity Number, you can expect reward through accomplishment, because as you reap, so you shall sow. Your 8 Maturity Number suggests you have the potential for mastery, but you must learn to find a balance between the material and the spiritual to achieve it. Your ability to see the big picture means you have the ability to lead others, but you must always work toward a clear purpose to achieve success.

Your true self will have to work hard to achieve anything, but this is part of what makes you strong. Directing and organizing is what you do best, because you're efficient, organized, capable, and most of all strong. You have to be strong to achieve balance between the two levels of life represented by the two loops of the 8—the material world and the spiritual world. Your life will be marked by ups and downs as

> **Easy as 1-2-3** _____
>
> Working for money or power alone won't do the trick with an 8 Maturity Number, because personal success is ultimately more important than financial reward. This number seeks recognition for excellence.

one or the other of these loops gains ascendance; but striving for mental strength will help you to achieve the inner power to see things universally and metaphysically.

Maturity Number 8s will work for the cause of humanity because they love the work, not for personal gain or recognition. At their best, they'll make easy connections between facts and feelings, and will be able to use their abilities to see things clearly to help others see them, too. Because 8 Maturity Numbers are self-reliant—and often the people in charge—they aren't always the best companions. They can, however, become great leaders and teachers of others, even great masters or mystics who others seek out for their wisdom.

In your later years you can expect to be called upon to direct or lead in some capacity right up to the end—for others see you as an authority. You will organize and be involved in business matters until the last nail is in the coffin.

If you've lived from a place of serving the greater good rather than from a place of ego gratification, you will be remembered as one of the great ones!

Maturity Number 9

With a 9 Maturity Number, you can expect that life won't always be easy. That's because you're learning to give up the physical world for the spiritual one, and you'll have to learn to let go of loving people in order to love humanity. At the same time, things will come easily to you, so you may mistakenly believe your gifts are meant to be used to attain the easy life, when in reality, they're given so that you can master this plane and move on.

> **Sixes and Sevens** _____
>
> It's not easy achieving perfection, and early in life, the 9 Maturity Numbers may appear inconsistent as they move from tolerance to detachment. Over time, people with this Maturity Number will learn to balance the needs of others with their own needs, and so move toward the perfection they're constantly seeking.

Your true self is both compassionate and humanitarian, but for you to be at your best, you must practice these qualities on an impersonal level. Your love of humanity can be a light for the world, but there is the danger of using it for personal gain, which can truly bring destruction to your own life—and the lives of those around you. The other danger is to ignore your sense of service. Your greatest joy is found in true universal love, because with this number of reward, the greatest good will come from the greatest giving.

The Maturity Number 9 will learn to let go of self to serve others, as well as to let go of attachments to outcome. You will learn to live in the flow. Surrender and release are the operative words at this time of life. Kind and generous, you'll need to beware of taking on too much responsibility, or trying to be all things to all people. Through your disappointments, you'll learn to help others without losing yourself. As a wise man recently told us, "The goal of every baseball game is to return home." Think about that: It's the lesson of the 9 Maturity Number.

You can expect to be more involved in the pursuit of the healing arts, metaphysics, the performing arts, writing, teaching, or philanthropic activities, if not in humanistic organizations that benefit large numbers of people. You have a compassionate heart and are willing to give your love to the sensitive, healing foundations of humanity. Like the Tarot's Hermit, in your later years you will hold your seasoned light of experience to illuminate the world around you.

Master Maturity Numbers

When a person has a Master Number as a Maturity Number, it gives possibility for mastership in handling human affairs. Remember to check your numbers before reducing them to see if you've got a Master Number as your Maturity Number. The Master Numbers are intense, highly intuitive vibrations. This means your energy is more vibrant, but that at the same time many people will pull back from the intensity of your energy when you have it on full force.

Master Maturity Number 11

This Maturity Number occurs when you have a combination Life Path and Destiny Numbers of 7 + 4, 8 + 3, 5 + 6, 9 + 2. Each combination adds up to 11.

At an early age, you'll have an unusual amount of self-understanding as well as the ability to see through emotional experiences to the truth within. With your higher knowledge, you demonstrate a wisdom beyond your years.

You'll need a good diet and rest with this highly nervous, intense number, and nervous system health issues are possible. You'll need companionship with built-in independence, and you may attain fame or move into the spotlight somehow.

Easy as 1-2-3

Maturity Number 11/2's mature years will provide opportunity to inspire in whatever field you choose.

> ### Merlin's Notes
>
> The 11 represents a high intensity energy, which can lead to moving into the realms of psychic phenomenon. With an 11 Maturity Number, you can get involved in other peoples' problems, and you may also tend to get involved with a nontraditional spiritual system. You're extremely sensitive to others' feelings, environmental conditions, various products, and even certain foods. This means that your lifestyle must be balanced, because you're a much higher vibration—pulsating at a more rapid frequency than most. To learn the depth and scope of your outstanding gift of intuition, you'll need to protect your immune system by following cleansing and detoxifying routines and by resting often.

If you're female, chances are you're strikingly beautiful and feminine, while if you're male, you're likely charismatic and refined, with exceptionally good manners. These are such extraordinary qualities in combination with a high level of intensity that others may find them *too* intense for everyday life. In that case, you'll return to the 2 and all that number entails.

As you grow older, you can expect to pursue spiritual interests (such as intuition development, clairvoyance, or a healing touch), and health and nutrition interests for purification. You'll have select relationships with those who share your psychic and intuitive wisdom, and you may find yourself in the role of mediator, arbitrator, or peacemaker. But more than that, you'll be called to inspire and uplift humanity, whether close to home or in the broad reaches of public service.

Easy as 1-2-3

As a Maturity Number 22, you'll find yourself in situations or jobs that demand multifaceted ability, and through these experiences you'll begin to see all that you've gained and accomplished over the years. You'll become an expert, because in spite of the restrictions, red tape, and negative thinking, you'll find a way to hold to your ideals and standards and to honor universal law.

Master Maturity Number 22

This Maturity Number means you have a combination of an 11/2 Destiny as well as an 11/2 Life Path.

With a 22 Maturity Number, you can expect to make things happen. While you'll encounter more obstacles than most, your masterful competency will allow you to overcome any barriers you might encounter in life. You'll be very, very successful, because you're the Master Builder.

Your true self is both a manager and a leader. You have an inner stability and inner power that stem from a firm rooting in universal principles, spiritual truths, and management know-how, and this power is what you draw upon when you encounter challenges. You're not as high-strung as the Master Number 11, most likely because you're grounded in practicality, competence, and know-how (the energy of the 4). Nonetheless, like all Master Numbers, you're bound to feel you're being tested many times in this life.

You may have some physical defect or health challenge that only strengthens your belief in higher principles and self-discipline. In your midlife, you'll go through a reexamination process …

1. To determine if living with such high ideals is truly allowing you to attain your goals. You may choose to give up your pursuit of these lofty goals because of a seeming lack of satisfaction, or because the "test" seems too hard.

2. To learn new mastery combining spiritual beliefs with material goals.

3. To allow for a new awareness of your true potential as a 22, a spark that emerges as the result of feeling the urge to work for the benefit of humankind, or, at the personal level, the feeling that you've got what it takes to achieve more.

In the second half of your life, you won't slow down much, and you'll always have a goal and a mission. You will require security, though, because the 4 aspect of this number says that stability and security are foremost priorities. You'll have to learn balance in all things—relationship, work, health, and a happy heart.

Master Maturity Number 33

This is an extremely rare combination of an 11/2 and 22/4 Life Path or Destiny for a combined total of 33/6.

This rare 33 Maturity Number can expect to benefit from long years of responsibility and service. Usually, the direction of a 33/6 in midlife will move to one of affection, joy, love, and the careful nurturing of these three. You can expect to serve humankind in some way through your highly developed skills of sympathetic understanding and problem solving.

Your true self lives from the heart and can know no limits when it comes to caring for others. Your abundant creative energy, coupled with your heartfelt care and nurturing of all those around you, is an extraordinarily healing

Easy as 1-2-3

Maturity Number 33 is a gift from heaven. You'll understand the balance between being responsible and taking responsibility for everyone else, between honoring your own needs and the needs of others, and between giving and receiving. You'll give your love openly, willingly, and intensely to those in need.

combination. Like all of the Master Numbers, you'll face many tests and obstacles unique to the numbers 3 and 6, yet you'll meet the challenge again and again. Also like the other Master Numbers, you'll be naturally drawn to higher principles, universal consciousness, and spiritual understanding.

Your extreme emotionalism will cause you to find a way to live in balance. This is the number that will struggle with reconciling what's right in your own heart with the needs of others. Codependence and failed marriage may be among your many tests.

> **Universal Law:** When it's right for you, it's right all the way around—trust this.

In your midlife years, you'll come to know love on a larger scale, where the strong emotional energy you feel so adamantly in your heart can be channeled into effective and appropriate outlets that benefit large numbers of people and heal humankind.

Later in life, you can expect to be sought after for your friendship, your creative energy, your sympathetic manner, and the healing energy of your love. You will learn how to protect your energy and your heart.

Looking for the Maturity Number in All the Right Places

Look for your Maturity Number in the numbers of your Numerology Profile and in others' profiles as well.

Some of your deepest experiences will come through those people who have your own Maturity Number in their Core Numbers. When this happens, there will be either an instant attraction or a strong sense of repulsion. That's because you're experiencing either the positive or negative energy of your Maturity Number when you meet these people.

Because your Maturity Number is such an important aspect of who you are, we're going to show you how your own number works with others who have your same number—from Soul to Pinnacles and Challenges.

The Maturity Number and Another's Soul Number

The deepest and most personal relationship will be when your Maturity Number matches the Soul Number of another person. When this occurs, there will be a deep and binding attraction felt by each of you, and from the beginning there will be a warmth and sense of understanding each other that will last even after there's been a separation. That's because this is a matching of heart energy (Soul Number) and true self (Maturity Number).

Usually, the situation or way in which the attraction occurs is unusual or peculiar, possibly even having a romantic flavor to it, although it's also possible to have an immediate antipathy for each other at first, because underneath all that, there's a deep attraction. Like attracts like, in this case.

It's much more than an ordinary acquaintance in this kind of relationship. That's because this relationship isn't meant for the material world or superficial matters, because it's a relationship that's the pathway to the soul.

The Maturity Number with the Personality Number

If your Maturity Number is the same as another's Personality Number, the relationship won't be as deep or lasting as a pairing with the Soul Number. That's because these two people will be drawn to each other because of something in their manner or appearance that appeals through similar tastes. When a close association is formed with this combination of numbers, there's apt to be unhappiness or disappointment. That's because there's no real foundation on which to base the relationship.

> ### Merlin's Notes
> It may be looks, or style of dress, or how someone comes across in a social situation that is attractive, but don't get carried away—it's not based on the solid stuff. For example, a man may see something attractive in the personality of a woman and fall in love with her, but what's really happening is that he's seeing in her the qualities that he's developing in himself—the qualities of his Maturity Number. But if it's just her Personality, it may all be an illusion.

This type of relationship teaches us that it's not wise to judge the book by its cover. Appearances don't go deep enough when we're dealing with the Maturity Number. Remember, this number is the essence of who you are, not just what you show to the outer world.

The Maturity Number with the Destiny Number

When someone has your Maturity Number as a Destiny Number, the association may not be long lasting, because the *relationship* may have more to do with a particular experience you're having than a true heart connection.

By the Numbers

Relationship is a broadly defined term. It can mean friend, lover, marriage partner, business partner, mother-in-law, or child, to name but a few. Think in inclusive terms, with broad application, when you read these descriptions.

Often the Maturity-Destiny combination may not go beyond a social or business contact. The person with the same Destiny Number as your Maturity Number may find you interesting or inspiring—or some other quality he or she can use as a stepping stone along the road to his or her own destiny. Because of that, when it's time, that person will be able to break the tie easily with no regret. This isn't a binding relationship!

In this case, it's the Maturity Number person who must make the effort, because that's the person with the lesson to learn and work out, and he or she must have the self-control. After all, this experience with a matching Destiny person is happening to help you move toward that ever-present calling, to move you in the direction toward which you are being called.

The Maturity Number with the Life Path Number

When there's an attraction and subsequent relationship between someone whose Life Path Number is the same as your Maturity Number, it's a deep link because it has to do with a past life connection. It may not, however, be the "land of milk and honey." Even though you may do some kind of important work together, the tie may not be harmonious. Oh, there will be love, but it is best not to get gooey over this connection.

CAUTION

Sixes and Sevens

The Life Path-Maturity Number relationship isn't a marriage made in heaven, because the Maturity Number person meets a strict teacher in the Life Path person and will have to conform to that person's requirements, while the Life Path person finds a difficult student in the Maturity person.

The person with the Life Path Number that matches your Maturity Number will find that things aren't quite balanced. The Life Path person will find this relationship a kind of test, because that person will be more fixed in his or her characteristics. (And why not? These are traits and skills brought in from past lives.) On the other hand, you, the Maturity Number, are just unfolding your character and are therefore not beholden to a certain path.

Shall that deter these two? Oh, no—this tie can be very hard to break. A real effort will have to be made on both sides and compromise for the good of both will be required.

Maturity Number to Maturity Number

How about when you meet someone who has your exact same Maturity Number? What kind of relationship can you expect?

This relationship can be very supportive, and the attraction to each other may result in much good, leaving a lasting mark upon the character of each. The tie here may be unusual, odd, out of the ordinary, or no tie at all in the normal sense, just a mutual sharing and pleasure in finding someone of one's own type with one's own interests.

If each unfolds at the same rate of development, then the tie may last a lifetime. However, if the spiritual development isn't equal, then the relationship is doomed. If you can work in common, it can lead to the most satisfying and meaningful relationship one can have.

Your Maturity Number and the Personal Year

A special situation occurs when you meet someone who is in a Personal Year (see Chapter 17) that is the same number as your Maturity Number. When this happens note it, because whatever takes place under these conditions will have more influence on your future than at any other time, or more than any other event in a nine-year cycle. Therefore, make the most of it. Take advantage of the opportunity to grow toward your Maturity Number.

> **Universal Law:** Life is what you make it—lemonade or finely aged wine.

A Few Words About Your Maturity Number and Midlife

Remember, the Maturity Number begins at approximately 40 years of age and becomes a stronger influence as you get older. By 50 years old or so, you should have your Maturity Number fully functioning. After you move through a midlife transformation, or slip past the midlife marker, you begin to reevaluate and, as anthropologist/psychologist Angeles Arrien says, to "re-vision your dreams." Your Maturity Number is an invaluable tool for helping you understand the direction for your later years in life.

It's important to remember that to have a fulfilled experience of life, you must embrace the Maturity Number. Its influence is felt throughout life, but will take the front seat in the second half of your life. This, then, will be the time when you can best live in harmony with your true self—your mature self. Look forward to it—it's the best!

The Least You Need to Know

- ◆ The Maturity Number is rightfully the fifth Core Number and an essential clue to manifesting your highest potential.

- ◆ Your Maturity Number reveals your true self and manifests as you grow older.

- ◆ Your Maturity Number is found by adding together your Life Path Number and your Destiny Number.

- ◆ Others whose Core Numbers are the same as your Maturity Number will be a strong attraction or strong test.

- ◆ When your Maturity Number is the same as your other Core Numbers, there will be special challenges and rewards.

Part 4

Divining the Future with Numerology

Your five Core Numbers are only half of the picture in numerology. Now that you know your true vibrational essence, we turn to the timing of things in your life. We look at the predictive indicators that come from your birthday numbers. We'll begin with your Pinnacle and Challenge Numbers and their meanings, then we'll move on to your Major Cycles, and finally to the easiest and most telling of all, your Personal Year and Personal Month Numbers.

Calculating Your Pinnacle and Challenge Numbers

In This Chapter

- Predictive numerology looks to the future
- Your Pinnacle Numbers reveal your potential for achievement
- Your Challenge Numbers pinpoint your potential difficulties
- All of us have four Pinnacle Numbers and four Challenge Numbers

Finding our way in life is one of our biggest challenges—we want to do it right and we want it to be successful. In the next three chapters, we tell you about a set of numbers that will help you navigate the course of life—in this chapter, how to calculate the Pinnacle and the Challenge Numbers, in the next chapter, what your Pinnacle and Challenge Numbers mean, in the following chapter, all about your Major Cycle Numbers.

All three of these sets of numbers, when executed fully, will yield a fully lived, fully engaged life. So come along and find out what your future holds, using predictive numerology.

Predictive Numerology

We now come to the phase of numerology that predicts when to do what. In this chapter, we look at two of the three predictive indicators in your Numerology Profile: the Pinnacles and the Challenges.

Your Personal Best

One set of numbers can guide you to your highest attainment, because they point the way for knowing what it is that can be achieved in a particular period of time. We're talking about the *Pinnacle Numbers*.

Pinnacles tell of the road ahead, as well as the name of the road you're on right now. It can be hard for any of us to understand a sudden, unexpected change in our lives, such as a time of uncertain finances, or a time when, no matter how you slice it, the marriage just seems to be falling apart. Each of these is part of the story of our lives, and knowing your Pinnacle Number can explain many a mystery.

By the Numbers

Your **Pinnacle Numbers** reveal your potential for achievement and success. These numbers show what is possible to attain at a given period in life.

The Pinnacle Number is one of the forecasting numbers in your profile. From it, you'll learn what to expect on the road ahead. Then, you can look ahead to what's coming for your life, as well as look back to see where you've been.

Pinnacles Equal Attainments

Easy as 1-2-3

Changing conditions may bring new horizons, but if you're in the middle of a change, the promise of something new is often no comfort. What you want to know then is what's happening and why. Now, you can know, because your Pinnacle Number (and your Challenge Number, which we'll discuss later in this chapter) alert you to your future, your present, and your past.

Each of us has four Pinnacle Numbers, each representing a distinct period in our lives that is governed by a singular theme. Each number shows the attitude and effort needed during the specified period, and all four of these numbers work together to help us work out our destinies. We'd suggest you view these Pinnacles in relationship to your Destiny Number.

Here are two important points to remember about your Pinnacle Numbers:

- Pinnacles are instructive on how to live with the least amount of resistance. They point the way toward manifesting your best.

♦ Each Pinnacle demands that you live up to the qualities indicated by the number on that Pinnacle. Circumstances will present themselves that will force you to live up to the elements of your Pinnacle Number.

Because they're based on nine-year cycles, Pinnacles can help you learn at exactly what age you should be doing what. Each of the four Pinnacles has a distinct meaning and a distinct length. The first and last Pinnacles are the longest, with the two middle ones being nine years each. Remember the concept of nine-year cycles, because it will come into play when you start to figure your Pinnacles. This is the significance of each Pinnacle:

1. The **First Pinnacle** is one of the longest periods. It covers approximately ages 0 through 27 (three nine-year cycles) at the least and can be up to 35 for some. The First Pinnacle varies in length for each person.

2. The **Second Pinnacle** is a period of blossoming and ripening. It's the period of responsibility and family. It's nine years in length.

3. The **Third Pinnacle** covers middle age and maturity, and is also nine years in length. It's a time of manifestation and reward.

4. The **Fourth Pinnacle** represents a time of aging and wizening, of retirement and reflection, and spiritual wisdom. It's the harvest cycle and lasts at least three cycles of nine years (roughly from age 50 to end of life). With new technology, however, some of us will have up to six cycles under this Pinnacle Number, up to age 104 or so.

Each Pinnacle is a time of development, each is accurately timed, and each is part of the blueprint of your life. It's all part of the master plan. Each pinnacle represents major growth for you that occurs along the lines of the designated number. Consciously or unconsciously, your Pinnacle Numbers are operative and with the knowledge of what your Pinnacle Numbers mean, you can achieve your goals, hopes, and dreams more fully and more quickly.

Finding Your Pinnacle Numbers

To find your Pinnacle Numbers you will simply use your birth date—but have your Life Path Number ready, too, because we'll be using it later. Finding your Pinnacles is easy—you just have to follow the directions carefully.

> **Numerology Rule:** Here are the formulas for finding your four Pinnacle Numbers:
>
> *First Pinnacle = month of birth + day of birth*
>
> *Second Pinnacle = day of birth + year of birth*
>
> *Third Pinnacle = First Pinnacle + Second Pinnacle*
>
> *Fourth Pinnacle = month of birth + year of birth*

A Walk Through a Sample Pinnacle Chart

Now, let's take it one step at a time. Using John F. Kennedy Jr. as an example, we're going to walk you through finding each of his four Pinnacle Numbers. As you read through the instructions and follow the steps, we'd like you to fill in the blanks for practice. When figuring the Pinnacle Numbers, keep in mind the following three guidelines:

1. Don't reduce Master Numbers.

2. Reduce all Karmic Debt Numbers.

3. Reduce all double-digit numbers, unless they are Master Numbers.

To find your Pinnacle Numbers, we will reduce all double-digit numbers, including any of the Karmic Numbers 10, 13, 14, 16, or 19. Karmic Numbers don't apply here in the usual way because Pinnacle Numbers show the potential for attainment, not a debt owed. However, if you find a Karmic Debt Number, you might want to note that a karmic influence is possible here.

Easy as 1-2-3

When figuring your Pinnacle Numbers, reduce all double-digit numbers except Master Numbers. When a Master Number shows up, it highlights the point that this is the time to show your mastery. Don't reduce Master Numbers for the Pinnacles.

When the result of your calculations is a Karmic Debt Number you will reduce it to the root number. With Karmic Debt Numbers in the case of Pinnacles, and later on with our discussion of Challenges, you might want to make a note. It might indicate that you could be dealing with people and past patterns during the cycle, but the main focus of the Pinnacle Number will be the single root number and what it means.

However, don't reduce the Master Numbers; rather, write them as usual: 11/2, 22/4, 33/6. Master

Number Pinnacles indicate that both the higher and lower vibration of the Master Numbers will be needed. The Pinnacle Number will show where your greatest opportunities lay as well as the nature of thought and effort that will be needed to satisfactorily work out your Destiny Number. A Master Number Pinnacle indicates you will have an opportunity to move into greater awareness and live more consciously.

Sample Chart for John F. Kennedy Jr.'s Pinnacles

1. John F. Kennedy Jr.'s birth date was November 25, 1960. First, we'll reduce all of the numbers in his birthday to single-digit numbers.

   Birth date: 11 + 25 + 1960

   Reduced to: **2** + **7** (2+ 5) + **7** (1 + 9 + 6 + 0)

   Note that each segment of the birth date has been reduced to a single-digit number, but make note that John Jr.'s Life Path is a 16/7, a Karmic Debt Number. For our purposes, we will use the reduced number 7.

2. Now, to find the First Pinnacle Number, simply add the month and day of birth together, arriving at a single-digit number. For example:

   Month of birth + day of birth = **First Pinnacle Number**

   2 + 7 = **9**

   So John's First Pinnacle was a 9. Write this number here.

   First Pinnacle Number: _____.

   Got the idea? Now let's try the second one.

3. To find the Second Pinnacle, add the day of birth to the year of birth.

   Day of birth + year of birth = **Second Pinnacle Number**

   7 + 7 = 14/5 = 1 + 4 = **5**

   So John had a 5 as his Second Pinnacle Number. (Note: John had a 14/5 or Karmic Debt Number here; however, for our purposes we will not use the 14, only the 5, to calculate his Second Pinnacle Number.) Write this number here.

   Second Pinnacle Number: _____.

4. To find the Third Pinnacle Number, add the number of the First Pinnacle to the number of the Second Pinnacle.

   First Pinnacle Number + Second Pinnacle Number = **Third Pinnacle Number**

   9 + 5 = 14/5 = 1 + 4 = **5**

So once again, John's Third Pinnacle Number is like his Second, a (14)5. Write this number here.

Third Pinnacle Number: _____.

5. To find the Fourth Pinnacle, add the month of birth to the year of birth.

    Month of birth + year of birth = **Fourth Pinnacle Number**

    2 + 7 = **9**

    So JFK Jr.'s Fourth and final Pinnacle is a 9. Write this number here.

    Fourth Pinnacle Number: _____.

So as you can see John F. Kennedy Jr.'s four Pinnacle Numbers are:

First Pinnacle Number = 9

Second Pinnacle Number = 5

Third Pinnacle Number = 5

Fourth Pinnacle Number = 9

Clearly his path was one of learning the lessons of loss, helping humanity through philanthropic service, development of creative ability (the 9s); and in his productive years he was learning to take risks, to work with uncertainty and confusion about life purpose, and to curb impulsive and irresponsible behaviors (the 5s). Since both of these 5 Pinnacles are also Karmic Debt Number 14, we would know that past-life patterns were in some way operative during this time.

By the way, the 5 just happens to be one of the numbers that rule publications, and we are reminded that during his 5 Pinnacle, John Jr. launched his own magazine publication. Wondering about the repetition of numbers 9 and 5? It's not unusual to see numbers repeated; it just means it takes some of us longer than others to get the lessons and achieve our goals. When a person ends his or her life with a 9 Pinnacle, it is thought to indicate that this period of time will be one of spiritual and material wealth. If John had lived, no doubt he would have finally reaped the rewards for all his previous challenges.

Finding Your Own Pinnacles

We've provided space for you to figure your own Pinnacles. Take your time, following the steps carefully.

1. Reduce each number in your birth date to one digit.

   Month of birth: _____ *11 . 2* *H 6*

   Day of birth: _____ *15 . 6* *1*

   Year of birth: _____ *1951 . 7*

2. Now, to find your First Pinnacle, simply add the month and day of your birth together, being sure to reduce the numbers to single digits—unless of course, you run across a Master Number. For Master Number sums, simply write the Master Number in the appropriate position as 11/2, 22/4, or 33/6.

It is possible to have a Master Number Pinnacle when you are adding to a single-digit total. For example, in calculating the first Pinnacle, if you were born in November (11 is reduced to 2) and your day of birth is the 9th, it will look like this:

11 = 1 + 1 = 2 (month) added to 9 (day of birth) = 11/2.

Your First Pinnacle Number is a Master Number, 11/2.

To add to a Master Number Pinnacle, use the 11, 22, or 33 for your next calculation. For example, if your First Pinnacle Number is an 11/2, and you are preparing to add the Second Pinnacle Number, use the 11 to add to the next number. *6*

Month of birth		+	day of birth *28*		=	**First Pinnacle Number**
11		+	*15*		=	*8*

Write this number here.

First Pinnacle Number: _____ *8* .

Got the idea? Now let's try the second one.

3. To find your Second Pinnacle, add your day of birth to your year of birth. Once again, remember to reduce your final sum to a single digit—unless you find a Master Number. For Master Number sums, simply write the Master Number as 11/2, 22/4, or 33/6 in the appropriate position; however, when you prepare to add your Master Number to the next Pinnacle, use the 11, 22, or 33.

Day of birth   +   year of birth   = **Second Pinnacle Number**

_____*15*_____   +   _____*1951*_____   = _____*4*_____
          6   *7*   *13*
Write this number here.

Second Pinnacle Number: _____*4*_____.

4. To find your Third Pinnacle, we do it a little differently. For this one only, add your First Pinnacle Number to your Second Pinnacle Number. You'll want to reduce this number to a single digit, too—unless it's a Master Number. For Master Number sums, simply write the Master Number in the appropriate position as 11/2, 22/4, or 33/6; however, when you prepare to add your Master Number to the next Pinnacle, use the 11, 22, or 33.

First Pinnacle   +   Second Pinnacle   = **Third Pinnacle Number**

_____*8*_____   +   _____*4*_____   = _____*3*_____

Write this number here.

Third Pinnacle Number: _____*3*_____.

5. To find your Fourth Pinnacle, add your month of birth to your year of birth. This number, too, will be reduced to a single digit. Remember, if your birthday is in November, the Master Number 11, reduce this number to a 2. If your year of birth adds up to 22, another Master Number, simply reduce this number to a 4 for this calculation. Both of these Master Numbers, then, are reduced to single digits in this position. You can, however, end up with a Master Number total. For Master Number sums, simply write the Master Number in the appropriate position as 11/2, 22/4, or 33/6.

Month of birth   +   year of birth   = **Fourth Pinnacle Number**

_____*11*_____   +   _____*1951*_____   = _____*9*_____
          2   *7*
Write this number here.

Fourth Pinnacle Number: _____*9*_____.

Once you know all four of your Pinnacle Numbers, the next step is to figure the length of each Pinnacle. Each Pinnacle will run for a specific length of time, so you can figure how old you'll be under each of these four numbers.

Figuring the Length of the Pinnacle

Here's where your Life Path Number comes in. The First Pinnacle lasts from birth to age 36, minus your Life Path Number. Hold on—we'll show you. It's easy, actually.

Let's use our same example to practice. JFK Jr.'s Life Path Number is 16/7 (a Karmic Number, you might want to note), but we'll use the reduced number 7 here instead of the 16 to determine how old he was when each Pinnacle Number was active. To find the length of each Pinnacle, we take his Life Path Number and subtract it from 36 (36 is the standard number used to figure the length of the First Pinnacle Number). The number 36 is not about your age, it is a number determined in the traditional Pythagorean system of numerology to be used to calculate the length of the First Pinnacle.

36 – 7 (John's Life Path Number) = **29 John's First Pinnacle Length**

Therefore, for John, age 29 was the end of the First Pinnacle, which means his First Pinnacle lasted from birth until age 29. We've started the following chart and filled in the first blank as 0 – 29. You can fill in the rest as we go along.

Pinnacles for John F. Kennedy Jr.

Pinnacle	Ages	Number to Add or Subtract to Find the Pinnacle Ages
First	0 – 29	36 – Life Path number
Second	38	Age at end of First Pinnacle + 9
Third	48	Age at end of Second Pinnacle + 9
Fourth	48 —	Age at end of Third Pinnacle, no addition or subtraction

To figure the age span for the Second Pinnacle, we add 9 (remember, the Second Pinnacle lasts one cycle of nine) to the number of John's First Pinnacle, in this case, 29. For John, we find that the Second Pinnacle is a nine-year span from age 29 until 38. Write these ages in the blank for John's Second Pinnacle.

The Third Pinnacle is like the Second, in that it, too, covers a nine-year span. Therefore, we'll simply add 9 to 38. John's Third Pinnacle, had he lived, would have taken place between the ages 38 to 47, so write these ages in the blank for John's Third Pinnacle. Just a note: John F. Kennedy Jr. died in the first year of his Third Pinnacle, which was actually a 14/5 Pinnacle. He was under a karmic influence associated with risk-taking behaviors at the time of his death. (Date of death was 7-17-1999.)

The Fourth Pinnacle age span is possibly the longest one we have, and is found by looking at the last year of the previous Pinnacle. For John, this figures out to age 47. We would then say that John's Fourth Pinnacle would have been from age 47 through the rest of his life. We write it as 47 with a dash showing that the Fourth Pinnacle goes from age 47 on.

Putting it all together, John F. Kennedy Jr.'s Pinnacle chart looks like this:

JFK Jr.'s Pinnacle Chart

Ages	Pinnacle Number
0 – 29	9
29 – 38	5 (14)
38 – 47	5 (14)
47 –	9

Some Pinnacles of Your Own

Okay, now it's your turn. We've provided the following spaces for you to calculate your Pinnacles, as well as a chart in which to write them down.

1. The First Pinnacle lasts from birth to age 36, minus your Life Path Number. This means you'll subtract your Life Path Number from the number 36.

   36 – _6_ (your Life Path Number) = _30_ (end of your First Pinnacle)

2. To figure the age span for your Second Pinnacle, add 9 to the age ending your First Pinnacle.

   _30_ (end of your First Pinnacle) + 9 = _39_ (end of your Second Pinnacle)

   Your Second Pinnacle runs nine years from the end of your First Pinnacle.

3. Your Third Pinnacle is like your Second in that it, too, covers a nine-year span. This time, add 9 to the end of the Second Pinnacle.

   _39_ (end of your Second Pinnacle) + 9 = _48_ (end of your Third Pinnacle)

   Your Third Pinnacle runs nine years from the end of your Second Pinnacle.

4. Your Fourth Pinnacle age span is possibly the longest one you have. The Fourth Pinnacle age span is found by using the last year of the Third Pinnacle.

   _48_ (end of your Third Pinnacle) + ? = ____ (the span of your Fourth Pinnacle)

Write this as the year ending your Third Pinnacle with a dash. Remember, John's last Pinnacle was written 47 –.

5. Fill in your four Pinnacle Numbers after each age.

Now that you've figured the length of your Pinnacles, fill in the following chart.

Your Pinnacles

	Pinnacle Ages	Number to Add or Subtract to Find Your Pinnacle Ages	Your Pinnacle Number
First	30	36 – Life Path	8
Second	39	Age at end of First Pinnacle + 9	4
Third	48	Age at end of Second Pinnacle + 9	3
Fourth	48	Age at end of Third Pinnacle, no addition or subtraction	9

Of course, you'll probably want to turn to the next chapter, which interprets the meaning of each Pinnacle Number. But hold on, the picture isn't complete until we've figured the Challenges John (and you!) will face in each of these Pinnacles. We discuss Challenges and how to figure them next.

> ### Merlin's Notes
>
> Let's do a quick review of some Pinnacle facts:
>
> ◆ The First and Fourth Pinnacles are the longest, spanning more than nine years each.
>
> ◆ The Second and Third Pinnacles are just nine years each.
>
> ◆ The age and length of the First Pinnacle are determined by your Life Path Number subtracted from the number 36.
>
> Go slowly, double-check your addition, and you'll do just fine!

The Challenge Number

Another predictive tool in the Numerology Profile is the *Challenge Number*. The job of becoming whole in this lifetime means we have to face and conquer our "sticking points," and there are four challenges we must meet in our lifetime.

Knowing your Challenge Number and understanding its meaning can make all the difference in your life. Instead of beating your head against the wall repeatedly, or continuing to bring grief into your life, if you know and face your Challenge Number, you'll find life flowing in a natural rhythm, rather than in jerking fits and failures. This is your opportunity to understand the major lessons you've come here to learn, and by doing so, you'll uncover the unique plan for your life, set in motion by your birth date—your own cosmic code for living this life well.

By the Numbers

The four **Challenge Numbers** outline for you what it is that you must face to reach the highest peak of your Pinnacle. You might think of your Challenge Numbers as doors you must go through to advance up the spiral staircase of your personal development.

Challenge Numbers are not meant to be *overcome*, but rather indicate what you must *become*. As in most challenging circumstances, we all would rather avoid the situation or resist what's presented to us in this challenging opportunity. However, resisting won't help, because this number demands that you pay attention and learn the lesson—even if you don't want to.

Your four Challenge Numbers go right along with your Pinnacle Numbers, and cover the same years you calculated for your Pinnacles as well. You can look back on the years past and see your mistakes, challenges, and lost ground in a new light. You get more information about what that period was about and possibly even have compassion for your struggle, now that you know the meaning of that period of time in your life. There are no mistakes—it is all part of your life path and purpose and it all leads you to higher ground if you choose to look and see.

Calculating Your Challenge Number

The Challenge Numbers are found in your date of birth, and we use the month, day, and year of your birth. The difference here is, where the Pinnacles are found by adding up the numbers in your date of birth, the Challenges are found by subtracting them.

Here's how you do it.

Numerology Rule: Here are the four formulas for finding your Challenge Numbers:

First Challenge Number = day of birth – month of birth

Second Challenge Number = year of birth – day of birth

Third Challenge Number = Second Challenge Number – First Challenge Number

Fourth Challenge Number = year of birth – month of birth

A Walk Through a Sample Challenge

As with the Pinnacles, to find the Challenge Numbers, we'll reduce all of the numbers first, then subtract.

Let's stay with our same example: John F. Kennedy Jr.'s birth date of November 25, 1960.

1. First we reduce all of the double-digit numbers:

   $11 + 25 + 1960 =$

   $2 + 7 + 16/7 = \textbf{7}\ (1 + 6)$

2. To find the First Challenge Number, subtract the month of birth from the day of birth.

   Month of birth – day of birth = **First Challenge Number**

   $2 - 7\ (1 + 6) = \textbf{5}$

   John's First Challenge was a 5, learning to adapt to change. Write this number here.

   First Challenge Number: _____.

   Note that when you are subtracting these numbers, it's okay to subtract a larger number from a smaller one. Remember, there are no negative numbers in numerology.

3. The Second Challenge Number is found by subtracting the day of birth from the year of birth. Again, it doesn't matter which number is bigger, because we'll simply convert a negative number to a positive one.

   Day of birth – year of birth = **Second Challenge Number**

   $7 - 7\ (1 + 6) = \textbf{0}$

   This means that John's Second Challenge was a 0, to learn to have faith in himself. Write this number here.

   Second Challenge Number: _____.

4. To find the Third Challenge Number, subtract the First Challenge Number from the Second Challenge Number.

   Second Challenge – First Challenge = **Third Challenge Number**

   $5 - 0 = \textbf{5}$

John's Third Challenge was also a 5. Write this number here.

Third Challenge Number: _____.

5. The Fourth Challenge Number is found by subtracting the month of birth from the year of birth.

Month of birth – year of birth = **Fourth Challenge Number**

2 – 7 (1 + 6) = **5**

Sixes and Sevens

It's not uncommon to have two Challenge Numbers be the same—it just means it takes some of us longer than others to learn the lesson.

So John's Fourth Challenge was a 5. This Challenge Number is all about learning to curb restlessness, impulsivity, and facing change in a responsible manner. Write this number here.

Fourth Challenge Number: _____.

Now that you've figured all of JFK Jr.'s Challenge Numbers, fill in the following chart.

John F. Kennedy Jr.'s Challenge Chart

Age	Pinnacle Number	Challenge Number
0 – 29	9	_____
29 – 38	14/5	_____
38 – 47	14/5	_____
47 –	9	_____

It's interesting to note that, had he lived, John would have experienced three Challenges of the number 5, through two different Pinnacle Numbers. All of the 5 Challenges mean he'd have been learning to adapt to uncertainty, changing circumstances, and working with risk-taking. In his Fourth Pinnacle he would have been making changes without the karmic influence of the previous two Pinnacles.

Numerology Rule: When subtracting the Challenge Number, it doesn't matter if the result is a negative number. In numerology, we ignore negatives and convert them to positives. For example, if your First Challenge Number is 3 and your Second Challenge Number is 8, you'll subtract the 8 from the 3 or the 3 from the 8, it doesn't matter which is bigger. There is no negative number.

Some Challenges of Your Own

Now, we're going to give you the opportunity to figure out your own Challenge Numbers. Don't worry—we'll take it one step at a time, just as we did with your Pinnacles.

1. Reduce each number in your birth date to one digit.

   Month of Birth   2   6

   Day of Birth   6   1

   Year of Birth   7   3

2. Now, to find your First Challenge Number, subtract your month of birth from your day of birth.

   Month of birth   – day of birth   = **First Challenge Number**

   2   –   6   =   4

   Write this number here.

   First Challenge Number: 4 .

3. The Second Challenge Number is found by subtracting your day of birth from your year of birth. Remember to convert any negative numbers to a positive, or don't worry about a negative number, just subtract the smallest number from the largest.

   Day of birth   – year of birth   = **Second Challenge Number**

   6   –   7   =   1

   Write this number here.

   Second Challenge Number: 1 .

4. To find the Third Challenge Number, we subtract the First Challenge Number from the Second Challenge Number.

   Second Challenge Number   – First Challenge Number   = **Third Challenge Number**

   1   –   4   =   3

   Write this number here.

   Third Challenge Number: 3 .

5. Your Fourth Challenge Number is found by subtracting your month of birth from your year of birth.

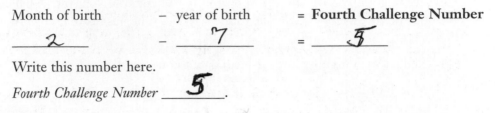

Month of birth   – year of birth   = **Fourth Challenge Number**

_____2_____   – _____7_____   = _____5_____

Write this number here.

Fourth Challenge Number _____5_____.

Now that you've found all your Challenge Numbers, you're ready to complete the following chart. Remember, you've already found the ages and Pinnacles earlier in this chapter. You'll want to fill those in along with each of your four Challenge Numbers.

Your Challenge Chart

Challenge	Age	Pinnacle Number	Challenge Number
First	0–30	8	4
Second	30–39	4	1
Third	39–48	3	3
Fourth	48–	9	4

The Cipher: The Zero

Note that, as we've seen, it is possible to have a 0 Challenge Number. Some numerologists believe that this indicates the person is an *old soul*. We would say that if one of your five Core Numbers is a Master Number and you have a 0 Challenge as well, then it is indeed an indication that you're an old soul. In our example of JFK Jr., he had an 11/2 Soul Number and a 0 Challenge, so we'd say, without a doubt, he was an old soul.

By the Numbers

Old souls are souls who have returned through many lifetimes. They're thought to be wizened in the ways of spiritual matters.

A 0 Challenge Number would indicate that the person will bring spiritual knowledge and universal law to assist him- or herself in working out of this 0 Challenge. A 0 Challenge Number also means that you can have all of the Challenges and none of the Challenges. That is to say, you can have all of the Challenges of the numbers 1 through 9 and have to work through each and every aspect of these numbers' negative and positive qualities, or it can mean that you have none of these Challenges. It's your choice—you can live Challenge-free.

The main thing to keep in mind is, as always, you have free will—and it's up to you what you make of this Challenge Number: You can make things a Challenge or not. This is a very heavy responsibility and obligation for a soul, and not to be taken lightly.

With a 0 Challenge, it'll seem as though somebody threw away the guidebook, so you'll have to make it up on your own. Should I let money be my challenge? Power? Relationship? Integrity? Love? If you have 0 in any one of the Challenge positions, the choice is yours—you have it in you to live life free from complexities and struggles that engage others during the 0 Challenge period of time. You've already mastered all of this stuff in the last life, now all you have to do is remember what you learned!

Putting It All Together

Pinnacles and Challenges in hand, it's time to learn what it all means. The next chapter is the place for that, so gather your numbers and turn the page.

The Least You Need to Know

- ◆ Predictive numerology looks to the future, using your Pinnacles and Challenges.

- ◆ Your Pinnacle Numbers reveal your potential for achievement through four different phases of your life.

- ◆ Your Challenge Numbers pinpoint your potential difficulties and problems along the path of your life.

- ◆ You have four Pinnacle Numbers and four Challenge Numbers.

less resistance

What Your Pinnacle and Challenge Numbers Mean

Potential Probs.

In This Chapter

♦ The meaning of Pinnacle and Challenges 1 through 9

♦ Your Pinnacles—from independence to endings

♦ Your Challenges—from standing up for yourself to sharing with everyone

♦ Some 0 Challenge lessons

Your Pinnacle Numbers represent the goals, attainments, and lessons possible in a given period of time at a specific age. Challenge Numbers represent your specific weak spots in attaining your Pinnacles. Knowing what's happening (or going to happen) in your life can make the difference between smooth sailing or canoeing without a paddle!

Either way, be sure to have your Pinnacle and Challenge Numbers from the previous chapter in hand as you navigate these waters.

The Meanings of Pinnacle and Challenge Numbers

Now that you've figured your own Pinnacle and Challenge Numbers, it's time to take a look at what they mean for your life. Note that we've grouped each number's Pinnacle and Challenge together, so if you're looking for the number 6 Challenge, you'll find it right after the number 6 Pinnacle.

Number 1 Pinnacle

A number 1 Pinnacle means that during this time in your life, you're striving to attain independence, self-reliance, and individuality. This is the main goal during this phase of your life, so all circumstances and people who cross your path in a significant way are teachers, who will help you move toward being independent.

If the 1 is the Third or Fourth Pinnacle, you're being groomed for leadership. Your greatest attainment will be to lead and understand all that it means to be thought of as a leader: integrity, vision, courage, drive, and determination.

Number 1 Challenge

When 1 is your Challenge, you're learning to stand up for yourself, be true to your own beliefs and ideas, be self-reliant, and, finally, find the courage to lead. You'll have test after test to see if you've finally learned to stand firm and not compromise yourself.

When the 1 is the First Challenge, you're learning to recognize that you have a self, while in the other Challenge positions, it means that you're learning to remain true to this self and have self-confidence.

Number 2 Pinnacle

If 2 is your Pinnacle Number, your greatest attainment will be to learn how to have harmonious relationships without sacrificing yourself. This is the number of unions, partnerships, patience, and keeping things fair. It's not a period of independence—the focus is on working as a team. You may be learning to cooperate, share, and be considerate of others.

Because the 2 has a natural talent for relating facts, gathering and perfecting details, and knowing what's correct and right, the 2 Pinnacle may well be a time where you will find attainment in fields of work where precision and detail are valued. With these same talents, you'll have an abundance of opportunities to use these attributes in perfecting the art of relating.

> **CAUTION**
>
> **Sixes and Sevens** _____
>
> There are extremely sensitive forces at work in the 2 Pinnacle. If you fail to identify and work with the complexities of relationships and partnerships, you will experience a good deal of pain as well as a devaluing your own self-esteem in the process. The 2 Pinnacle causes a person to turn to spiritual principles and to learn to trust his or her own intuition. It's a time to achieve harmonious relations within and without.

Number 2 Challenge

The number 2 Challenge is one of the most common ones, for it emphasizes sensitivity to all human relations. In its negative form, the 2 Challenge can be about fear, timidity, or lack of self-confidence, making this Challenge very painful. There might be a struggle with subordination or undue attention paid to what others think. The value of this Challenge is that you become sensitive to the feelings and nuances of others—their needs—but do not suppress your own needs at the same time.

Another aspect of the 2 Challenge is that it requires a constant vigilance to stay balanced, because, remember, the 2 is the symbol for duality. This Challenge says you're trying to juggle two seemingly opposing forces. Eventually, you'll learn where the balance point is, and then it's up to you to maintain that evenness. What you must become is balanced and sensitive, and learn to live in harmony—both with yourself and with others.

Number 3 Pinnacle

Here's a Pinnacle that opens the door for personal expression—more than any other Pinnacle. This period of life deals with the emotions, the imagination, and the creative spirit. In early life, this Pinnacle is about pursuing a creative career, and in later life, a 3 Pinnacle is about friends, joy, the pleasures of life, and creative expression. In the middle Pinnacles, this is a time to deal with your emotions and to learn to say what's in your heart.

The 3 Pinnacle has a natural attraction for money and the easy life. It's also a highly creative period, when you're meant to encourage and inspire others. You'll learn that your energy can be easily scattered with this vibration, so discipline will become an issue under this number.

 **Easy as 1-2-3** _____

Overall, the energy of the number 3 Pinnacle is calling you to find joy and happiness. It invites you to live with a positive, optimistic outlook on life.

Number 3 Challenge

When 3 is your Challenge Number, you're learning to identify your feelings and to speak from the heart. You may be critical with your words—especially critical of yourself—and this is one of the things the 3 teaches: Your words have a profound impact on your life. Instead of addressing the truth of what's in your heart, you may tend to use humor (or criticism) to cover your feelings. This is because when the 3 is in the Challenge position, it's the negative uses of the 3 that must be overcome: superficiality, exaggeration, gossip, scattered energy, self-centeredness, moodiness, and talking just to hear yourself talk.

What you're invited to achieve under the 3 Challenge is to use your creative energy to create a loving, encouraging, positive, and joyful spirit. It's particularly sad to waste the 3 energy, because it's what we all long for: pure, unadulterated happiness.

Number 4 Pinnacle

The 4 Pinnacle is the time for building your life with solid, stable foundations that will last. Usually this means it's a time of building a home, career, and family. Endurance, hard work, and patience are all part of what you're learning in this Pinnacle, and planning, organizing, setting up systems, orderliness, and moving ahead methodically are all part of this 4 energy as well. It's a time of practical application, of putting ideas into form, and of crafting a place for yourself in the material world. It's also a demanding time, requiring discipline, recognition of limitations, and a serious attitude. It's definitely not a time of leisure.

> **Easy as 1-2-3**
>
> The 4 Pinnacle is an especially important learning period if you have prominent 5s and 1s in your Numerology Profile, because you're learning to ground your energy, build something of lasting value, and stick with it. Money, timelines, and things that limit you are your teachers under this Pinnacle.

The 4 Pinnacle teaches that it's the effort one makes that counts. You'll find reward, lasting throughout your life, for the effort that's made during this period. When children have this as their First Pinnacle, they tend to be serious and are often influenced by their parents' financial limitations.

Number 4 Challenge

When the 4 is your Challenge Number, you're learning the value of discipline, organization, thrift, practicality, and hard work. This is a difficult challenge, and restriction and limitations are usually present in this period. The Challenge is to learn how to work within these boundaries. You are also learning to set boundaries with others. It's a time for learning to curb impatience, stubbornness, narrow-mindedness, and self-righteousness.

Number 5 Pinnacle

If you have a 5 Pinnacle, get ready for change and uncertainty. Ultimately, this period is about loosening up restricted patterns of the past to bring you freedom and liberation. However, because it's a time of the unexpected, and change is not everybody's favorite, it can be an unsettling time. This can be a period of restlessness, activity, public life; but it also favors sales and promotion.

Change is the constant in this pinnacle. Attitudes, career directions, and business decisions that are forward thinking and progressive do well under this 5 energy. This isn't a domestic or homey sort of Pinnacle, because you'll find yourself being drawn into the public world. You'll be learning to avoid impulsive, hasty decisions, especially the urge to pack it in and run. The main lesson here, and the major attainment, is to learn to be adaptable and flexible, and to trust that everything always works out in the end. And it does—as you'll learn under this Pinnacle.

Number 5 Challenge

During a 5 Challenge, you'll discover that the love of changing rules can bring impatience and restlessness and a desire for freedom in some way. If you've been stuck in a rut (usually the 4 energy), it's a great time to loosen up.

Change and all that it brings may cause fear, holding back, or confusion. But taking a risk and being flexible are encouraged under the 5 Challenge Number. You're learning to free yourself from limiting behaviors that are restricting your creative energy. Change, baby, that's the name of game with this one—but it's timely change for the better that is the true Challenge.

> **CAUTION**
>
> **Sixes and Sevens**
>
> During a number 5 Challenge, there may be a tendency to quit something before it's completed, to choose love affairs that don't last (usually because they were based on sex, not love), and to overindulge in food, drugs, drinking, gambling, or sex. Don't forget—this is the Challenge Number of the one-night stand!

Number 6 Pinnacle

When you have a 6 Pinnacle in any of the four positions, it's a time for love, duty, and responsibility to family. These are the years of responsibility, when you're to care for others, and the usual dominant choices for this period are teaching, counseling, and marriage. Your lesson is to learn to think of the needs of others and to work with balancing your life. If you do all the giving, are responsible for everyone else, and do all the work, you'll learn the difficult lesson of having to love not only others but yourself as well. You'll learn to give to and care for yourself. This number demands that balance be restored at home and within the family.

This is very much the Pinnacle of home, children, and beautifying your surroundings. The 6 also carries with it the energy of community and humanitarian service, so in your 6 Pinnacle, you may find that your work centers on giving to the community, children, and animals. There is money to be made and happiness to be had when you focus your energy on some kind of service, although some of your money may need to be spent on family or loved ones under this Pinnacle. Under a First 6 Pinnacle, young people will tend to marry too early and feel a tremendous responsibility to the family.

This is the love and marriage Pinnacle, the Pinnacle of babies and home. It can also be a period of divorce when commitment and responsibility to the marriage can no longer be sustained. You're ultimately learning about responsibility—when it's required and when enough is enough. This is a time for honoring what's in your heart— because it's there that you must be truly responsible.

Number 6 Challenge

When 6 is your Challenge, the lessons are about responsibility for others or feeling burdened by family obligations. You're learning to serve others and to find the balance between honoring your commitments to family and honoring those you make to yourself. You can't avoid giving and caring for others with this Challenge, however.

Merlin's Notes

If you have a number 6 Challenge and idealize beyond reasonable limits, you'll find unhappiness and the loss of family and marriage. There's a tendency with this Challenge to be too stubborn and set in your opinions—especially on parenting issues. The lesson you're learning is to move the energy from the negative qualities of the 6 to the positive: to create warmth, beauty, nurturing, and love in your environment and home.

The number 6 Challenge is also about codependency and giving for the wrong reasons. Under the 6 Challenge Number, you'll learn when you're taking care of others in an unhealthy way. But no matter what, this Challenge is a domestic one. Because 6 idealizes things, you may be challenged to discover when loyalty, obedience, the desire to be the head of household, and even love, have gone too far.

Number 7 Pinnacle

With a 7 Pinnacle, you're in a time of study, research, introspection, or soul development. Under this Pinnacle, education, scientific interests, study, and specialization are not only favored but strongly recommended. There's a quality of the individualist, separatist, and the loner present under this number, and it's a time to be reclusive, and focus on the inner landscape.

Country living is excellent during this period—or anywhere you'll have time to learn to be alone, learn about yourself, do research for areas of specialization, learn about mystical thinking, and understand the principles of right living. This Pinnacle brings much wisdom, and people come to you for your wisdom, because you develop a talent for explaining the unexplainable. Specialization in a field brings good money.

As a First Pinnacle, the 7 can be difficult, because it usually means you feel alone or isolated. Unusual circumstances bring you to a deeper understanding of life's mysteries, and you may have talent or special ability in technical or scientific fields. (The stereotype of computer nerds comes to mind with this Pinnacle.) In addition, you'll be very selective about friends.

> **CAUTION**
>
> **Sixes and Sevens**
>
> During a 7 Pinnacle you most likely will feel the urge to withdraw, be left alone, and have privacy, so it can be a difficult time for marriage because of your high need to be alone, think, and contemplate. Unless, of course, your sweetie has 7 in a prominent place in his or her Numerology Profile!

As a Second and Third Pinnacle, this 7 offers a chance to refine or specialize your skills—to move deeper in your chosen direction while, at the same time exploring the meaning of life on the inner planes. As a last Pinnacle, the 7 brings spiritual development. This is a quiet, reserved time of inner analysis and gaining of knowledge, which eventually you teach to others.

Number 7 Challenge

The 7 Challenge, like the 4 Challenge, is one of the most serious times in your life. Feelings of aloneness and isolation must be overcome by turning the energy inward to the rich, vast interior world of meditation, soul development, spiritual awakening, and the contemplation of the meaning of life. The lesson you're learning is to recognize that your inner self is searching for experiences that will allow you to grow.

Often there can be a big test or serious repression under this Challenge Number. Holding yourself in reserve, hiding feelings, or acting in secrecy only further isolate and separate you. There can be some kind of a secret, or something that happened within the family life, which is kept hidden or considered an embarrassment.

> **CAUTION**
>
> **Sixes and Sevens**
>
> Withdrawing, whether through drugs, alcohol, or by spending your life on the Internet, will not allow you to meet the Challenge of the 7. You are to become safe in being alone, to find meaning in your analysis of the mysteries of life, and to understand that all things in life are connected and in relationship.

The Challenge is to learn to discern reality from false notions. By being more real yourself, connecting to others, and learning to listen within for inner guidance, you'll cultivate those keen powers of analysis and observation that are particular to the number 7. The 7 Challenge promotes inner awareness through enhancing your intuitive skills, examining philosophical and metaphysical material, and learning the universal laws of nature.

Number 8 Pinnacle

This is the Pinnacle where you learn to deal with the business world and authority of any kind, and to find your own sense of personal power. It's the Pinnacle of authenticity and mastery, and you learn about money, power, and authority. Organization, responsibility, leadership, management of financial affairs, and efficiency are the essential elements of this number 8.

Under an 8 Pinnacle, your judgment is tested repeatedly, and the activities of this period of life bring you the opportunity to manage property and business and to advance your career. Achievement and recognition for your efforts are significant under this number.

Home life may be of less importance under this Pinnacle, because career and success are usually your top priorities. This is not an easy Pinnacle—it requires a constant shoulder to the wheel, and you're required to demonstrate strength and courage, with no time for weakness.

Often, there's a big expense to pay under this Pinnacle, but careful management of financial affairs, coupled with hard work, should bring reward—both monetarily and in satisfaction of a job well done. This is not a time to trust luck or to be misguided in placing your trust. The lesson you're learning under the 8 Pinnacle is to become your own authority, and to understand your true power and how best to use it for the good of all. You are developing self-mastery and authenticity under an 8 Pinnacle.

Number 8 Challenge

When the 8 is in the Challenge position, you're clearly being called to step up to the plate and achieve. You'll be challenged on material issues, either to have more or to get some—money is what we're talking about. Striving for material gain alone will not reap the rewards you're hoping for. Instead, the 8 Challenge Number says that you're learning to look beyond the dollars to the true meaning of life. Integrity, right living, and moral motives are some of the qualities you're called to incorporate in your manner of doing business in the world.

This is not an easy Challenge. Any attempts to misuse your power, to falsely claim authority, or to abdicate your power will only delay success and advancement. When the 8 shows up in the Challenge position, it often signals that this individual needs to stop giving away his or her power. It's a period of development where you're meant to take back your power and to learn to empower others, rather than defer to authority or dominate others.

Number 9 Pinnacle

When you have a 9 Pinnacle, you'll be expected to show a great deal of tolerance, compassion, and love, and you're meant to inspire and uplift others with your wisdom and deep loving nature. The 9 Pinnacle is known for emotional crises, partly because you'll have to end and release any matters in your life that have no further energy for you—no matter how scared you are. This Pinnacle is the time for maturation—and working through your emotions seems to be a part of this growth process.

This is not considered an easy Pinnacle, partly because of the inherent endings, but also because it's not easy to have to be loving and tolerant all the time. However, tolerance and compassion will have to be learned or this Pinnacle becomes one of great disappointment. You're meant to develop a philosophical attitude—grounded in global consciousness, universal principle, intuitive knowing, and a great love for your fellow human.

Merlin's Notes
With the 9 Pinnacle there are many rewards, even the potential for money and fortune; but the lesson you're learning is to yield and surrender to the universal order of all things, and in doing so you begin to receive rewards beyond your most imagined expectations. You're learning that you'll have to give and expect nothing in return in order to receive, and that includes the love you so dearly desire.

The 9 is not a personal number, and this is a period when you'll be called to think big—beyond your own comfortable little world. You're in a period of understanding and working with the human condition, and the following areas are where you might find your best success: the arts, drama, writing, higher education, healing work, spiritual pursuits, philanthropic projects, international travel and business, and anything that advances global awareness and giving.

As a First Pinnacle, this may be a time of early losses that bring early maturity. In the middle Pinnacles, it's a time of integration and giving back to the world. As a last Pinnacle, the 9 brings completion and material and spiritual wealth. But on all of the Pinnacle positions, the number 9 requires that you forget the self and grow into a true humanist.

Number 9 Challenge

There is no 9 Challenge possible using the simple numerology system we've described in this book because 9 is the highest number and all other numbers are subtracted from it. Instead, use the 0 Challenge Number, which we discuss next.

By the Numbers

The **Cipher Challenge** is another name for a zero (0) Challenge Number. It contains all or none of the other Challenges, depending on how you look at it—and how you live it!

Easy as 1-2-3

There's nothing holding you back with a 0 Challenge Number except yourself. It's up to you—the possibilities are limitless. Meditation, prayer, and positive visualization will assist you in creating your ideal world.

The 0 Challenge

This number is also called the *Cipher Challenge;* it stands for all or nothing. As a symbol for the circle, the 0 Challenge contains all things: It can be full and empty at the same time. With this number, you have full free will—you have the right of choice—to drift in life or to rise above the problems of life to achieve greatness. You have the choice to create your own world as one filled with love, compassion, integrity, responsibility, vision, and to do great works.

When a period of your life is governed by the 0 Challenge, it should not be taken lightly, for some kind of selection must be made, and it should be done with clear consideration of your Destiny Number and the higher laws of universal order. Your test and Challenge, like the number 9, is to nurture a desire to make the world a better place. There's a great deal of responsibility with the 0 Challenge Number.

Metaphysics teaches that the soul migrates from past life to present life, and it's thought that a person who has a 0 Challenge is an old soul, especially if this same person is carrying a master number as his or her Soul Number. As an old soul, this person is thought to have lived many lifetimes and is open to utilizing soul knowledge in this lifetime. Under this 0 Challenge, a person is expected to make choices that honor this higher awareness and that foster spiritual growth on the material plane. There's a much greater chance for profound growth with this Challenge Number. The various tests and lessons encountered in this life are meant to advance your understanding of the meaning of life.

Master Number 11/2 Pinnacle

This Master Number Pinnacle may also be reduced to its lower vibration, the 2, and for many, this Pinnacle will be experienced and lived as a 2. It's only when you're working at the level of the 11, the higher vibration (which emphasizes the metaphysical, spiritual, and philosophical, rather than the material), that you'll be addressing the unique qualities of this number.

> **Easy as 1-2-3** _____
>
> With an 11/2 Pinnacle, there's a great possibility you'll become famous or be thrust into the spotlight. Sudden changes often occur under this vibration as well, and marriage is possible now—as long as you aren't so famous that you have no need for a partner. Work that's favored under this number includes art, psychology, poetry, public speaking, media work like film and television, or work that entails visionary, futuristic focus.

An 11 Pinnacle is a challenging time because you will be at the high point of your intuition and sensitivity. Because this is a time of extraordinary sensitivity, you'll have to take measures to ensure balance under this volatile number. There's a wide-open channel with the number 11, and it stretches between your personal consciousness and the realms of higher consciousness. This means that you will experience intense revelations, enormous personal and spiritual growth, and a compelling sense of being different, and you'll develop an uncanny ability to see into the soul of things. In an 11/2 Pinnacle you have a message to deliver to people, and you'll have the desire to inspire, uplift, and share your revelations with those in your sphere.

If the 11 is too intense a vibration for you, then you'll revert to the energy of the 2 and the issues that will dominate this Pinnacle are those of the 2. But either way, sensitivity is one of your major tests, and a radical change in consciousness is at hand.

Master Number 11/2 Challenge

The Challenge of the 11/2 is to honor the demands of both the 11 and the 2. A constant vigilance is required to stay in balance physically and emotionally. Under this Challenge, a person is called to step up to the leadership role of the 11 using spiritual principles, and in some way this presents an opportunity for growth. At the same time, the 11/2 Challenge presents all of the opportunities of the 2: lessons of partnership and relationship.

Master Number 22/4 Pinnacle

The 22/4 Pinnacle is fairly rare and usually occurs only after having two preceding Pinnacles of 11/2. Because of these preceding Pinnacles, you'll most likely have undergone a radical change in consciousness and may have even experienced some kind of handicap or health issue. But now, with a 22/4 Pinnacle, you're given the chance to do something truly great that will affect the masses on a national and even international scale.

This is a time of building something of lasting value and it calls you to do good work that will benefit humankind. Your keen organizational and managerial skills will be fully utilized under this Master Number. You will learn to apply practical solutions to problems. All that you've done in your life prior to this 22/4 period will be realized as experiences you've accumulated, so that now you can execute these masterful plans. This is a highly productive time; it's also a testing time, but you have the necessary endurance and vision to see yourself through any challenging periods.

Because the 22 is also the vibration of two 2s, you'll want to take time to live fully balanced in your personal life, because, like the 11/2, you're subject to extreme sensitivities. One of your tests will involve learning to limit your workaholic capacity and to find the balance between your visions for making the world a better place and your need to manage boundaries for your own health. People look to you as an example under this Master Number vibration.

Master Number 22/4 Challenge

At this time, numerologists do not recognize the 22/4 as a Challenge Number. Instead, the 22 is reduced to the 4 and read as a 4 Challenge.

Master Number 33/6 Pinnacle

The 33/6 Pinnacle is fairly rare and usually occurs only after having two preceding Pinnacles of 11/2 and 22/4. Because of these preceding Pinnacles, you'll most likely have undergone a radical change in consciousness and now you're given the chance to do something truly great that will affect people on a larger scale. All that you've done in your life prior to this 33/6 period will be realized as experiences you've accumulated, so that now you can demonstrate your mastery. This is a highly productive time; it's also a testing time, but you have the necessary endurance and vision to see yourself through any challenging periods. This is a time of service and brings great opportunity to master emotions. It will require self-sacrifice and numerous opportunities to elevate your own consciousness and the consciousness of humankind. You will be working with all aspects of love as an energetic force for change. A 33/6 Pinnacle is a time of teaching; you will find you are the teacher of teachers. Your sensitivity to the suffering of others and the needs of the planet will call for your courage and inspiration, which in turn will inspire others. There is great responsibility at this time in your life; however, you will be both protected and guided.

Master Number 33/6 Challenge

While numerologists do not recognize this number in the Challenge position, we would offer to those of you who might find this number as a Challenge that the 33/6 is the vibration of healing oneself and others using spiritual principles. It is through teaching love and understanding the responsibility of love that you will move through any Challenge this Master Number brings.

In Appendix B we offer a Numerology Profile worksheet to figure your Pinnacles and Challenges as well as all of the numbers of your Numerology Profile. The last third of the predictive numerology triad is the Major Cycles. We'll be devoting the entire next chapter to their timing and lessons.

The Least You Need to Know

- Your Pinnacles show you how to achieve your destiny.
- Understanding your Challenges can help you stop being your own worst enemy.
- The 0 is called the Cipher Challenge.
- Pinnacle and Challenge themes are told in the numbers.

Chapter 16

Numerology's Major Cycles

In This Chapter

- ◆ Major lessons are shown by your Major Cycle Numbers
- ◆ Your Major Cycles show you the timing for your life
- ◆ Three Major Cycles: formative, productive, and harvest
- ◆ You work your way through the three numbers of your birth date

Another aspect of predictive numerology is your Major Cycles, which, like your Pinnacles and Challenges, are found within your date of birth. From your formative beginning, through your productive midlife, to your completion in your harvest cycle, your Major Cycles can help you understand the particular rhythms of your own life.

In this chapter, we'll be looking at three of numerology's Major Cycles, as well as the interpretation of each number as a Major Cycle. Once you learn your own rhythm, you will better understand and be able to interpret the major events and transitions of your life. After you understand your Major Cycles or the big picture, we will turn to your Personal Year which will be covered in the next chapter.

Major Cycles

Another predictive element in your numerology chart, the *Major Cycles,* also comes from your date of birth. Here's how it works: We work our way through our birthday—the month, day, and year of our birth—and find three distinct cycles with approximately 28-year chunks in each. The *number* of the month of your birthday is the First Major Cycle, the *number* of the day you were born is the Second Major Cycle, and the *number* of the year you were born is the Third Major Cycle. It's as simple as that.

By the Numbers

Your **Major Cycles** show the major lessons you are learning at specific times in your life. They're found in the date of your birth.

The Major Cycles have great influence on our lives and our approach to life, and they also have a great deal to do with our destiny. Each cycle has its own distinct theme. The number of your cycle tells of the conditions and lessons you'll need to meet that will advance you down your path (Life Path Number), and assist you in meeting your destiny (Destiny Number).

Getting the Timing Right

Like all good stories, your story has a beginning, a middle, and an end. Your story is told in the three large cycles of your birth date, and each cycle governs a distinct period of time in your life.

◆ **First Major Cycle.** This is your formative cycle. It governs approximately the first 28 years of your life, and its theme is found in the number of the *month* you were born.

◆ **Second Major Cycle.** This is your productive cycle. It governs approximately the middle years of your life, and its theme is found in the number of the *day* you were born.

◆ **Third Major Cycle.** This is your harvest cycle. It governs the later years of your life, and its theme is found in the reduced number of the *year* you were born.

We'll be figuring the exact ages of these three cycles in this section. But first, there are a few things you should know about the Major Cycles.

The rule of thumb in figuring the length of the Major Cycles is that your First Major Cycle starts at birth and lasts for approximately 28 years. The Second Major Cycle runs for approximately the next 28 years, and the Third Major Cycle lasts from the end of the Second Major Cycle for the rest of your life. Lost? The following chart may help, because the Major Cycle is calculated using your Life Path Number. In the chart, find your Life Path Number to identify the ages at which your Major Cycles will start.

Timing of Major Cycles Chart

Life Path Number	First Cycle Start	End of First Cycle, Start of Second Cycle	End of Second Cycle, Start of Third Cycle
1	0–26	26–27	53–54
2 and 11	0–25	25–26	52–53
3	0–33	33–34	60–61
4 and 22	0–32	32–33	59–60
5	0–31	31–32	58–59
6 and 33	0–30	30–31	57–58
7	0–29	29–30	56–57
8	0–28	28–29	55–56
9	0–27	27–28	54–55

The change from one cycle to the next can be almost unnoticeable and easy, or it can be very dramatic and life changing. Big changes can occur as you move from one Major Cycle influence to another, especially if the numbers of those cycles are not harmonious, such as moving from a 3 to a 4. You always begin a new Major Cycle in your 1 Personal Year (see Chapter 17 for a discussion of the Personal Year).

This is where we can see how all of these predictive numbers fit together. The Major Cycle is the grand theme and major lesson for a given period of time in your life (in 28-year chunks), and the Pinnacle and Challenge Numbers, which happen during a Major Cycle, are subthemes to the major theme. Underneath the Pinnacle and Challenge theme is the Personal Year theme, which tells you on a year-by-year basis what the focus is. It all weaves together to guide you to an expression of your higher and best self.

Easy as 1-2-3

The advantage of knowing about the three Major Cycles and their influence is that you can prepare for them in advance, make sense of what's happening presently in your life, and, finally, piece together the story of your life with its many lessons.

Calculating the Major Cycles

This one is easy: To find the number of your Major Cycles, look no further than the month, day, and year you were born.

The First Major Cycle is the number of the month you were born. For example, if you were born in July, your First Major Cycle Number is 7. If you were born in December, your First Major Cycle Number is 3 (1 + 2 = 3).

> **Numerology Rule:** The First Major Cycle Number is found in the reduced number of the month you were born.

Here's a chart for quick reference in finding your *First* Major Cycle, a major growth cycle and the time of formation as you begin to form who you are.

First Major Cycle Reference Chart

Month	First Major Cycle Number
January	1
February	2
March	3
April	4
May	5
June	6
July	7
August	8
September	9
October	1
November	11 (a Master Number Major Cycle)
December	3

The number of your birth month tells the theme of your first 28 years (approximately) of life.

The Second Major Cycle—the *productive* years or achievement years—is found in the number of the day you were born. If, for example, you were born on the 8th day of the month, then your Second Major Cycle Number is an 8, which tells us that this period of time in your life is all about the issues of money, power, and success. You will learn your lessons in the business arena during an 8 Major Cycle.

> **Numerology Rule:** The Second Major Cycle Number is found in the day you were born. If you were born on a double-digit date (such as the 17th, 23rd, or 30th of the month, for example), reduce these double-digit numbers to a single number unless you were born on a date that is a Master Number—the 11th or 22nd of the month. Don't reduce these Master Numbers; they have special significance.

The number of your day of birth tells of your Second Major Cycle theme.

The Third Major Cycle Number—the harvest years—is found in the year you were born. If you were born in 1964, you will add these numbers together to get the single reduced number of 2, which is the vibration and theme of your last Major Cycle.

> **Numerology Rule:** The Third Major Cycle Number is found in the reduced number of the year you were born.

The reduced number of your year of birth tells of the theme for your last Major Cycle.

Some Predictions of Your Own

It's time to calculate your own Major Cycle Numbers. The steps are as easy as 1-2-3.

1. The First Major Cycle Number is the reduced number of the month you were born. (You can look up your number in the First Major Cycle Reference Chart we gave you earlier.) Write your number here:

   Your First Major Cycle Number: __11/2__.

2. The Second Major Cycle Number is found in the reduced number of the day you were born. If you were born on the 11th or 22nd of the month, don't reduce these Master Numbers. Write your number here:

   Your Second Major Cycle Number: ___6___.

3. The Third Major Cycle Number is found in the reduced number of the year you were born. If the year you are born reduces to a 22, you have a Master Number Major Cycle. Don't reduce the 22 any further. Write your number here:

   Your Third Major Cycle Number: ___7___.

4. Now, look up the timing of your Major Cycles in the Timing of Major Cycles Chart we showed you earlier in this chapter. Find out when your Major Cycles begin and end and then start filling in Your Major Cycles Chart that follows. Transfer the numbers you found in steps 1 through 3 and you've got yourself a complete Major Cycle chart.

Your Major Cycles Chart

First Major Cycle	Second Major Cycle	Third Major Cycle
Age at the end ____	Age it begins ____	Age it begins **57-58**
Cycle Number **2**	Cycle Number **6**	Cycle Number **7**

The Meanings of the Major Cycles

So what do these numbers mean? Each of the three Major Cycles coincides to a period of life: the beginning, the middle, and the end of your life. Which Major Cycle Number you have during each one can help you understand the lessons to be learned and the heights to which you may rise during that period of time. The three Major Cycle themes together point the way for you to live your life to its fullest potential.

Major Cycle Number 1: An Active Cycle

When the 1 is your First Major Cycle, you'll gain independence and build self-confidence, although you may feel lonely or different. You'll need to stand for what you believe in. If you have 1 as a Second Major Cycle Number, however, you'll find increased confidence, leadership, or entrepreneurial enterprise, but will also learn to deal with loneliness, and proving that one person can make a difference. You'll demonstrate resilience and strength and may even start a new business. If the 1 is your Third Major Cycle (your harvest cycle), you'll be assertive and proud. You'll discover new ways of doing things, maintain your independence, and work on issues of integrity and self-discovery.

Easy as 1-2-3

Your 1 Personal Year Number dictates the beginning of a new Major Cycle. We discuss the Personal Year Numbers and cycles in the next chapter.

Major Cycle Number 2: A Slow Cycle

As a First or Second Major Cycle, this is a period of slow, patient development. Your natural gifts of gentle persuasion and peacemaking will be utilized often. You're learning how to cooperate with others, how to be part of the team. Under the 2, partnerships of any kind are important, and the lessons will be around learning the skills of tact, diplomacy, and compromise, while gaining a clear understanding of how relationships work. This is a gentle vibration and teaches gentleness, support, and harmony, and encourages you to seek out beauty and harmonious environments. Discord and disruption are not tolerated well under this number's energy. As a Third Major Cycle, the 2 means that patience and cooperation will be the hallmarks of your mature years.

Easy as 1-2-3

In all three Major Cycles, the 2 means cooperation and partnership.

Major Cycle Number 3: A Time of Self-Expression and Joyful Living

With a 3 as your First Major Cycle, any ability you possess in the performing arts, and especially writing, will be met with great reward. The emphasis is on creativity and the expression of that creative self. As a young adult under this cycle, you may choose to use your creative expression to entertain friends and live the party life. In the Second or Third Major Cycles, the 3 emphasis encourages the delight of living and warmth of many friends. The Second Major Cycle requires discipline and focus to harness the considerable creative energy pulsing through your life at this time. As a Third Major Cycle, the 3 means your harvest years will be both creative and rewarding, and you'll enjoy the pleasures of life.

Major Cycle Number 4: A Time of Putting Things in Order

In all cycles, the 4 brings a time of hard work and building foundations for your life. It's the practical things of life that will dominate this period of time: work, career, family, buying a home, building a solid community. Money matters are of top priority now, as you build a sound financial plan for your life. The Third Major Cycle for the 4 is a time of discipline, order, economy, and self-motivation; it means that your harvest years will be both stable and secure.

Easy as 1-2-3

A 4 Major Cycle is a time for learning how to set boundaries and to maintain good health.

Major Cycle Number 5: A Freeing Cycle

Rapid progress and change characterize the 5 Major Cycle in any position, and travel, moving your residence, and changing jobs are all part of this cycle's energy. During this period, you'll be free of the burdens of responsibility seen in some of the other cycles, such as the 4 and the 6, because it's a time for promoting yourself, seeking new opportunities, and there's the prospect of visiting foreign lands, discovering other cultures, and having exciting new adventures. Seeking change, taking risks, and facing new adventures will bring great satisfaction. You're learning the lessons of freedom, which, if managed well, will show you the excitement of life, and, if managed poorly, will teach, as Janis Joplin sang, that freedom is a metaphor for recklessness, for nothing left to lose.

Easy as 1-2-3

A 5 Major Cycle means your major lesson is to learn to change, adapt, live with uncertain finances, and explore.

Major Cycle Number 6: A Cycle for Marriage, Family, and Responsibility

Under this Major Cycle, the issues of commitment, marriage, family, and responsibility all dominate, so this is the best cycle for marriage, because when one is committed and can live with acceptance and respond lovingly, this is the cycle of happy heart and happy home. However, if commitment cannot be made deeply or is broken, then divorce and separation will punctuate this cycle.

This is also a time that favors starting a business—especially one that is service oriented—in the home or a family-run business. Under this cycle new opportunities for self-expression are found as well—gardening, painting, music, especially singing, decorating, or writing. Family or the lack of family, home, and children also play a large role in this Major Cycle. You're learning the power and problem of responsibility. When 6 is the number of your Third Major Cycle, you can expect to be surrounded by family, content with your home and garden (it is the time of harvest, after all!), and active in community service. It's a perfect time for all those Cancer Sun signs out there—or for anyone who's ready to become a homebody!

Easy as 1-2-3

A 6 Major Cycle is a time for learning the lesson of codependence, that is, to not subjugate your needs for another's and not go overboard with responsibilities.

Major Cycle Number 7: A Cycle for Delving Deeper

The 7 Major Cycle emphasizes study and research of some kind, investigation, spiritual seeking, and gaining skills, and generally centers on scientific, technical, intellectual, religious, or metaphysical fields. This is the time for analysis and

contemplative thinking—reflecting upon
the deeper questions of life, and it's also
the time of specialization. Here, intuitive
skills are enhanced, the inner life becomes compelling, and wisdom is developed.

Easy as 1-2-3

A 7 Major Cycle is a time for
study, specialization, and sharing your wisdom.

Relationships require understanding partnership during a 7 Major Cycle, because a
great sum of your energy will be spent in time alone or in introspection. You're called
upon to share your knowledge and wisdom with others through teaching, counseling,
writing, or conversation. As a Third Major Cycle, the 7 brings spiritual development,
and a quiet, reserved time of inner analysis and the gaining of knowledge—people
will come to you for your wisdom.

Major Cycle Number 8: A Cycle of Money and Recognition

The 8 Major Cycle is an excellent time for work, career, success, and financial reward.
It's the hard work and ability to overcome obstacles and setbacks that bring your true
success. This is a time of competent management, good planning, and acute organization, because you develop the gift for seeing the broader picture and boldly carrying
out that vision.

Business and career dominate the 8 Major Cycle. It's not uncommon to gain financial
freedom, because there's a compelling drive to take control of your work and bring it
to new heights of achievement. You're viewed as an authority during the later stages
of this cycle, and others deem you power-
ful. If 8 is the number of your Third
Major Cycle, you'll know monetary reward, with the possibility of inherited
money. You won't really retire; instead, in
some way, you'll utilize your skills as "the
boss" to the last breath you take!

Easy as 1-2-3

An 8 Major Cycle is a time for
learning about power, money,
and success in the business
world.

Major Cycle Number 9: A Cycle of Selfless Service and Reward

Under this cycle, you develop compassion and tolerance, a broad view of humanity,
and a sincere concern for the welfare of your fellow human. Obviously, it means
you'll have to bring the lessons of all the other numbers to bear upon this humanitarian cycle.

Under Major Cycle 9, there's an element of sacrifice, of letting go, of forgiveness, and
of surrender to the mystery of life. It's here that you finally make the connection

between human existence and the spiritual energy of all that is. Intuition is enhanced and much personal and spiritual enrichment is found. It's a rewarding cycle for those who live selflessly and altruistically. You're learning the lessons of giving and loving in this cycle, as well as the lesson of completion. This can be an emotional time until you understand that all things are a part of the great cosmic plan, and that when something ends, it makes room for something new to move in. You will learn to let go.

Easy as 1-2-3

A 9 Major Cycle is a time to learn the lesson of letting go, developing intuition, and trusting in the universal order of all things.

You grow toward your ideals of perfection, an expanded view of love, and selfless service. Your work is directed toward the improvement of the world, the planet, the unfortunate, and the healing of others. Creative talent is enhanced under this cycle, especially if your efforts encompass a larger social purpose or message.

Major Cycle Master Number 11/2: A Cycle of Illumination

If you have this Master Number as one of your Major Cycles, it means you were born either in November or on the 11th of the month, or you were born in 1901. The 11 is a cycle of growth and understanding of higher human ideals, and it's a time of inspiration, self-improvement, and hard-won revelations about how life truly works.

But it's only through a deep personal transformation and improvement of self-expression that you'll be able to bring forth these revelations, because you were born to illuminate others and share with your community. The more willing you are to work on yourself, the more good you will do the larger world. The 9 in any Major Cycle position requires courage, determination, and strength to delve deeply into a higher consciousness of universal principle and spiritual interconnectedness.

In an 11/2 Major Cycle, you may have to relearn the lessons of the 2: partnership and cooperation. As an 11, if you accept the path of the "spiritual messenger," you will find great reward, including financial support, even fame. If the energy of the 11 is too intense or too demanding, you will revert to the energy of the 2, where the issues of sensitivity, cooperation, and relationship will dominate your days. Either way, this is a period in your life where you will have to learn to find harmony within yourself while you learn to lead.

Major Cycle Master Number 22/4: A Cycle of Enormous Potential

A cycle with this Master Number can occur only if you were born on the 22nd of the month or in a year that reduces to 22/4, so it appears only in the Second or Third

Major Cycle positions. The 22/4 Major Cycle is a time of tremendous potential for establishing lasting institutions, monuments, and/or teachings that will benefit others.

Generally, the 22/4 Major Cycle is rewarding financially and spiritually, because you will be called to build things for your society that reflect your understanding of spiritual principles and the material world. It's the weaving of these two together that is your true mastery.

Easy as 1-2-3

The 22/4 Major Cycle is learning the lessons of integrity, balance, and responsibility to a larger purpose.

During this time, your level of mastery as a builder, organizer, and visionary is at its peak; you're filling a great human need. It's an all-consuming role that you must play, requiring great sums of energy and focus. In return, you're rewarded with the satisfaction of knowing you've made a lasting contribution to the betterment of the Earth and humanity, and have left a legacy for generations to come.

Major Cycle Master Number 33/6: A Cycle of Cosmic Love

The number 33/6 can occur only if you were born in a year that reduces to a 33, so it appears only in the Third Major Cycle position. We did not see this Master Number denote a Master Cycle position in the twentieth century. The first time this number will occur is over 100 years away—in the years 2103, 2112, 2121, and 2130. What does this tell us? Perhaps that we have a long way to go before we are ready to have a 25+ year Third Master Cycle on the personal level where love is the dominant theme.

In the new millennium with its vibration of the 2 (as in 2000), we will need to work and live in partnership and harmony. This is the groundwork that will have to be done to prepare the way for a 33/6 Master Cycle harvest.

The Least You Need to Know

◆ Your Major Cycles show you the timing for your life.

◆ Your First Major Cycle is the formative cycle.

◆ Your Second Major Cycle is the productive cycle.

◆ Your Third Major Cycle is the harvest cycle.

Your Personal Year Number

In This Chapter

- Every year has a theme and lesson
- You can have a Personal Year Number from 1 to 9
- Calculating your Personal Year Number
- The nine-year cycle and you
- Finding your age vibration

Now that you've learned how to find your five Core Numbers, Pinnacles, Challenges, and Major Cycles, it's time to take a look at the Personal Year Number and how you move through the cycles of your life. Each of the nine numbers represents a year in a nine-year cycle, and each year carries its own unique vibration, identity, and demands.

Each month and even each day have their own special numerological vibration as well. We'll be adding those in the next chapter. But first, let's take a look at your Personal Years.

What Is Your Personal Year Number?

Your *Personal Year Number* is a number that tells you what's happening for you, personally, this year. Every year has a number and carries with it an

By the Numbers

Your **Personal Year Number** represents where you are in a nine-year cycle of personal growth. It's found by adding your month and day of birth to the current year.

energy that vibrates to that number. If you know how to read this energy—that is, if you know the number of your year—then you can direct your affairs for the best possible result!

Your Personal Year Number can show you how to avoid difficulties, position yourself for what's coming, and, in addition, what you can expect during this 12-month cycle. As one of the predictive numbers in numerology, your Personal Year Number is one of the most easily recognized numbers at work in your life.

By knowing your Personal Year Number, you can know in advance what to expect, what obligations might lie ahead, and how best to prepare for this year. Once you know your Personal Year Number (or someone else's), events and situations make more sense, because you can put them in the context of the predicted pattern for the year.

The Personal Year starts on January of any year, and runs through the entire 12 months. Each Personal Year has a theme, so you'll have nine Personal Year themes in a cycle (because Personal Years run in nine-year cycles). Some people feel the thrust and purpose of their Personal Years more toward their birthdays, especially if their birthdays are in the summer or fall, rather than at the beginning of the year.

Each year has both an identity of its own and certain demands. We're told there's a time for everything under the sun, and wise men and women will succeed (where others may fail) by reading their Personal Year Numbers and planning accordingly. Your Personal Year Number is one of the most significant numbers in your life, so it's worthwhile to spend some time getting to know your Personal Year Number and what it means.

Figuring Your Personal Year Number

It's quite simple to figure your Personal Year Number. Just remember one tip: You'll be using the *current calendar year* when you figure the Personal Year Number. Plus, you'll want to be sure to use all four digits of the year to get the right reduced number—no shortcuts allowed! You'll want to use 2000, not 00, or 1999, not just 99. Also, Master Numbers and Karmic Numbers do not apply to the Personal Year.

Numerology Rule: This is the formula for finding your Personal Year Number: *Month of birth + day of birth + current calendar year = Personal Year Number.*

Let's say you were born April 10, and that you want to know what this year's Personal Year Number is. Just add 4 (April) + 1 (10 reduced) + the calendar year.

If you were figuring the Personal Year Number for the calendar year 2006, you would simply add:

(handwritten) 2+6+5
11 15 5 2012 = 4

4 + 1 + 8 (2006 reduced) = 13 = 4 (3 reduced)

This means that anyone born on April 10 in the year 2006 is in a 4 Personal Year. Get it? Let's try another example.

Sixes and Sevens _____

One mistake frequently made when calculating the Personal Year Number is to use your year of birth instead of the current calendar year. It's the current calendar year that you need to figure your Personal Year Number. You drop the year you were born when figuring the Personal Year Number—and replace it with the current calendar year.

If you want to know what year you were in for 1999, you would add 1999 together (1 + 9 + 9 + 9 = 1) to get the single-digit number 1 and then add that number to your month and day of birth (leave out your birth year). If you were born December 23, for example, it would look like this:

Month of birth	12 (reduced to 1 + 2) = 3
Day of birth	23 (reduced to 2 + 3) = 5
Calendar year	1999 (reduced to 1 + 9 + 9 + 9) = 28 = 10 = 1

Now add the reduced numbers together:

Personal Year: 3 + 5 + 1 = 9

So this person would be in a 9 Personal Year, a year of endings.

Days of Your Life

Now it's time to figure your own current Personal Year Number. Fill in the number in steps 1 through 4 and see what you find.

1. Your month of birth: ____11____ (reduce if necessary) = ____2____ = _____

2. Your day of birth: ____15____ (reduce if necessary) = ____6____ = _____

3. The current year: __2012__ (reduce this number) = ____5____ = _____

    Be sure to use the *whole year*. For example, use 2005, not 05.

4. Add together the numbers from steps 1 through 3, and this is your Personal Year Number: ___13=4___

My Personal Year is for ___4___ (current calendar year)

Now circle the number of your Personal Year in the following chart. That's where you are in the nine-year cycle.

Table for Personal Year Cycle								
Personal Year Numbers: 1	2	3	4	5	6	7	8	9

How the Personal Year Fits into the Nine-Year Cycle

We're all living under nine-year cycles, from a numerology standpoint. Somewhere in that cycle of nine is where you are.

Once you've found your own Personal Year Number, circle the number in the preceding chart that shows where you are now in this nine-year cycle. This will also allow you to see what year you were in last year and what next year will bring as well. You may want to tab this page for future reference, so that you can find all your Personal Years.

The Rhythm of the Years

Each year has its own natural rhythm and flow, and fits into a larger flow of the nine-year cycle. Here's the pattern of flow for each Personal Year:

The Flow of the Nine-Year Cycle

Personal Year Number	What It Means
1 Personal Year	A time of new beginnings, planting seeds; an active year
2 Personal Year	A year of cooperation, sensitivity, and relationship; a slow year
3 Personal Year	A year of creative ideas, having to say your truth, expressing yourself; an active year
4 Personal Year	A year of putting down roots, hard work, discipline, health, and putting into form the ideas of the 3 Personal Year; a productive year—must persevere

Personal Year Number	What It Means
5 Personal Year	A year of change, unpredictability, risk taking, and freedom, getting unstuck from the 4 Personal Year; an active year
6 Personal Year	A year of tending to domestic affairs, family obligations, nurturing others; constant effort is required
7 Personal Year	A year of turning inward, rest and rejuvenation, contemplation and pursuit of spiritual quest; will spend time alone, can study and read this year
8 Personal Year	A year of respect, achievement, recognition; business matters dominate, especially financial management; an active, busy year where you must administrate
9 Personal Year	A year of completion, release, forgiveness, and transformation; a quieter year, a time to rest, but can be busy in the first half

You can trust these Personal Year Numbers; they're uncanny in their accuracy in terms of describing the events that show up under each number, and how the year will play out.

Merlin's Notes

Personal Year Numbers are very accurate. Kay cites a client who learned that next year she would be in a 6 Personal Year, a year of duty and responsibility to family. The client had broken away from her family and couldn't see how the year could possibly be about family as she had no children or husband. Then, in June of her 6 Personal Year, she called to say, "I can't believe it, you were right. I've had to help my family deal with my brother who is troubled and has had a near-death experience, my mother has died suddenly, and I've just found out I have a brother I haven't known about in my 46 years."

Each Personal Year Number has its own characteristics. The number tells the tale.

Personal Year Numbers

So what year's best for having a baby? For buying a house, or moving to another apartment? Do you want to go into business? Get married? Ditch it all and hitchhike across Europe (or Nepal)? Your Personal Year Numbers can help you determine all kinds of things.

If you miss out on a Personal Year Number because you didn't know about it, weren't able to focus on it, or whatever, don't despair—out of the 12 months of each year, you will have at least several opportunities to deal with the number (and theme) you have missed. That's because each month of the year has a personal theme and personal number. We get to the Personal Months in the next chapter.

Personal Year Number 1

This is the year to begin any project. Begin it now because the flow is with you, and anything begun in a 1 year is favored and in synch with your natural rhythm. It's also a time for independence, courage, taking charge, and applying yourself. Unlike last year (which was a 9 year, a time of letting go), now is the time to start anew. Everything you do now will affect your future: You're planting seeds this year for your whole nine-year cycle.

The 1 year means it's time for you to focus on yourself. Use this year to take self-improvement classes, change your image, and/or focus on your personal goals. More than any other year, this is the time to become acquainted with the needs of your self. Here's the seed for all of the new beginnings that might be planted this year. It's time for a new you, and if you don't take time for yourself this year, you won't really get another full year to devote to this energy for nine more years, when you'll have another 1 Personal Year. However, each year you will have a chance to work on missed opportunities when you are in your 1 Personal Month. We discuss the Personal Month in the next chapter.

Personal Year Number 2

This is the year to back up and regroup. It's a time to listen to others, and perhaps even defer to them. A time of waiting and delays, this isn't a year for getting things done, but you will be more sensitive to the nuances of relationship and the needs of others. Unlike last year, this year your own needs will be secondary now. People often move in a 2 year, because this is a year of adaptability and balance.

The 2 year means it's time for you to relate to others. Cooperation is the lesson. Use this year to listen, be sensitive, and take the time for others. More than any other year, this is the time to compromise and seek harmony in all that you do. It's time for taking things slowly, and if you don't take your time this year, it will be another nine years before you have a full year to devote to this energy. However, each year you will have a chance to work on missed opportunities when you are in your 2 Personal Month. We discuss the Personal Month in the next chapter.

In a 2 Personal Year, you often find a quiet, soothing rhythm to life, and may even truly experience a sense of peacefulness.

Personal Year Number 3

A 3 year is one of the hardest to understand, but no matter what, it won't be like your 2 year. Because the number 3 is supposed to be about joy, fun, and socializing, it may be hard to understand the agony experienced during this year. So many times Kay has heard students say, "What's fun about this 3 year?" The truth is, you may be working the emotional aspect of the 3: learning to say what's in your heart; finding words for what you feel; and having to go out into the world and speak your truth. This can be a very painful part of the 3 year; however, once you've conquered this milestone, the creative juices just seem to flow. Then it's time for fun, creative endeavors, and playing with friends. Of course, if you had a heads-up last year, the 2 year, you probably took care of those relationships so this year you don't have to do the hard work emotionally.

 **Easy as 1-2-3**

The 3 Personal Year is the year for projects that involve writing, artistic flair, inspiration, public speaking, or a dramatic flair. In a 3 year the creative juices just flow more freely—provided you're not an emotional basket case from struggling with having spoken your truth!

The 3 year means it's time for you to express yourself. This is the year to write, keep a journal, paint, sing, dance, or have that heart-to-heart discussion—anything that allows you to speak and express your truth creatively. More than any other year, this is the time to use your imagination. It's time for playing and being with others, and if you don't take time to express yourself and your emotions this year, it will be waiting for you in your next 3 year—nine years away. However, each year you will have a chance to work on missed opportunities when you are in your 3 Personal Month. We discuss the Personal Month in the next chapter.

Personal Year Number 4

This can be a year to manage things, especially your health. It's a time to set things in order, set up systems, and lay down solid foundations for your future. Getting a home, having a family, getting insurance—all of these are the foundation pieces for our life. Needless to say, a 4 year takes a lot of hard work.

Another facet of the 4 Personal Year that you may be working on is going back into the roots of the family dynamic in order to sort out your relationship to the early childhood drama. This work is usually called "family of origin" work, and (so fitting for the 4) it's about getting to the root of the problem. For this reason, this year may feel like the year from hell; it's very hard work to dig deep and reset the foundation pieces of your adult life.

The 4 year means it's time for you to build for the future, lay a foundation, or put down roots. Use this year to make lasting decisions and put these into action. More than any other year, this is the time to make things secure. It's time for stability and reliability, and if you don't take time to build your life this year, it will be another nine years before you will have a full year to devote to this energy. However, each year you will have a chance to work on missed opportunities when you are in your 4 Personal Month. We discuss the Personal Month in the next chapter.

Personal Year Number 5

This is the year of personal transition, as opposed to the 9 year, when you'll be working on transformation. The 5 is a time of change—change in attitude, change of work, residence, and change of direction. Travel is good during this year, and you may do a lot of it. Because the 5 is curious, you may find yourself delving into metaphysics, taking classes, or investigating some new subject.

The 5 year means it's time for you to take some risks. Use this year to make big changes in your life. More than any other year, this is the time to move, change jobs or careers, or even try unconventional things you haven't tried before. It's time to be curious, and if you don't take time to investigate new things that interest you this year, it will be another nine years before you will have a full year to devote to this energy. However, each year you will have a chance to work on missed opportunities when you are in your 5 Personal Month. We discuss the Personal Month in the next chapter.

Sixes and Sevens

Marital issues move to the forefront in a 6 Personal Year, too, and you'll either recommit to your relationship or decide not to, thereby putting in motion an end to the marriage. It may take you until your 9 year, when the energy is about truly ending something, to finalize the divorce, however.

Personal Year Number 6

If you have elderly parents, this is the year for them. In an uncanny way, you'll become needed by your family this year more than any of the other years. It's also a year that demands that you balance your domestic life with your work life, and you'll be shown many opportunities to get your work life in balance—even if it means getting another job.

The 6 year means it's time for you to pay attention to your family duties and responsibilities. Use this year to nurture and serve those you care about.

More than any other year, this is the time to balance the needs of others with your own needs. It's time for generosity and sympathy, and if you don't take time to give to your family, or to nurture your own needs, it will be another nine years before you have a full year to devote to this energy. However, each year you will have a chance to work on missed opportunities when you are in your 6 Personal Month. We discuss the Personal Month in the next chapter.

Personal Year Number 7

This is a time to move inside yourself. You'll need alone time and rest as you reexamine your goals, relationships, and the very direction for your life. Often, during a 7 year, you're drawn to the study of spiritual, mystical, or metaphysical subjects, and it's not unusual to find you need spiritual direction, and so look to a counselor or healer who can help further your quest.

This year is also a time of body purification, so diets, cleansing, and detoxifying programs may become of interest now. The 7 rules legal affairs, so it may also be the year you get that insurance settlement finished, or any matter where legal papers are involved. But no matter what, you'll need and seek solitude, because this is the time to be alone and quiet.

The 7 year means the time is favorable for you to take a sabbatical, or do a vision quest. More than any other year, this is the time to be quiet and listen to your inner guidance. It's a time for seeking counsel from both yourself and others, as well as learning about what will help you find your own particular peace. Don't miss your chance for this introspective time, because you don't get another 7 year for nine more years! However, each year you will have a chance to work on missed opportunities when you are in your 7 Personal Month. We discuss the Personal Month in the next chapter.

Personal Year Number 8

This is a year to learn about your own power, to deal with authority issues, and to become the boss, because people will look to you this year for your executive ability or to act as an authority in some respect. This is the year where you'll be challenged to take the lead, to stand up as an authority, and in that way to begin to empower yourself with your full sense of power.

The 8 year means it's time for you to be thrust into the role of the leader, boss, or authority and to tend to business. Use this year to administrate something—the family estate, the school auction, or the company's overseas spring tour. More than any other year, this is the time to deal with the energy of power, money, and success, and to achieve something. You'll want to make the most of your opportunity this year because it will be another nine years before you have an 8 year again. However, each year you will have a chance to work on missed opportunities when you are in your 8 Personal Month. We discuss the Personal Month in the next chapter.

Sixes and Sevens

In an 8 Personal Year you can have some kind of big expense, but money will be good this year. Money flows toward you in an 8 year—as long as you're working for the good of all, and not just for personal profit. Still, as the money flows in, it flows out at almost the same rate. You must keep your head on and manage your financial affairs well this year. It is not time for extravagance or to get carried away with your emotions.

Personal Year Number 9

The tide is out in a 9 year, but the harvest is in! This is the year of rewards for all the effort you've made in the past eight years. This is the end, the conclusion of your nine-year cycle, so the seeds you planted in your 1 year are now harvested.

When the tide goes out, it means that the ending of a cycle is at hand, and the energy of this year is more about letting things go, finishing, and dreaming about the next nine years. It's time to revision, dream, and envision once again how you would like your life to proceed, to allow things to conclude, and wait, because the beginning that you sense is coming is next year. This is also a time for healing and dreaming on both a figurative and literal level. Have a massage and pay attention to your dreams.

Sixes and Sevens

Sometimes, the 9 Personal Year can be emotional, because you're letting go of the old so the new can come in. For others, the 9 year is a transformational year: A large piece of their life story is healed or released, and with it, an end occurs.

On another note, this is a good money year, because efforts of selfless giving and loving are favored and rewarded this year. Of course the inverse can be true as well. If you're behaving selfishly and needing to revamp your money picture, the 9 Personal Year may be a trying time for money. Don't despair; next year is a 1 year and starting anew is always favored under a 1.

The 9 year means it's time for you to forgive and forget. Use this year to complete things and bring things to closure on every level. More than any other year, this is the time to follow your intuition and seek to perfect what was begun eight years before.

It's time for tying everything together, and if you miss this opportunity for finishing things this year, you will most likely find your unfinished business lurking about and needing to be faced, again—in nine years. However, each year you will have a chance to work on missed opportunities when you are in your 9 Personal Month. We discuss the Personal Month in the next chapter.

Looking Back

Now that you know your Personal Year Number, you'll find it fun to look back and see what was happening for you nine years ago, when you were in the same Personal Year as you are now. You may want to look at the entire nine years of the past with this new tool—or you may even want to look back at your whole life! You'll be surprised at how true to your life each Personal Year Number's vibration is, and once you do see it, you'll want to calculate the future, of course.

Nine Years Ago

Personal Year Numbers move in nine-year cycles as we have said; however, nine years ago you may have been in a different Pinnacle than the one you're in now—and had a different Challenge Number, too. Check your Pinnacle Number to see what you were trying to attain when you last had this Personal Year Number. You'll also want to check your Challenge Number from nine years ago to see what lesson you were working on during this Personal Year.

Even though you repeat the Personal Year every nine years, the experience is not exactly the same. That's because you were working on a different facet of this personal number last time around. Still, upon close examination—and with a good memory (or good journal)—you'll see that it was, to cite a few examples, a time of new beginnings if you were in a 1 year, a time of duty and responsibility to the family if you were in a 6 year, or a time of study and wanting to withdraw if you were in a 7 year.

> **Easy as 1-2-3**
>
> Your Personal Year is influenced by your Pinnacle and Challenge Numbers.

Numbers Are Like Crystals

Each number is like a multifaceted crystal. When you look at each number as a crystal, you're actually viewing only one facet of the crystal at a time. When you've finished with one aspect of a number, you'll move to the next facet of the number.

Someone else may be looking at the same number (or crystal), but will be viewing a different facet.

We're not all the same; each of us is working our way through our own blueprint for life, but all of us will go through nine-year cycles, one Personal Year at a time. That's why, when you and your friend are both in an 8 year, you may not be working on the same thing. While each of you will be learning about the basic characteristics of the 8, you'll experience it differently, because whatever Pinnacle or Challenge you're in during your 8 year will influence and color that year.

Study the basic meaning of each number, and you'll begin to see that each number has many facets. You're currently working on some facet of a particular number right now. For example, the number 6 is about nurturing and caring for others, service, romance, marriage and divorce, duty and responsibility, and balance. If you're currently in a 6 Personal Year, you may be working on caring for family members, while when you were in a 6 Personal Year nine years ago, you may have been working on marriage and/or divorce, or attracting a new love interest.

This is what we mean by facets of the number: When a certain number comes up, you'll naturally be involved with issues of that number. We work our way around the facets of the crystal—the number crystal.

Don't Miss Your Chance

What happens if you pay no attention whatsoever to your Personal Year Number? Well if you didn't know about your Personal Year before reading this chapter you already know that things will happen anyway! Whether you're aware of it or not, whether you choose to pay attention or not, your life is proceeding in a distinct pattern, and moving through these cycles of personal growth. It's when you pay attention that you can make the most progress and gain a sense of mastery.

Now that you've got this key, however, there are certain things about certain Personal Year Numbers you won't want to miss. You won't want to miss the 1 year, for example, because it's the time to put yourself into a new start. A new time is forming.

Merlin's Notes
Things *begun* in a 9 Personal Year don't tend to last; they're not supported by the natural energy flow of this number. Instead, if you start something in a 9 year, you are beginning when the tide is going out. Of course, there is another way to look at this: If you get married, or finally begin that novel, it may be a time of rewards—what's long been waited for. Then the new beginning is really more of an end to a long cycle of events.

You'll know a new start when it shows up—if you're paying attention. You'll feel the highly active energy of the 1, as opposed to the more subdued energy of the 9, which feels quiet and reflective.

Another year you won't want to miss is the 5 year. In a 5 Personal Year, change is afoot. This is a very significant time for personal transition, and setting yourself on a course of action that will affect the next four years (the rest of the nine-year cycle).

Still another year you don't want to miss is the 7 year—it's the only full year you'll have in nine years to devote to turning inward and reevaluating. At the very least, you'll want to devote a good portion of this year to reevaluating where you're headed with your life. The 7 year requires that you pull back from others and have time alone. Solitude, nature, the woods, and the mountains all provide sacred places and quiet energy to restore you and allow you to listen within. Of course, you'll have a 7 month every year, so if you miss the boat in this 7 year, at least you'll have a chance to do the 7 thing once or twice each year. (We'll tell you all about your Personal Months in the next chapter.)

The Age Vibration: Harmonic Resonance

A subtheme to your Personal Year is found in the age you'll be during a particular Personal Year that is called your *age vibration*. Simply stated, how old you are during a Personal Year has a subtle influence on your year.

To figure your age vibration number, just determine how old you'll be in the given year. If, for example, your birthday is March 30, 1948, and you're figuring your Personal Year age vibration for the year 2004, simply subtract 1948 (year of birth) from the current year, 2004: 2004 − 1948 = 56.

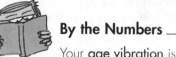

By the Numbers

Your **age vibration** is the way your age influences your Personal Year.

Most of us are two ages in a given year. So, if you were born in March, you'll live almost four months of 2004 as 55 years old, and then on your birthday (March 30), you'll be 56. So we then say that in 2004 you were both 55 and 56.

Sixes and Sevens

Don't forget—whenever you're figuring the year, you must use and reduce *all four digits* to come up with the right number. So use 2004, not 04, and 1995, not 95!

We find your age vibration by taking these ages and adding them together. In other words, for this example, we add 55 + 56 to get 111, which we reduce to a single digit, or 1 + 1 + 1 = 3. During the year 2004, you would have an age vibration of a 3.

It's important to look at the age vibration in relation to your Personal Year theme. Let's say you're in a 5 Personal Year and you have a 2 age vibration. The 5 means change and the 2 means relationship, so we might conclude that you will experience change along the line of relationship during the year. It also means that partnerships of all kinds are up for change. See how it works? All of the numbers work in relationship to one another.

What if your birthday's in January? Well, you won't have many days of being two different ages so if you have a January birthday, just calculate the one age you'll be. For example, if you're turning 34 in January, just add 3 + 4 = 7, which means that you'll have a 7 age vibration that year.

The Least You Need to Know

- ◆ Every Personal Year Number—from 1 to 9—has its own special message and demands.

- ◆ Finding your Personal Year Number is as easy as adding your month and day of birth to the current year.

- ◆ Knowing where you are in your own nine-year cycle can help you plan for the future—and understand the past.

- ◆ Your age vibration adds a secondary influence to your Personal Year Number's vibration.

Your Personal Month Numbers

In This Chapter

- ◆ The natural rhythm of the months of the year
- ◆ Finding your Personal Month Numbers
- ◆ Laying out your year
- ◆ A word about Personal Day Numbers

In addition to finding Personal Year Numbers, you can also find your Personal Month Numbers—even your Personal Day Numbers! Personal Year Numbers have the strongest influence, but laying out your year month by month can help you understand the natural rhythm of your year.

According to its number, each month's theme has a rhythm of its own, and, once you know the meaning of your Personal Month Number, you can use it to know which tasks will go best in which months. In this chapter, we'll show you how to do just that.

You've Got Personal Month Numbers, Too

So what exactly is a *Personal Month Number?* Personal Month Numbers are found by adding the number of the calendar month to the number of your Personal Year.

By the Numbers

Each **Personal Month Number** has a theme that is part of the rhythm of your Personal Year. The Personal Month Number is found by adding the number of your Personal Year to the number of the calendar month. You have 12 Personal Month Numbers for each Personal Year.

In terms of emphasis, the Personal Year is the most significant number. You can think of it as the main theme of the year. The Personal Month Number represents that month's particular influence within the greater Personal Year vibration. Every Personal Month Number has its own special energy, which infuses that month of the year with its unique opportunities and potential. For example, October may be your 7 Personal Month in a 6 Personal Year. In this case, the 7 Personal Month represents not only the opportunity to go within during your nurturing 6 Personal Year, but also provides a sneak preview of the energy and issues surrounding your upcoming 7 Personal Year.

Figuring Your Personal Month Number

Figuring your Personal Month Number is easy, once you know your Personal Year. (To review the calculation of the Personal Year, see the previous chapter.) You'll simply add the number of your Personal Year to the number of each calendar month. We won't be using Master Numbers or Karmic Numbers for the Personal Year Month calculations. Most numerologists don't consider them applicable. Master and Karmic numbers are more important when working with the Core Numbers. Here's a chart of the numerical equivalent of each month to get you started.

The Numbers of the Calendar Months

Month	Number
January	1
February	2
March	3
April	4
May	5
June	6

Month	Number
July	7
August	8
September	9
October	1 (1 + 0)
November	2 (1 + 1)
December	3 (1 + 2)

As an example, let's say 2001 was a 5 Personal Year for you. Look at the following chart to see how each Personal Month for that year is calculated.

Personal Months for the Year 2001 and a 5 Personal Year

Month	Month Number	+	Personal Year Number	=	Personal Month Number
January	1	+	5	=	6
February	2	+	5	=	7
March	3	+	5	=	8
April	4	+	5	=	9
May	5	+	5	=	10 = 1
June	6	+	5	=	11 = 2
July	7	+	5	=	12 = 3
August	8	+	5	=	13 = 4
September	9	+	5	=	14 = 5
October	1	+	5	=	6
November	2	+	5	=	7
December	3	+	5	=	8

Numerology Rule: This is the formula for finding your Personal Month: *Personal Year Number + calendar month number = Personal Month Number.*

Easy as 1-2-3

Finding your Personal Month Numbers for any given year is really simple. Remember, just add your Personal Year Number to the number of the calendar month!

Personal Month Meanings

When she does clients' personal Numerology Profiles, Kay likes to lay out their Personal Months for them, using a template that she fills in. We've created just such a template for you to calculate your Personal Month Numbers.

Your Personal Month Numbers

To find the numbers of your Personal Months, add the number of your current Personal Year to the number of the month. Do your calculations and fill in your numbers in the following spaces:

ie July 7 + 4

0   For the calendar year __2012__, which is my Personal Year Number
     ___4___, my Personal Month Numbers are: (+4)

Jan. __5__   Feb. __6__   Mar. __7__   Apr. __8__
May __9__   June __1__   July __11/2__   Aug. __3__
Sept. __4__   Oct. __5__   Nov. __16__   Dec. __7__

So what month are you in right now? You'll find that each Personal Month Number has its own particular theme.

Personal Month Number 1

Easy as 1-2-3

As we were finishing this chapter, someone we know well started a job with a new company—after 15 years with another. He was in a 1 Personal Month—and a 5 Personal Year. He couldn't have timed it better if he'd tried!

A 1 Personal Month is a lot like chili pepper—it will make you sit up and take notice. That's because a 1 Personal Month is the month of beginnings, when you'll tackle new projects, take charge, take over, and just plain get things rolling. It is a month to set goals and intention.

This month comes on the heels of a 9 Personal Month, which was good for tying up loose ends and finishing things up, so it will be only natural during this Personal Month to have the time and energy to want to start new projects.

Personal Month Number 2

A 2 Personal Month requires attention to detail. It is a time for taking care of all the bits and pieces of your life. It is also the Personal Month when the seeds you planted during the 1 Personal Month will begin to take root. You'll seek the help and advice of others, and work with them cooperatively on their projects as well. Cooperation is key to this month. That's because this is a month for relationships, for paying attention to others after the "me first" spirit of the 1 month.

Personal Month Number 3

A 3 Personal Month gets the creative juices flowing. Ideas come in abundantly. This is the month where you get to add those creative touches and you may find that you are expressing yourself verbally, emotionally, and artistically during this Personal Month.

A 3 Personal Month can be playtime, but this means personal playtime as much as playing with others. This means it's a great time to go shopping, buy gifts, go out to lunch, or buy yourself that sterling silver pin you've wanted since last Christmas. It's also time to play with color and design—so redesign your bedroom, put up new wallpaper in the bathroom, and do whatever gets your creative juices flowing.

> **Merlin's Notes**
>
> The 3 is considered the lucky number, so when you're in a 3 Personal Month, things may just be easier for you. The 3 month can also be an opportunity to express yourself—you know, speak up about that issue you've been reluctant to mention.

Personal Month Number 4

A 4 Personal Month is where you'll find yourself having to be practical and disciplined, and tending to the hard work. This is a good month to make sure your goals are on track, building for the future, and creating a solid foundation. You'll work hard in a 4 month, but you'll be doing that work to ensure that your project's security and stability are assured. You may also work hard on family issues this month to make sure that your life is standing on solid footing—with no dry rot.

The 4 Personal Month is also a time to attend to health matters—go get that checkup, see that therapist, get a massage, get that juice maker, or investigate the proper vitamins/minerals for yourself and your family. In some manner, create a solid foundation for your health program this month—and that includes getting the right insurance program. This is the month to attend to these tasks, because this is the natural rhythm of the 4 month—to put down roots, secure things, get a plan, or build a foundation of stability for the rest of your Personal Year.

oct

Personal Month Number 5

A 5 Personal Month can bring something unexpected. Everything can change this month—your life may take off in a new direction or you may decide to abandon something entirely. This is the month of transition, which favors travel, adventure, and dealing with uncertainty.

A 5 Personal Month is also a good time to network, promote yourself, or sell, because you'll be more apt to communicate with others with enthusiasm, excitement, and magnetism in this month. The change you may feel in a 5 month is that of being willing to finally take a risk—that certainly will change things!

> **Sixes and Sevens**
>
> It's natural to want a change during a 5 month—after all, you've been following the same path step by step since you began in the 1 month. The trick is to realize this change is taking you to the next step. It's not time to panic; just make the necessary change.

Nov

Personal Month Number 6

In a 6 Personal Month, you'll be feeling a sense of duty and responsibility, so taking care of mom, the grandkids, and family issues, or visiting relatives, all might be on the agenda now.

This month you'll probably want to stay home and be with your family or putter around the house doing little home projects. A 6 Personal Month is a great time to tend to matters at home: Repot those plants, trim out the yard, add a little paint to the front door—it's the natural time to beautify the home. Of course, you may find it beautifying to just clean the house! It's a great time to just be family oriented: Go to that soccer game, make the trip to the zoo, go visit your parents this month.

Personal Month Number 7

A 7 Personal Month is a month for R & R, for studying the esoteric aspects of your life that you may not have previously pondered. You may want to schedule a retreat this month, because you'll feel the need to be alone to reflect and consider how things are going. It's natural during a 7 month to seek solitude, because you'll feel introspective and want to reevaluate where you've been—and where you're going.

The 7 month is a great time to go to the woods, to the mountains, or to the ocean to be restored by nature. Curling up with a good book or investigating a website or two are also activities for a 7 month. It's the one time in the year when you'll want to pay attention to your need to be by yourself and have time to think.

Personal Month Number 8

No nonsense in an 8 Personal Month! It's time to take your life by the reins and lead with your sure power and strong authority. At this point, you're certain of your direction and you'll want to assume command so that everything goes the way it should. You'll want to make sure that everything's taken care of in an 8 Personal Month—and you will.

An 8 Personal Month is a time to get down to business—all manner of business. Whether it's about speaking to the neighbors about their barking dog, calling the phone company about a new fax line, paying the taxes, handling those divorce papers, or making an investment; this is the month for taking charge of your life and manage things.

It's also a good time to organize your financial affairs, and this month also favors business deals and making arrangements for expanding into new markets. It's about money, power, and management this month!

Personal Month Number 9

In a number 9 Personal Month, you get to reap what you've sown—and you get to harvest all that you have done in previous months. You've earned the reward for all your hard work, and, whether it's monetary or spiritual, you'll know it was worth the effort.

A 9 Personal Month is a time to clean out, let go, and release. This is the month of endings. Something wants to draw to a close in this month, so you may feel like cleaning out file drawers, closets, or old girl/boyfriends, or putting an end to your credit card. This month's energy is inviting you to finish up, let it go, and make room for the new that is coming in next month.

Putting the Month in Context with the Personal Year

It's important to remember that the Personal Year has the strongest influence—the main theme for the whole year. The Personal Month adds its own particular twist. For example, a 3 Personal Month in a 4 Personal Year won't be as much fun as a 3 Personal Month in a 5 Personal Year.

If we were to list the subtle Personal Month influence on every Personal Year, we'd have 144 things to show you! Instead, to make things easy, we thought we'd set up a chart that lists an accent for each month. Each accent characterizes the mood or activity of a particular month, which you can add to any Personal Year.

To use this table, you'll need to have a good understanding of what each Personal Year's emphasis is. (You'll find what you need to know in the previous chapter where we talk about your Personal Year Number.) Now have a look at the key accents for each of your Personal Month Numbers and see how they can modify or enhance your Personal Year.

What Those Months Mean, Every Year

Personal Month Number	Accent
1	Seed something, begin it
2	Cooperate, be patient
3	Have fun, be with friends
4	Work hard, tend to health
5	Make a change
6	Nurture, beautify your home
7	Take some R & R
8	Take charge, deal with money
9	End it, get your reward

Learning to Work with Your Own Natural Rhythms

You've probably heard of *biorhythms*, which are your own natural physical cycles. Personal Years, Months, and Days act a lot like biorhythms, moving you through your own particular metaphysical cycles, and helping you to understand them and how to use them to work, play, or rest, at the times when these activities are best for you.

By the Numbers

Biorhythm is the name for any biological cycle that involves periodic change. Because biorhythms are cyclical, like numerological cycles, they can be predicted.

This is not to say that you can't begin something in a 5 month or even a 9 month—but it does suggest that things begun in a 1 month will more closely follow your own natural rhythm and therefore have a greater chance for success. If you must be social during a 7 month, something will probably feel "off"— just as if you try to have fun during a 4 month—or work hard during a 3 month.

Knowing your Personal Months can help you time when to begin things and when to end them, and it can also help you understand why sometimes, something just doesn't feel right or seems harder than it should.

Matching Your Day with Your Number

The *Personal Day Number* is the least emphasized of the three numbers: Remember, the Personal Year Number, which provides the theme for the year, has the strongest influence, while the Personal Month Number adds its unique accent. Some people don't feel their Personal Day Numbers at all—but there are places where you should pay attention.

By the Numbers

Your **Personal Day Number** adds a certain number's subtle energy to every day of your life. It's found by adding the number of the calendar day to the number of your Personal Month.

When your Personal Day Number matches your Life Path Number or your Soul Number, you should pay attention, because its subtle influence is added to what's already a strong influence in your life. These days will resonate more for you than other Personal Days.

The important thing to remember about Personal Days is that every Personal Day Number does have a subtle energy that it adds to the mix. These energies are more like little charged ions that add a certain spark to any given day. We've listed these sparks for you in the next chart.

What Your Personal Day Number Means

Personal Day Number	A Day To
1	Begin things, focus on self
2	Be patient, attend to details
3	Be creative, be with friends, communicate
4	Get organized, attend to your health
5	Make a change, network, and promote
6	Pay attention to work, family or home
7	Rest and reevaluate, time for quiet solitude, meditate
8	Handle money, take charge
9	Finish up, use your intuition

You can create an easy guide for finding your Personal Days. Write the number for each day directly on your regular calendar, once you've got them calculated. Simply add your Personal Month Number to the calendar day and write in your Personal Day Number. You might want to use a pocket month-at-a-glance calendar just for this purpose, keeping it as a handy reference for your Personal Days year round.

For example, if you are in a 7 Personal Month, using your calendar, the first day of the month will be an 8 day for you (7 + 1 = 8). Write the number 8 on the calendar for the 1st of the month, then write in your Personal Day Numbers for each day thereafter. Remember, this 7 month and 8 day belong to your Personal Year theme. Look to see how they fit together. What are you learning this month?

The Personal Months are indicators of the natural flow of your Personal Year theme. And like we've said before in this chapter, your Personal Month and Personal Day Numbers are guideposts for your journey throughout the year.

The Least You Need to Know

- ◆ Each Personal Month Number has a resonance that is part of the rhythm of your whole Personal Year theme.

- ◆ The Personal Month Number = the number of the calendar month + the number of your Personal Year.

- ◆ Laying out the Personal Months in your year can help you understand the natural flow for the year.

- ◆ The Personal Day = the number of the Personal Month + the calendar day.

Part 5

Living by the Numbers

Now that you've learned the basics of numerology, it's time to apply it to your own life. We'll show you how to map your relationships by the numbers, how to find the hidden information in a name, and how the numbers on your house or apartment affect your life.

Relationships by the Numbers

In This Chapter

- ◆ Looking to the numbers of relationships
- ◆ Finding compatibility with others—and with yourself
- ◆ The numbers next to each other can cause friction
- ◆ Concords: harmony in numbers

While your Personal Year Number can help you navigate the 12 months of the year, we thought you'd like to have some information to help you swim in the waters of relationship. By now, you've probably figured out that your relationships can be better understood when you look at what numbers you, your sweetie, and your family or friends have in common. How you and someone else will act and react in a relationship can be determined if you know how to read the numbers. Understanding the numbers helps reveal whether your relationship is likely to sink or float.

Some numbers have natural relationships as well, and some of you may already know these numbers. The Concords of numerical harmony are the 3, 6, and 9; the 1, 5, and 7; and the 2, 4, and 8. Each of these triads (group of three numbers) has a special emphasis, one more numerological aspect that you can learn to use to your relationship advantage.

Finding Your Soul Mate

There are some really simple formulas to use when it comes to finding the best relationships by the numbers. For example …

♦ When it comes to close, heartfelt relationships, you'll want to look to the Soul Number.

♦ For understanding what you can count on with someone, you'll look to the Life Path Number and the Birthday Number.

♦ To see if you'll get along with someone, the Personality Number is the one to check.

♦ If you're curious about growing old together, look to the Maturity Number for clues about late-life compatibility.

♦ If you want a spiritual relationship, look to the Soul Number—and especially for numbers 7, 9, or 11/2.

♦ If you want a partner you can count on to bring home the bacon and put a roof over your head, then look for a 4, 6, or 8 Life Path Number, or a 4 Destiny Number.

♦ If you're looking to play, live in a creative environment, and laugh your way through life, then look for a 3 Personality Number or a 3 Soul Number.

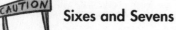

Sixes and Sevens

The Personality Number gives you an idea of how someone behaves and comes across in public life, but don't go signing on the dotted line when you're looking for a deep, soul-mated relationship. For that look to the Soul Number.

All kinds of things will affect your relationship choices, including karmic lessons and the Major Cycle and Pinnacle Numbers, which will show what the climate is for settling down for life. In addition, the Challenge Number will tell you what Mr. or Ms. Right is struggling with, and ultimately what he or she must learn and grow into.

When it comes to compatibility, look at the five Core Numbers as indicators of the essential elements of the person you want to understand. If you are trying to *find* somebody who is compatible, look to a person's five Core Numbers as well. If you want to know if the timing is right, or what the future holds, look at the Pinnacle, Challenge, Major Cycle, and Personal Year Numbers.

If you want to know if your new love interest can be loyal, open-minded, and appreciative, look to the numbers in both the Personality Number and the Soul Number. A 4, 6, or 9 would be nice for these qualities, for example. If, on the other hand, you want someone who'll be compliant, supportive, and loving, find yourself a 2 Personality or Soul Number.

Sixes and Sevens

People who share a Master Number can have many similarities, but they will also both share the intensity and sensitivity of the Master Number. It might not be a match made in heaven.

When you look at compatibility, there are several ways to examine your compatibility quotient. The most compatible of all is when you're evenly matched—Soul to Soul.

Every number can be counted on to have specific needs, and once you understand what each number's special needs are, you'll understand your potential for compatibility with a person who has that number. Here's a chart to help you evaluate the compatibility of each number.

Choose one of your Core Numbers and look to the table for the interpretation of what that number needs in relationship. Now choose one of your partner's numbers and see what he or she needs in relationship. Do this for all of your Core Numbers and do the same for your Pinnacle and Personal Year.

Number	Needs
1	Needs to be an individual and can be willful
2	Needs cooperation and peace
3	Self-expression is a must and is compelled to pursue its creativity
4	Will work hard and expects discipline
5	Wants change and to feel free
6	Needs to feel responsible, to be of service, and to feel needed
7	Focus is on gaining wisdom and is detached, introspective, and silent
8	Focus is on power and achievement
9	Needs to express compassion, is altruistic, and has strong emotions
11/2	Needs to inspire others and is intense
22/4	Needs to have a purpose, to be building something, and is intense
33/6	Needs to be saving the world, rescuing lost souls, teaching others through love, and is emotionally intense

Karmic Numbers are not used for this section except to say that when a Karmic Number shows up, it usually indicates you are dealing with a past life pattern or person in this relationship.

Master Number Relationships

Master Numbers are thought to be more charged, with a stronger energy present. To say the least, a Master Number is intense. Therefore, the person with the Master Number most likely won't remain at the intense level of the higher vibration (11, 22, or 33), but will revert to its lower vibration (2, 4, or 6). By operating at the lower frequency, the Master Number person will be easier to live, work, or be friends with, but, be forewarned, that person must address these master level energies, so it will be a life of constant ups and downs.

Merlin's Notes

If you have a Master Number as one of your five Core Numbers and want to team up with someone else with a Master Number, expect the relationship to be both intense and volatile. On the other hand, you two will share an understanding that's not available to those who don't have a Master Number in their profiles. Most likely, a two-Master-Number relationship will be spiritually connected, and you both will be leaders. It could be the most alive, high-energy, intense experience of your life!

When Core Numbers Match Up

In this section, we'll be talking about matching numbers, that is, when your number *matches* the number of someone else who has your same number in the same place in the five Core Numbers.

Easy as 1-2-3

It's simple: If you're looking for someone to be your lifetime companion, choose someone with your same Soul Number. Matching Soul Numbers are the most significant of all of the compatibility indicators. The trick is finding him or her!

If it's a permanent, committed relationship you're looking for, or one where you feel truly understood, then you'll want to look for the Soul Number. Remember, the Soul Number is also called the "heart's desire" number, and it's precisely the matter of the heart we're talking about here.

When the Soul Number is the same for both of you, there's a strong emotional tie. It suggests that you both want the same things in your heart of hearts. When you have the same Soul Number as another it strongly suggests a long-time love relationship, and even though other circumstances may cause problems or separation, the bond here goes on, because the tie between two similar Soul Numbers is a spiritual one, and possibly even a past-life relationship.

However, just because you have found a matching Soul Number, doesn't mean the relationship won't have its bumps. If your mate's Personality Number conflicts with your Soul Number, you may both want the same thing, but won't necessarily act on it in the same way.

Note that if you have a similar number in your Numerology Profile to one of your mate's, but not in the same Core Number position, then there's still a good degree of compatibility, because you both understand each other's energy through the characteristics of that number.

Life Matches

The next most important number to consider for compatibility is the Life Path Number. When two people share the same Life Path Number, it points to a happy relationship with many shared interests, provided you are both living the higher vibration of this number. This association may have its roots in work or social interests connected to work, because the Life Path Number indicates successful use for your inherent talents. With similar Life Path Numbers, you and your partner can expect to find similar talents and abilities. Look to the specific number for details.

Your Life Path Number tells of the path you'll travel in this lifetime, and with a love interest who has the same Life Path Number, you might expect to share a similar journey in life. While this attraction may lead to marriage, however, it doesn't promise smooth waters, because it's what's in your hearts (your Soul Numbers) that will determine the depth of understanding.

Destiny Matches

The next important number to consider for compatibility is the Destiny Number. When two people share the same Destiny Number, the relationship may be comparatively happy because they live on the same level, have similar backgrounds, come from similar environments, and are headed in a similar direction. Even though this can be a comparatively happy marriage or partnership, there will need to be other similar points of attraction for the union to last a long time and develop to its fullest potential.

Sixes and Sevens

While we wouldn't recommend basing a union on matching Personality Numbers, we would strongly recommend that you look at your partner's Personality Number anyway, because it will tell you a lot about what it will be like to live or work with this person.

Maturity Matches

The last significant number to consider in finding a true partner is the tie between two who share matched Maturity Numbers. Usually, when this is the matching number, it suggests a late-life marriage or some kind of culminating partnership, so you'd want to either share this number or have a compatible number with your mate if you're wondering about the later years of life and the ultimate goal for your lives.

Personality Matches

The Personality Number isn't considered an indicator of successful love relationships because this number shows the external person, rather than what's in the heart. Relationships based on Personality Number compatibility may feel great at first, but generally don't have the staying power of the other combinations. You know the old saying, "Don't judge a book by its cover"? Well, we want to encourage you to follow this advice, and to look more deeply than the Personality Number for your soul mate.

Compatibility by the Numbers

What if you add up your numbers and your partner's and find that each of you have all different numbers? Naturally, you're wondering about the degree of compatibility you share. The secret is in the differences—the *mathematical* difference in your numbers.

Numerology Rule: When figuring the compatibility differences between two people, subtract the numbers to find the key to resolving the difference.

Some numerologists call this number the *Stress Number*, because it shows the nature of the stress in a particular combination. Finding the Stress Number can help you understand which energies you need to focus on to improve your relationship. For example, if you have a 2 Soul Number and your partner has a 9 Soul Number, the stress will be the issues around the energy of the 7 or the difference between these two numbers (9 − 2 = 7). The Stress Number here is 7. Therefore, you'd want to explore the number 7 to understand the ups and downs of this energy and to determine how you can work with it.

Most likely, a lower energy vibration is being expressed if there's conflict between you, so you would want to look at the lower energies of all of the numbers involved, such as the 9, 2, and 7 in our example, and then look to the higher vibrations of each of these numbers and begin to emphasize the positive aspects, particularly the higher vibration of your difference number, in this case, the 7.

Let's look at an example. Let's say you have a 4 Soul Number and your partner has a 5 Soul Number. The difference between these numbers is 1 (5 − 4), so the key to resolving differences will be in understanding that you must work together to honor the characteristics of the 1: independence, desire to lead and do things your way, a need to be self-reliant, and a need to assert yourselves. These are the traits you'll want to foster in each other for the 4 Soul to feel secure, and for the 5 Soul to feel free to change things.

Of course, it will help enormously if you study the characteristics of each number. For this, please review the chapters in Part 2 on the meanings of each of your numbers. In addition to self-knowledge, you can gain valuable insight into your partner's needs. For example, if a 5 Soul doesn't understand that security and stability are vital to the 4, then you won't experience the connection you might long for—at least not on issues such as a steady income, accountability, and doing what you say.

Using Your Differences to Your Advantage

So what's the difference? Once you know, you can use it to your advantage and to the advantage of your relationship, whether the relationship is one of love, family, work, or play. If you have a 2 Soul Number and your partner has a 5 Soul Number, 3 is the difference. Look to the 3 to show you how to resolve your soul-related differences. Consider the following for differences between any of the numbers in your Numerology Profiles:

- **When 1 is the difference.** You'll need to honor the need for independence and individuality in the relationship.

- **When 2 is the difference.** You'll need to be sensitive to the person with the 2, and minimize conflict in the relationship. Honoring each other's sensitive points and working together as a team is key.

- **When 3 is the difference.** You'll need to communicate honestly, with no pushing anything under the rug. You'll have to say your truth and make it safe for the emotions that have been locked away to surface.

- **When 4 is the difference.** You'll need to resist the urge to be inflexible and rigid, especially if you happen to also have a 4 in your Core Numbers. Instead, this relationship will be about learning to set good boundaries, and keep them, with love and kindness. There's hard work here, and you'll have to discipline yourselves to make this relationship work.

◆ **When 5 is the difference.** Change is required here—honest, well-thought-out change. One or both of you may have an extreme need for freedom, and, with this number, you'll have to find a way to give each other that sense of freedom without compromising the integrity of the relationship.

◆ **When 6 is the difference.** You'll have to give up stubbornness and dogmatic opinions. Something's out of balance when a 6 is the difference number. Restore the balance immediately for love is at stake. You may also be learning about the depth and commitment of love and about being truly responsible.

◆ **When 7 is the difference.** You'll need to honor the need to be alone, to have private time, and to examine the spiritual or lack of spiritual consciousness in the relationship.

◆ **When 8 is the difference.** There are power struggles with this number, and you'll need to empower each other rather than struggle with who'll be the boss. You'll want to work on softening your response to each other, and to find a new plan for the business of this relationship.

◆ **When 9 is the difference.** There are no 9 differences!

Compatibility with Others

For love relationships, the Stress Number between your Soul Numbers is the one to examine first. When it's not a love relationship you're analyzing, but rather you're curious about other types of relating, such as sibling relationship, mother/daughter, father/son, father/daughter, mother/son, boss/coworker, or even best friend relationships, examining the other person's numbers will give you tremendous insight into what you can expect (and what you can't expect) from this relationship. You can determine how compatible you'll be with others by looking at the five Core Numbers of someone's profile and comparing them to your own. You'll also want to identify the Stress Number and look at its higher and lower energy vibrations for clues to your potential relationship peaks and pitfalls.

Use your differences to your advantage by understanding your numbers. If your differences are similar, there will be a greater basis for understanding and sharing complementary attitudes about life.

Looking at What's Going On in Both Your Lives

After you have your five Core Numbers and your partner's figured out, it's time to look at where each of you are in life. You might then want to look at how this time in life is going: What goals are important, what challenges need to be faced, and what Personal Year each of you is in now. It's especially fun (and informative, to say the least) to look to the following as indicators of what's cooking for your person of interest:

- ◆ **Personal Year.** This number tells what the immediate issues are, as well as what this year has in store for the other person. Compare this number with your own. Are you able to commit to that person when he or she has this kind of year coming up? What about next year?

  For example, if your guy has a 6 year coming up, or is in a 6 year, and you aren't talking marriage yet, you'll want to note two things: First, marriage or making a commitment may be coming up on the agenda for this 6 year; second, if marriage isn't what you're looking at (or for), then you should know that this 6 year will require your partner to give most of his or her time and energy to the family, because family obligations and responsibilities govern this year. And no, it's not negotiable.

- ◆ **Pinnacle.** For compatibility purposes, it's very valuable to look at what your partner will need to expend his or her energy on in this cycle in life. Remember, a Pinnacle is at least nine years long. You'll want to consider what's to be achieved, as well as how to time certain events and plans. For this, consult the Pinnacle Number of your partner. If the number you find on the current Pinnacle is the same as yours, then you'll have greater understanding and similar goals. But if the number is different, then you'll want to study the meaning of your partner's Pinnacle for clues about what to expect.

  For example, if you're in a 7 Pinnacle and your love is in a 7 Pinnacle, too, you'll know that this will be a cycle of introspection, soul searching, and a carefully evaluated direction for both of your lives. You shouldn't expect this to be a time for raising a family, building an empire together, or entertaining hordes of people. Instead, it's a quiet time, and anyone with a 7 Pinnacle will be moving toward more solitude, time alone, and quiet activities—at least that's the natural flow of energy. Now, if that's not the way one of these 7s is living it, then you can expect that person to be out of sorts, and possibly to develop health issues.

  It is also important to note that other numbers influence this Pinnacle Number. Look to the Major Cycle Number, the Challenge Number, and the Destiny Number for clues about other influences.

Merlin's Notes
If you're in an 8 Pinnacle and your sweetie is in a 7 Pinnacle, you'll have to make some adjustments. The 8 Pinnacle will be moving out into the world to work toward accomplishing recognition and material success, while the 7 won't find these pursuits to be his or her cup of tea. Find the difference between your numbers and work from there. For the 8 and 7 Pinnacles, the difference is a 1, the number of individuality, so let the 8 have its independence to pursue the business world, and let the 7 pursue its introspective analysis. The key is to honor the individual path each of you is on.

Personal Compatibilities

We're sure you'll want to set up your own chart for major relationships, so we've provided a blank form here to do just that.

Five Core	Your Number	Your Partner's Number	Stress Number (the Difference)
Life Path	_____	_____	_____
Destiny	_____	_____	_____
Soul	_____	_____	_____
Personality	_____	_____	_____
Maturity	_____	_____	_____
Plus:			
Birthday	_____	_____	_____

Concords

In numerology, there are certain groups of numbers that naturally belong together. These are called *Concords*, and there are three of them. Each Concord has three numbers in it, three numbers that have similar characteristics. For this reason, Concords are another measurement of compatibility.

The Concords, three separate groups of numbers that belong together, tell of a natural affinity for one another. Because these numbers go together naturally, it's useful to consider the Birthday Number of a would-be partner to see what group or Concord his or her number belongs to.

The three Concords are:

- 3, 6, 9
- 1, 5, 7
- 2, 4, 8

Look at these three Concords and select the one that includes your reduced Birthday Number. This is your Concord, your own number group. It is here that you will find like-minded kindred souls and compatible friends. For example, if your Birthday Number is a 6 or reduces to a 6 and your friend, love interest, or partner is born on the 12th (1 + 2 = 3) of any month, both of you belong to Concord group 3, 6, 9. This suggests that you will have shared interests in the artistic, creative, and inspirational, and both of you will approach life from an emotional perspective.

By the Numbers

Concords are three sets of three numbers that naturally belong together. The concords are 3, 6, 9; 1, 5, 7; and 2, 4, 8. Concords tell where friends can be found.

The Concords

Each of the three Concords is a set of three numbers:

9		7		8	
3	6	1	5	2	4

Now that you have found your Concord, let's look at the meaning of these number groups.

The Numbers 3, 6, and 9: Inspirational, Spiritual, and Artistic

These are the motivational teachers, the artists, the creative arts people, and the spiritual directors of our world—the numbers of those who resonate to matters of spiritual and artistic interest. Inspired by others with these numbers as well as inspirational themselves, these numbers are creative and emotional. You'll want to look to those who share these numbers for a heartfelt connection.

Numerology Rule: Anyone with a 3, 6, 9, 12, 15, 18, 21, 24, 27, or 30 Birthday Number will find comfort and kinship in the Concord **3, 6, 9.**

The Numbers 1, 5, and 7: Scientific, Intellectual, and Technological

These are the thinkers, the intellects, and the analytical ones, and they all share an innate love of learning, are curious, and want to be informed. Look to these numbers for the analytical types, the science guys and gals, the techies, and the computer whizzes. But even without a specialized field, these numbers crave mental stimulation. Look to those who share these numbers for good stimulating conversation—and someone who thinks like you do. When they're at a loss for words, just give them a good book to read—they'll love it.

> **Numerology Rule:** Anyone with a 1, 5, 7, 10, 14, 16, 19, 23, 25, or 28 Birthday Number will find like minds here in the Concord **1, 5, 7**.

The Numbers 2, 4, and 8: Business, Money, and Management

These are the workers of the world, and they own, operate, manage, and build the business world. Stable, efficient, and business minded, these are the practical ones. In addition, they're the ones who have trouble expressing their emotions. Look to those with these numbers for compatibility in business, for feeling grounded, for stability, and for career considerations. When your life needs order or you need to get back on track, the numbers in this Concord will help you refocus. Members of this Concord find solace in each other's no-nonsense approach to life.

> **Numerology Rule:** Anyone with a 2, 4, 8, 11, 13, 17, 20, 22, 26, 29, or 31 Birthday Number will find similar practical ability and temperament in the Concord **2, 4, 8**.

No matter which of the three Concords you belong to, you will find likeness and similarity with others in your number group. Concord compatibilities share similar approaches to life.

If you and your partner aren't in the same Concord, don't despair. There are plenty of ways to share common ground; they can be found in your Core Numbers, Pinnacles, Major Cycles, and Personal Year Numbers.

Figuring Your Own Compatibility Quotient

Here's a worksheet for you to see just how compatible—or incompatible—the two of you are. You may want to copy this worksheet to use for more than one relationship.

Compatibilities Worksheet

Concords

My Birthday Number (reduced) is: _____

My **Concord** group is _____. My most compatible group is: spiritual/artistic, intellectual, or business (circle one).

My partner's **Concord** is _____. Most compatible group: spiritual/artistic, intellectual, or business (circle one).

Compatible Cycles

Pinnacles: Mine   1st _____   2nd _____   3rd _____   4th _____

His/Hers   1st _____   2nd _____   3rd _____   4th _____

Areas of concern:

_____

Areas where we match:

_____

Challenges: Mine 1st _____   2nd _____   3rd _____   4th _____

His/Hers   1st _____   2nd _____   3rd _____   4th _____

My lesson and challenge for this cycle are:

_____

_____

My partner's lesson and challenge for this cycle are:

_____

_____

continues

Major Cycle

My **Major Cycle** at this time is: _____

My partner's **Major Cycle** at this time is: _____

My next **Major Cycle** is: _____

My partner's next **Major Cycle** is: _____

Personal Year

At this time I am in a _____ **Personal Year.**

My partner is in a _____ **Personal Year.**

Five Core Numbers

My **Life Path Number** is: _____

My partner's **Life Path Number** is: _____

The difference between our numbers, our **Stress Number,** is: _____

My **Destiny Number** is: _____

My partner's **Destiny Number** is: _____

The difference between our numbers, our **Stress Number,** is: _____

My **Soul Number** is: _____

My partner's **Soul Number** is: _____

The difference between our numbers, our **Stress Number,** is: _____

My **Personality Number** is: _____

My partner's **Personality Number** is: _____

The difference between our numbers, our **Stress Number,** is: _____

My **Maturity Number** is: _____

My partner's **Maturity Number** is: _____

The difference between our numbers, our **Stress Number,** is: _____

Now that you have filled in the Compatibilities Worksheet, you can see the strengths and weaknesses of your relationship. Keep in mind that all of the numbers have higher and lower vibrations. In any partnership, the goal is to understand the essence of each individual in the duo. Once you know both of your numbers, you can begin to balance your differences and make better unions and better choices.

Numerology is only one of a vast array of resources you have available to you to discover how to read the signs for compatibility. Still, using numerology will help you form healthy relationships. Try it and see!

The Least You Need to Know

- ◆ Looking to the numbers of relationships can help you find the best matches.

- ◆ Finding compatibility with others is one more potent aspects of numerology.

- ◆ Stress Numbers help you find common ground for resolving differences with others.

- ◆ Concords are numbers that have a natural affinity for each other.

20

Names by the Numbers

In This Chapter

- ◆ Your name is an energetic force
- ◆ Your first name: physical and mental abilities
- ◆ Your middle name: your emotional side
- ◆ Your last name: your spiritual nature
- ◆ Maiden, married, adopted, family, and business names
- ◆ Choosing names by the numbers

Not only do your numbers give you good information about your relationships, they also reveal the nature of your name. *Harry Potter and the Order of the Phoenix, James Bond Agent 007, Macbeth,* McDonald's: Whether it's a book title, play, movie title, business, or your own personal moniker, names have meanings. You may think of a name as just so many words, but there's far more to a name when it comes to numerology. All names have energy and a special vibration, and that means *your* name, too.

We invite you to think of your name as an energetic force field that carries your family heritage, your lessons in consciousness, your destiny, your personality traits, and your soul vibration. Each name given to you at birth provides information about your inherent strengths and weaknesses.

In this chapter, we'll look at what's in your name, including what the first vowel and consonant mean in your name. We'll also show you ways that you can choose names for babies, businesses, and even yourself—to maximize your success.

What's in a Name?

Have you ever met someone whose name just seems "wrong" for that person? Or does your own name feel as if it should belong to someone else? When it comes to names, a perfect fit can be as important as the right pair of running shoes or finding the right relationship.

When we look at a name numerologically, we can explore the form and the fit. Each part of your name tells of three different levels of information.

Numerology Rule:

◆ Your first name tells of your physical conditions and mental acuity.

◆ Your middle or second name tells of the emotional aspect of your life.

◆ Your third or last name tells of your spiritual consciousness.

Merlin's Notes

What if you haven't got a middle name? If that's the case, your last name carries the combined story of your emotional and spiritual consciousness. If, on the other hand, you have more than one middle name, for this part of our numerology analysis, you'll treat them as one long middle name, which will give insight into your emotional life. Last, if you have more than one last name, string them together into one long last name while working with this section. This name will tell of the level of spiritual consciousness you're dealing with. The main thing is to consider each name separately for its own individual energy.

With that background in mind, let's look at what's behind each of the names given to you at birth. If you figured your Destiny Number in Chapter 10, you already know the numbers of your first name, middle name, and last name, and you can use them in this chapter to further explore the significance of each name. We've also provided instructions and space to do the figuring in this chapter.

Your First Name

Numerologically, your first name tells us many things, including ...

◆ The physical and mental influence of your direction for growth.

◆ How predictably you think, act, and behave.

◆ How you will interpret life's experiences.

To understand this information, you'll look to the individual numbers that make up your name as well as the number total. For example, let's consider the first name Anna-Stina. This hyphenated name is considered as one whole first name.

A	N	N	A		S	T	I	N	A			
1	5	5	1		1	2	9	5		1 = 30 = 3		

What can we tell about this person from her first name? First of all, notice that there are four 1s in this name. This suggests that she's going to be a very independent person, and, with three 5s, she'll want her freedom. The 2 and 9 tell us that she has mental ability that is good with both details (the 2) and the big picture (the 9). The first name total 3 indicates a happy disposition, humorous, quick wit, creative, an emotional nature, and someone who's good with words.

The total from your first name also gives us your *Growth Number.* The Growth Number, as the name suggests, helps you know how to further grow as you move along your life path. We look at this Growth Number in relationship to the Life Path Number. For example, with a Growth Number 3 (we've added up the total letter value of this first name), Anna-Stina can expect to use her special gifts of creativity, self-expression, and way with words to assist her along her Life Path (an 11/2), which is about inspiring and uplifting others. This is a nice match.

To find your Growth Number we've provided space for your calculation. We're repeating the "Letters and Their Numbers" chart to make this easier for you.

By the Numbers

The **Growth Number,** sometimes called the Key, tells of the growth and development you can expect with this number. This single-digit number total is found in your first name. It's found by adding together the numerical value of the letters of your first name and reducing to a single number total (unless it's a Master Number—remember, we don't reduce Master Numbers here). Karmic Numbers aren't used here.

1. Write down your first name and assign the appropriate number to each letter.

   First name: Kent ___ ___ ___ ___ ___ ___

   Numbers: 2 5 5 2 ___ ___ ___ ___ ___

2. Add the numbers together and reduce to a single digit = **Growth Number.** If you have a Master Number 11 or 22 as your final number, don't reduce it.

5   Joseph

Letters and Their Numbers

1	2	3	4	5	6	7	8	9
A	B	C	D	E	F	G	H	I
J	K	L	M	N	O	P	Q	R
S	T	U	V	W	X	Y	Z	

So what's your Growth Number? Following is a quick reference guide to the interpretation of Growth Number energies. Whatever your Growth Number is, it indicates where the greatest potential for self-actualization will be as you journey down your Life Path. You will want to read the meaning of your Growth Number in relation to your Life Path Number. Remember, your Life Path Number is calculated using the numbers of your date of birth. (See Chapter 9 for an in-depth look at your Life Path Number.)

Growth Number	Meaning
1	Your greatest growth will be along the lines of asserting yourself and being the individualist.
2	Your greatest growth will be relationship with others.
3	Your greatest growth will be the way you use your words and creativity.
4	Your greatest growth will be around issues of fear and security.
5	Your greatest growth will be around responsible use of freedom.
6	Your greatest growth will come through love.
7	Your greatest growth will come from knowledge of mystical and spiritual wisdom.
8	Your greatest growth will come from management of money and responsible use of power.

7

Growth Number	Meaning
9	Your greatest growth will come from compassion and forgiveness.
11	Your greatest growth will come from teaching spiritual truth and balancing your energy.
22	Your greatest growth will come from leading with intuition and practical application of universal principles.
33	Your greatest growth will come from mastery on the emotional level concerning self-sacrifice without becoming a martyr.

It is believed that the ancients thought that the soul entered the body on the vibration of the first vowel of a name. That's not surprising because the Soul Number is calculated from the vowels in a name. No matter what, however, numerologists agree that the first vowel of your name holds great significance.

The first vowel of your first name reveals valuable information: This is the letter that describes your natural and innate approach to life. The first vowel is considered your soul vibration, because it reveals character traits such as creativity, sensitivity, willpower, and determination. Will you approach life with timidity, tenacity, or as a pleasure seeker? The first vowel is thought to describe your spiritual approach to the experience of life as well.

Easy as 1-2-3

Is your name "Yves" or "Yvonne"? If so, that "Y" is the first vowel of your first name. If your name's "Yolanda" or "Yancy," however, that "Y" is a consonant.

Let's consider the first name Sandy. The first vowel is an "a." When we check the vowel interpretation chart that follows, we find that "a" means that Sandy will innately approach life creatively and independently, demonstrating the value and importance of the individual. Sandy's spiritual approach will be to seek a belief system where individuality is highlighted. All of this is told in the number 1, which is the number of the first vowel (the "a") in Sandy's name.

What's the first vowel of *your* name? Use the following chart to see what it means.

Vowel	Number	Interpretation
A	(1)	Highlights individuality, creativity, leadership, and the value of one
E	(5)	Highlights curiosity, investigation, fascination with the mystery of life, resourcefulness
I	9	Highlights a deep emotional nature, a humanitarian approach, a global consciousness, creativity, a highly developed intuitive skill, and the desire to help and heal
O	6	Highlights concealed feelings, loves deeply, accepts responsibility, sentimental, protects family and home, mission is to beautify
U	3	Highlights sensitivity, inspired creativity, enthusiasm for life
Y	7	Highlights thoughtful analysis, intuition, observation, uses an investigative, possibly skeptical approach, seeks divine guidance, pursues the metaphysical and philosophical for truth and wisdom

Like Sandy and Anna-Stina, or for that matter, Christina, Theresa, Tommy, Susan, and Alphonso—no matter what your name—you can use this chart to determine the meaning of your first name vowel. Simply match the vowel letter to the appropriate number, and then find the meaning for that number.

The first vowel in my first name is ____*e*____.

The matching number for this letter is ____*5*____.

The meaning of the first vowel of my first name is

____*Curiosity / resourcefulness / Investigation*____

This vowel number indicates how I will think and act predictably, as well as my spiritual and philosophical approach to life.

Your Middle Name

Your middle name is thought to govern your emotional life and reveals your likes, loves, emotions, attraction to certain hobbies, and marriage suitability. It is a resource you can draw upon. Add together the numbers of the letters that make up your middle name. The reduced total number tells the story.

Just as for your first name, note that if you have a Master Number as your middle name number, do not reduce it. When you're ready, turn to Part 2 of this book to find the meaning of Master Numbers and any of the reduced numbers—1 through 9—of your middle name. We do not consider Karmic Numbers for this aspect of name analysis.

The reduced number total for my middle name is _____.

The meaning of my middle name number is

_____.

My middle name number indicates my emotional approach to life as well as my likes and dislikes.

Your Last Name

Your last name, whether it is your birth name, adopted name, or married name, reveals the inherited traits of the family. The letters of your last name reveal your spiritual nature, that is, your inner, subconscious response to life. Some letters in your last name are more conducive to spiritual growth than others. Again, we recommend examining the letters and number equivalents for your last name and then interpreting the meaning of the numbers you find here.

Your Family Name

For many of us, the family name is our last name, which naturally carries with it a history and linkage to ancestral traits. In your family name are certain strengths and inherent weaknesses. It may seem odd, but just as we can inherit genetic characteristics like hair color and nose size, we also inherit vibrational traits like attitudinal and ancestral history through our family names. If there are different spellings of your family name, you will want to consider the original spelling, and how many generations ago the original spelling was changed. A family name will have grown into its full vibrational force after three or four generations have held the name. Numerologically, inherited traits are calculated in the same way we figure any name, except that we work with only the last name at birth.

Let's look at two famous names of our times to see what each has inherited. Here's the first one:

```
K   E   N   N   E   D   Y
2   5   5   5   5   4   7 = 33/6
```

In the Kennedy name, we see the traits of cooperation (2); sudden unexpected change (all those 5s); determination, hard work, and a sense of patriotism (4); and a sense of privacy and intellectual analysis (7). When the Kennedy name is added up, we find a Master Number 33, which reduces to a 6. This, then, would be a name that promotes family closeness (6), while at the same time demands that those who carry this name endure the tests of a Master Number (33).

Here's a second family name we've all come to know:

G A T E S

7 1 2 5 1 = 16, which reduces to 7

In the Gates family name, we see the traits of the loner, the perfectionist, the desire to know everything and anything, the analytical mind, the need for privacy, the eccentric, and an aloof demeanor (7); independence and self-starting initiative (1); teamwork and partnership (2); the need for freedom and progressive thinking (5); and assertive leadership (1). The Gates family name adds up to inventiveness, intelligence, and yes, specialization in technology (7). As a 16/7, those born to the Gates name will also carry traits of being strongly opinionated (6) and the tendency to impose one's ego on others (1). Because the last name indicates the spiritual nature, we want to note that the Gates name is a Karmic Debt Number revealing a family history of learning through wake-up calls to develop a philosophical, spiritual, or metaphysical consciousness. Greatness can be achieved with this name and number as long as the ego isn't the motivating force.

Figuring Your Family Name

Let's examine your family name.

1. Write down your family name here and assign the appropriate number to each letter.

   Family name: ___ ___ ___ ___ ___ ___ ___ ___ ___ ___

   Numbers: ___ ___ ___ ___ ___ ___ ___ ___ ___ ___

2. Add the numbers together and reduce to a single digit ___ = **Family Name Number.**

Here's a quick guide for checking out what your Family Name Number means:

Family Name Number	Meaning
1	You inherit an independent spirit, a forceful nature, a strong will, and the ability to come up with original ideas.
2	You inherit a peaceful nature, the desire to reduce conflict, a sensitivity to things, a gift for detail, a love of gathering things, and a loving nature.
3	You inherit a fun-loving, optimistic nature, a sense of humor, and a creative spirit.
4	You inherit a belief that hard work is the right way to work, a sense of cautiousness, thoroughness, and self-discipline.
5	You inherit a belief that you shouldn't be fenced in, for you are a free spirit. Restrictions, limitations, routine challenge you. Travel and change are easy for you, and you are innately curious and a risk taker. You inherit a sexual magnetism.
6	You inherit a conservative attitude that sees helping others is the responsible thing to do. You are an excellent problem solver and, of course, are family oriented. You may have inherited a stubborn streak as well as strong opinions.
7	You inherit a desire for knowledge, you value learning, and you respect quality, facts, and theories, as well as a need for spiritual understanding. Your family traits will be those of observation, analysis, perfectionism, and the desire for privacy.
8	You inherit an attitude about money and power that will cause you to seek recognition in business and finance. Your family name brings you the qualities of leadership, organization, a high value placed on success, competency, and doing a job well, as well as a possibly inflated ego.
9	You inherit an artistic flair, a concern for others, an emotional nature, generosity, a sense of needing to serve, a philanthropic nature, and an attitude of looking for what is possible.
11	You inherit the ability to uplift, encourage, and inspire others. Your family name brings with it a sensitivity to others and the desire for spiritual living. You will learn from life through many tests that illuminate certain universal truths.
22	You inherit the ability to build things that will benefit the masses or a large group. Your family name brings you the skills of leadership, management, a good solid work ethic, and the

continues

continued

Family Name Number	Meaning
	ability to gain material wealth. You have the endurance to bounce back after many difficulties.
33	You inherit an ability to teach others in a masterful way. Your family name brings a keen sense of responsibility, love for your fellow human, and a desire to serve. You will learn, just as your family has learned, to overcome the many setbacks life will put in your path.

Your Maiden Name

A woman's maiden name is her family name. It is part of her original birth name and therefore part of her original cosmic code and blueprint for life.

Whether you use your maiden name now or not, the energy present in that name will be with you all of your life. When you give up your maiden name in favor of a married name (or any other name you may choose), you cannot deplete the energy of your maiden, or family, name, for it is your essence and belongs to your energy field. Any new name you assume will merely be an add-on—additional energy you bring to your experience of life. But it won't change the essence of who you are—or the story that your maiden name tells.

Your Married Name

In numerology, we look at the married name as an additional energy. For some, it will be a number that's missing in the original birth name, and in that case, it would also be one of your karmic lessons. If that's the case, the married name may be assumed to be bringing you a karmic lesson which you've needed to round out your learning experience while you are here on Earth.

The married name does not replace your original birth name. The essence of who you are is determined by the name given to you at birth, which determines your major five Core Numbers.

To determine the meaning of your married name, follow these instructions.

1. Write down your married name and assign the appropriate number to each letter.

Married name: __ __ __ __ __ __ __ __ __ __

Numbers: __ __ __ __ __ __ __ __ __ __

2. Add the numbers together and reduce to a single digit ___ = **Married Name Number.**

To interpret the meaning of your Married Name Number consult the chart showing Family Name Numbers and meanings we gave you earlier in this chapter. This will tell you what new energy you've brought to yourself by assuming your married name. It usually will bring another energy to your original name and vibration and often is one of your Challenge Numbers or karmic lessons.

So, let us say it again, your original birth name is the most significant name: It tells of the essence of who you are. That never changes—not even if you add a married name or drop your original birth name.

A word about divorce and name changes: If you marry but do not take your husband's name, you might ask: am I "rejecting" that energy, or does it add to my name whether I take it officially or not? The answer is: If you divorce and go "back" to your maiden name, you may be rejecting the energy of your husband's name intentionally because you found it incompatible with your own vibration. You may be rejecting this energy and wanting to be free from it. On the other hand, you may have gotten what you were supposed to learn from this energy and now you are finished with it and it is time to move on. For a name to have an impact on you, you have to take the name for yourself and use it every day for its energy to be felt.

What if you divorce but keep your married name? Kay has kept her past husband's name, Lagerquist, because it brings her 8 and 3 energy, both of which have changed her life. Her maiden name, which she will not divulge, is powerful but lacks the energy needed to create and manifest in the world. So Kay has kept her married name to enhance her professional persona and the quality of her life. Besides, you've got to love a Swedish name like Lagerquist!

Your Adopted Name

While we discussed the adopted name briefly in Chapter 10 on your Destiny Number, we want to go into a little more detail here. If you were given an adopted name early on in life, it may be the only name you have known. If that's the case, figure your Numerology Profile on your adopted name, although if you are privy to your original name, for our purposes, the original name is best to use.

An adopted name may sometimes replace your original name, as in the case of your mother remarrying and your stepfather adopting you. For example, if you were born David Yale Krug and your mother remarried your stepfather, whose last name is Baker, and he adopted you, your new name would be David Yale Baker. For numerology purposes, your entire Numerology Profile would be figured on the original name David Yale Krug, but we would want to examine the new name Baker to discover what new energy has come in.

> **Sixes and Sevens**
>
> When calculating a married name, Mrs. is never used—just as Mr., Jr., Sr., or the Third (III) aren't used either.

Let's look at this situation more closely.

D A V I D	Y A L E	K R U G	
4 1 4 9 4	7 1 3 5	2 9 3 8	
22	16	22	
22/4	16/7	22/4	Totals for each name

Now we can see that this name has two Master Numbers, and he also has a Karmic Debt Number 16/7 as a middle name energy. This original birth name is very powerful. What happens when he changes his name?

The adopted name then becomes Baker instead of Krug, and we figure it like this:

David	Krug	B A K E R
22/4	16/7	2 1 2 5 9 = 19 = 1 (1 + 9)

Several things need to be pointed out in this situation. First, as we've said, the original name remains as the essence and the basis of the Numerology Profile. David's Soul, Destiny, and Personality Numbers, and eventually his Maturity Number, will all be figured from his original name, David Yale Krug. However, with this new adopted name, a new energy comes into play, the energy of the 1 (Baker).

So we might say that David has an additional positive vibration of independence, innovation, and self-reliance that comes to him through his adopted name. This new energy will serve him as long as he carries the name of Baker and lives up to the demands of this new name. Of course, free will determines whether the energy is used at a higher or lower vibration. The lower use of this new energy would be to use the 1 to bully, dominate, be aggressive, and operate from an ego-centered point of view.

Merlin's Notes

It's interesting to note that David Krug's new name of Baker is a 19, which is also a Karmic Debt Number. This means that he now bears two Karmic Debt Numbers (16 from his original name and 19 from his new name)—and all that those numbers imply. While he has increased his debt load, in keeping with universal law, it would seem that there's no mistake. David must have needed to work with this kind of energy (both the 19 and the 1) to advance his spiritual development. Nonetheless, he can't ignore the energy of his original name which bears two Master Numbers: 22/4. His life will demand that he live up to his name.

The message is the same for adopted names as it is for married names. You'll use your original birth name and then figure your new names separately. However, you'll want to note your original last name, for it tells of inherited family traits, strengths, and weaknesses.

When you have no other name except an adopted name, then all of your calculations will be done with the adopted name. This name represents the energy you're presently experiencing and the strengths and weaknesses that will accompany you through life. Note that there's less of an energetic impact if you change an adopted name than there is if you change your original birth name.

Nicknames

While our nicknames or pet names bring a certain personal response, and carry a vibrational frequency, these names aren't to be considered part of the original five Core Numbers. Like any name you may add to your original set of birth names, it's just that—an add-on. So consider the nickname as an added energy you have brought into your sphere of energy. Of course, it is valuable to figure the number for this nickname and the meaning of that number, just as we have figured the married name or the family name. The nickname is an added energy and is figured separately from your original birth name.

If you were named William but are called Bill or Billy, you might have fun calculating these name numbers to see how the energy changed for you at those times in your life when you went from being one name to being another.

Let's look at a famous William who has taken the nickname Bill: Bill Gates Jr., founder of computer giant, Microsoft. Born as William, let's see what energy he has added by using the name Bill instead of William.

```
W  I  L  L  I  A  M        B  I  L  L
5  9  3  3  9  1  4        2  9  3  3
7                          17 or (1 + 7) = 8
```

As you can see, Mr. Gates bears the energy of the 7 in the name William, the number of the loner, inventor, specialist, analytical technician (and dare we say nerd?). Yet, when he took the name Bill as his nickname, he added the energy of the 8, the number of power, money, and success. For a computer industry mogul, the combination of both the 7 and the 8 seems to be a nice fit. The 7 could have remained isolated and only a researcher, but the 8 brings forward the demand for doing something powerful and financially successful with his specialized field. Nicknames can add energy to your original energy pattern.

Choosing a Name

At some point in our lives we all have to choose a name—either for a child, a new business, a pet, an e-mail name, and even a new surname (that's your last name) when the old one wears out for one reason or another. As we mentioned earlier in the book, the ancients believed that a name is a mystical code for the essential character of a person, and, because your birth name is your destiny, name changing should not be entered into lightly.

Sixes and Sevens

A new name can bring a new advantage, and even a special purpose, because it's a new tool for the enhancement of your original capabilities and consciousness. But beware—changing your name means you're changing your power. Obviously, you'll want to select your new name with a great deal of care.

Things to Consider When Changing Your Name

There are several things you'll want to consider when changing your name. For example, there's a mistaken notion that a new name will mean a new life. The main thing to keep in mind if you're going to change your name is that you'll have two sets of numbers operating simultaneously. The first and most significant set is the numbers in your birth name—you're never without this cosmic code and vibrational pattern. The second is that a new name has a vibrational pattern also, and, with careful choice, this new name can enhance your original name energy.

If you're changing your name, keep these things in mind:

◆ Choose a name that feels right rather than a name that is cutesy, popular, or honors a relative or friend. When we say "feels right," we mean using your intuition. Is this a name you would enjoy using today and in 10 years? Does your energy rise when you think or hear this new name? Use your inner sense of knowing to guide you in a new name choice.

◆ Choose a name that will attract favorable experiences—not more tests, karma, or aggravations. To do this, you'll have to calculate the meaning of this new name using the same steps we've outlined for you in Chapters 10 through 12, especially if you are changing more than one of your names. You'll want to be aware of what your new name means and what kind of energy you're bringing to your life. You'll want to know what the vibration is for your Soul, Destiny, and Personality Numbers. Invest time in this important decision and take your time—you'll be glad you did.

◆ Avoid choosing a name that adds up to one of your Challenge Numbers or a Karmic Lesson Number, unless you've already conquered these Challenges. The same is true for a Master Number name—be sure you're willing to live up to the additional demands of the Master Number.

◆ For best results, select a name that has the same Soul Number and Destiny Number as your original birth name—so the inner motivation and general direction for your life will be the same as your original blueprint.

◆ A new name carries the potential for new opportunities, but it takes approximately five years before the energy of this new name is fully integrated. 5 is the number of change, remember.

> **CAUTION**
>
> **Sixes and Sevens**
>
> Then again, maybe your original name isn't so bad, and through careful calculation, you'll learn a new appreciation for it. After all, you could have been born with the name Romeo Montague—and "A rose by any other name might not smell as sweet."

◆ Choose a name that harmonizes with your Life Path Number (your birth date). If you have a strong Life Path Number, you won't want to choose a weaker name number—it won't bring you the success promised in your birth date. Choose a new name whose vowels add up to a number that's compatible with your Life Path Number, and then also calculate the total name number (consonants and vowels) to harmonize with your Life Path Number. Taking care to work out these numbers will pay off—you don't need to make life any harder than it already is!

◆ Have fun with your new name but remember, you're expected to live up to your new name vibration as well as your original name. Name changing isn't for the faint of heart. Be sure you understand your original name's meaning before you give it up: You'll want to know who you really are before you become someone else.

Finally, if you're in doubt about choosing a new name, consult a professional numerologist.

Naming Your Baby

Choosing the name for a baby is a very important step. You're choosing for another soul the pattern for his or her time on Earth. Needless to say, this must be done with careful consideration.

Some numerologists refuse to influence the naming of a baby. The child's purpose and destiny in life aren't meant to be put in the hands of a numerologist or a stranger. Instead, it's generally felt that the responsibility for naming the baby is solely the parents'.

It's hoped that the chosen name for the baby will be an inspiration coming from the parents. That's because it's believed that the parents have chosen to be a channel for this baby's birth and life on Earth, and if they'll only tune in to their own inner guidance, and listen to their intuition, they'll come to a name that's just right for their newborn. This is all part of the great mystery, the secret of creation and belongs to the souls of those directly involved: the new baby and the parents. In other words, we don't recommend that you work on getting the numbers right for your unborn child—the number that results from the name you choose will be the one that's right for that soul!

Easy as 1-2-3

We strongly recommend that the final selection of the name for the new baby not be made until you're in the presence of this incoming spirit. If you can still the inner clamor, the baby will help you to know the perfect name to choose.

Parents who each have kept their own last names and need to decide which name to give the baby might want to work out the family name of each parent. To interpret the number of each family name, you can use the chart showing Family Name Numbers and their meanings that we provided earlier in the chapter. If both family names are desired, you might want to hyphenate the baby's name.

In the meantime, prior to the baby's birth, we suggest you find a time every day to sit quietly and listen in your own heart and mind. When the right name comes to you, you will know. Your energy will rise when you've hit upon the right name, and your intuition will signal that this is it—you've got the right one. The surname is usually the family name, which brings the new soul into alignment with the family inheritance—traits of similarity—that the newborn will share with those in his or her clan. In this way, a newborn can be held in the family vibration while the child begins to establish his or her own individual vibrational pattern.

Naturally, after the baby is born, we recommend that you set up a full Numerology Profile for your baby to examine the meaning of the name you've chosen for your infant. But we don't recommend you try in advance to select a name that means "money and power" or that sort of thing. In addition …

- ♦ Don't pick a name for the qualities you hope to create with this name, but instead, choose a name that feels right and know that this little soul's path will be just the right one for him or her.

- ♦ Trust the universal law that says everything works out perfectly and at the right time. The soul of this incoming child knows what it needs.

- ♦ Don't block your inner guidance, your inner sense of knowing, by trying to force a name to fit a certain number. When a name comes to you that feels right, trust it.

The time to check on the numerology of the new baby's name is after you've decided upon a name.

Naming Your Business

The name of a business is equally important. Careful consideration of your business name will pay off because your business name gives off a vibration—and you want the right "vibe." When choosing the name for a business, you'll want to consider the nature of the business. Whether it's a product business, service business, research firm, educational institution, or business for the arts, keep in mind that it's the nature of your enterprise that should resonate to the number of the name.

Here's a quick way to see numbers best suited for your type of business:

- ♦ Product businesses = 2, 4, 8
- ♦ Service businesses = 2, 3, 6, 9
- ♦ Research businesses = 2, 7, 9
- ♦ Educational businesses = 6, 7, 9

- ◆ Arts businesses = 2, 3, 6, 9

- ◆ Music businesses = 2, 6

- ◆ Entrepreneurial businesses = 1

- ◆ Advertising, promotional, and publishing businesses = 5

- ◆ Financial businesses = 8, 9

- ◆ Health-related businesses = 4, 7

Use the same tenets for choosing the name of your business as you would use for naming a baby (after all, your business is your baby, right?). Let your intuition be your guide, and choose a name that feels right first. Only then should you look to see what the name means.

Here are a few other pointers:

- ◆ Don't use "Inc." or "Corporation" in the name calculation.

- ◆ Examine the Soul Number for this business name as well as the Destiny and Personality Numbers. (See Chapters 10 through 12 for an in-depth discussion of how to calculate and interpret these three Core Numbers.)

- ◆ If your business is family owned, the name should harmonize with the Family Name Number.

- ◆ If your business is a sole proprietorship, then the business name, Soul, and Destiny Numbers should harmonize with your own Soul and Destiny Numbers.

- ◆ If the business is a partnership, then you'll want to consider the Soul and Destiny Numbers for each partner and look for a business name that resonates with each of these.

Easy as 1-2-3

The Personality Number of the business name shows its public image (how others will view this business), so you'll want to choose a Personality Number that spells the greatest attraction!

Utilize the steps we've outlined for choosing a name and you should be able to create a successful choice for your business name. We wish you the very best of luck with your new enterprise. May the numbers guide you to your highest and best!

Names have meaning, whether it is a business name, a family name, a married name, or a child's name. There are many resources available for choosing names, and some give numerical meanings for names as well. All names have number equivalents, and all names have a vibrational frequency. Rely on your intuition—but let the numbers guide you as well.

The Least You Need to Know

♦ Your name is an energetic force that reflects your nature.

♦ Each of your three names—first, middle, last—presents a different dimension of who you are.

♦ Your baby's name reveals its soul and destiny vibration and careful selection brings success.

♦ Married, adopted, family, and business names each tell of special meanings.

♦ Choosing names by the numbers should be undertaken cautiously and judiciously.

Chapter 21

House or Apartment, It's the Number that Counts

In This Chapter

◆ Figuring your house or apartment number

◆ The challenge of each house number

◆ The meaning of your street name   *city*

◆ The meaning of your phone number

Our lives are surrounded by numbers. Some are more important than others. Your house, apartment, phone, and city are among the most significant numbers in your life and have an impact on your daily experience. Like all numbers, these numbers have meanings. Some people swear by the number on their house. One of Kay's colleagues considered it the sole deciding factor when she made a move. If you're a very busy career type with a good deal of stress, for example, a 5 house isn't the place for you. If you're having financial difficulties, start to turn them around by moving into an 8 house or apartment. And, if you're in a place in your life where you want to focus on studying or working on your spiritual path, a 7 house is perfect.

Whether for a house or an apartment, it's important to calculate the number *before* you move in. Naturally, there are many considerations in choosing a home, but your residence's energy, like your phone and city, is important and should resonate to your own personal energy. These numbers are significant factors in living your life consciously!

This chapter is all about the numbers of where you live. We'll show you how to figure the numbers for your house and street. We'll also explain the meaning behind the number of a house or apartment and even tell you about the challenges of each number. Next we will figure your P.O. box number, the number of the town where you live, and finally your phone number. Beyond the numbers of your Numerology Profile, the numbers that influence your life most directly are where you live and those constantly used digits—your phone number.

Figuring the Numbers of Your House or Street

In this section we tell you about house numbers and street numbers. If you live at 421 Long Ears Lane, both the house number and the street name affect you. The same is true if you live on a numbered street. However, the number on the house will have the strongest effect.

House numbers tell the essence or energy of the house. The street name (or number) tells the essence of the neighborhood. When the number of the house is reduced to a single digit, that number tells of the characteristics of the house and what goes on there.

To get you started on seeing how this works, here's a sample address: 5717 16th N.E.

First, we figure the house number like this:

5 + 7 + 1 + 7 = 20

When we reduce this 20 to a single root number (the final reduced single digit you get after adding together all of the numbers of any name or address), we find the house number is 2 + 0 = 2. This 2 house, then, tells us that sharing and cooperation will be important for people who live there.

Next, the street number is figured:

1 + 6 = 7

So 16th is a 7 kind of street: quiet, private, everyone pretty much keeping to themselves.

N.E. = 5 + 5 = 10 = 1

Together then, 16th (7) N.E. (1) as a street bears the energy of the 8. This is a street where money is made (good for real estate!), but you will be surrounded by independent, private neighbors.

See? It's easy.

Let's try another example: 578C Sunlight Beach Rd.

Here's how to calculate the number for this house. First, the house number:

5 + 7 + 8 + 3 (for C) = 23

The 23 is then reduced to a 5 (2 + 3). The 5, then, is the number of this house.

Any time your address has a letter on it, convert the letter to a number using this handy letter chart.

Letters and Their Numbers

1	2	3	4	5	6	7	8	9
A	B	C	D	E	F	G	H	I
J	K	L	M	N	O	P	Q	R
S	T	U	V	W	X	Y	Z	

Next, calculate the street name separately. This gives you the neighborhood's number. Let's look at how the street name appears *exactly* on the street sign.

    S U N L I G H T   B E A C H   R D
    1 3 5 3 9 7 8 2   2 5 1 3 8   9 4 = 70

Reduced, 7 + 0 = 7. So we have another 7 neighborhood, but with a 5 house. The 5 house will be full of activity, much coming and going, and full of change. It will probably be a bit too active for the rest of the quiet, refined 7 street!

The Numbers on the House

When we consider the numbers of a house, the reduced total number is only part of the energy of the home. The rest of the numbers that make up the house's address are important as well. Using our 578C Sunlight Beach Rd. address, we notice that the house number is comprised of a 5, a 7, an 8, and a 3 (the C). From these numbers, we note the following:

Easy as 1-2-3 _____

Occasionally, a house will be renumbered. If that happens, the change in numbers will also change the energy field of a home.

◆ The 5 is active, the 7 reclusive, the 8 brings success and money, and the 3 brings social and creative influences.

◆ The busy 5 main energy of this house is enhanced and accelerated by the 8 and the 3.

◆ The 7 allows for research or study at the house, but rest and retreat will be overshadowed by the more dominant active energy of the 5, 8, and 3.

Needless to say, if you need quiet to study or just to be yourself, forget this house!

The Street Where You Live

As we've mentioned, the full meaning of your place of residence is made up of both the house number and the street name or number. To calculate the meaning of either the name or number of the street, we suggest the following steps.

Easy as 1-2-3 _____

To figure the street name, use what is actually on your street sign. Look for Rd. for Road, Ave. for Avenue, and Ln. for Lane, for example.

For a named street …

1. Write the name exactly as it appears on your street sign.

2. Assign the corresponding numbers from our Letters and Their Numbers chart.

3. Add the numbers together.

4. Reduce the numbers by adding them together until you reach a single number.

5. Check the meaning of the number in The Meaning of Numbers Quick Reference Guide in Chapter 3.

6. Make note of Karmic Numbers 10, 13, 14, 16, and 19 and Master Numbers 11, 22, and 33.

Sixes and Sevens _____

Karmic Numbers give us a chance to go back and get it right. Each Karmic Number has a special theme and task. For a full discussion of Karmic Numbers—10, 13, 14, 16, and 19—turn to Chapter 8. You have to be ready for the lessons if you are going to live under a Karmic house number!

For example, Log Cabin Rd. (use Rd. instead of Road if it is written that way on the sign) corresponds to …

Log = 3 + 6 + 7 = 16 (1 + 6) = 7

Cabin = 3 + 1 + 2 + 9 + 5 = 20 (2 + 0) = 2

Rd = 1 + 3 = 4

Taking the final sums of Log, Cabin, and Rd., you get …

7 + 2 + 4 = 13

1 + 3 = 4

Log Cabin Rd. is a 4 street. But, look again: Log Cabin Rd. is a 13/4 street. It's a Karmic Number. A lot of hard work there! Karmic work!

For a numbered street use only the number, not the word "Road" or "Street" unless it is clearly present on the street sign, because the street number is usually the name of the street. Look at this example: The street is 23rd and most often would be referred to as just 23rd rather than 23rd Street.

23rd = 2 + 3 = 5

We might say then, that 23rd Street is a 5 street—a lot of change here!

Okay, now let's try a famous address. Let's look at the address of the Twin Towers in New York City, both destroyed in the terrorist attacks of September 11, 2001: the North Tower, 1 World Trade Center, and the South Tower, 2 World Trade Center.

First let's start with the name World Trade Center:

W O R L D	T R A D E	C E N T E R
5 6 9 3 4	2 9 1 4 5	3 5 5 2 5 9
27	21	29
(2 + 7) = 9	(2 + 1) = 3	(2 + 9) = 11/2

So 9 + 3 + 2 = 14 (1 + 4) = 5.

The number of the name of the World Trade Center is 14/5. Here we see a karmic influence present with this infamous building. The 5 is appropriate as the number of change, travel, and communication, and the karmic number 14 suggests that karmic energy was present here as well. The karmic 14 is "one of the great destroyer and transformation vibrations," as Jeanne points out in her book *Numerology: Spiritual Light Vibrations* (see Appendix A). This karmic vibration, like all of the Karmic Debt Numbers, suggests an awakening to a new way and an opportunity to finish some task or situation that was left undone was part of the vibrational force of this building.

It is significant as well to note that the World Trade Center complex had its own zip code in New York City: 10048. This zip code reduces to a 13/4, which is also a Karmic Debt Number, indicating an additional transformational vibration.

Each individual Tower had its own vibration within the general complex of the World Trade Center.

N O R T H   T O W E R   1

5   6   9   2   8   2   6   5   5   9

50   27

$5 + 9 = 14/5 + 1 = 15 = 1 + 5 = 6$

S O U T H   T O W E R   2

1   6   3   2   8   2   6   5   5   9

20   27

$2 + 9 = 11/2 + 2 = 13/4$

As a result, the address of the World Trade Center North Tower 1 would be 14/5 (World Trade Center) + 6 (North Tower 1). To add the two together, we reduce the 14 to 5, its root number, and add it to the 6 (5 + 6 = 11/2). The North Tower then was the master energy, the "Spiritual Light" energy, standing as a beacon of inspiration.

The address of the World Trade Center South Tower 2 would be 14/5 (World Trade Center) + 13/4 (South Tower 2). To add the two together, we reduce the 14 to its root number 5 and we also reduce the 13 to its root number 4. Adding the two, we see that the South Tower's address was the vibration of the 9 (5 + 4), the energy of broad-minded thinking, global concern, and service to humanity.

Metaphysically, it is a sad loss for everyone to have these two energies removed from our world.

No Number—Only a Name

If you live in a named house, work out the letter-number equivalents and reduce them to a single-digit number. For example:

M A R S H   H O U S E

4   1   9   1   8   8   6   3   1   5 = 46

Reduced, 4 + 6 = 1. So Marsh House is a place of independent, creative energy, where leadership will be learned and expected.

Finding the Number of Your House

We thought you'd want to find out what number your own house represents, so we've provided space here for you to do just that.

On the first line write down the numbers of your house address. That's all of the numbers on the house. We will show you how to calculate your apartment number in a moment.

The numbers of my house are: _____2763_____

These numbers add up to: _____9_____

On the next line, write down your street name exactly as it appears on the street sign. Then translate each letter in your street name to a number, and on the following line write down each number directly under the letter it corresponds to:

Street name letters:

_____Sonoma   St_____
1 6 5 6 4 1   1 2
Corresponding numbers:

_____

Now, add all the numbers of your street name together and reduce to a single-digit number. Write that number here.

My street name number is: _____8_____

Or, if you have only numbers in your street address, add only the numbers together here, then reduce to a single number. Note that if your street name is a number, you should write down *only that number*. For 23rd Street, for example, write down only 23 and ignore all the other letters.

My street number is _____ and it adds up to: _____

So what's the number of your house and what's the number of your street?

Total house number = _____. Street total _____

(We do not add these together, but view them in relationship to each other.)

Merlin's Notes

We realize you often have no choice in the address of your home. So we want you to know that every number vibration has its own beauty, and that the number on your house or apartment is exactly what you need at this time. We believe there are no accidents in where you live. You'll gain valuable insight from the number on your house, which will help you to orchestrate a fulfilling life. Remember, the more you know, the more you grow. Knowledge is power.

Universal Law: Life happens as it should. There are no mistakes and no accidents. Its all part of the lessons of life directing you to your destiny and higher purpose.

Your Apartment Number

Not only does a house number have influence in your life, but your apartment number adds or subtracts to the harmony of your life as well. Let's calculate the apartment number now.

Easy as 1-2-3

If your apartment has a letter as well as a number, or is just a letter, use the Letters and Their Numbers chart shown earlier in this chapter to convert it to a number. For example, apartment 3B equals a 5, because B is a 2, and 3 + 2 = 5.

Usually, there are two addresses for an apartment. One is the building address, the other is the actual apartment number. Both numbers have significance. Figure each one separately, and then view them in relationship to one another. The number that will have the most influence will be the number of your apartment. For the meaning of the apartment number, you can use the meanings for house numbers, which we discuss next.

Remember, if you're living in an apartment, your apartment number tells what is expected of you personally, under that number.

The number (and letter) of my apartment is: _____

My apartment numbers add up to: _____

The address of my apartment building is: _____

My apartment building address adds up to: _____

I live in a _____ apartment which is in a _____ building.

The number on the building tells what type of building it is and the overall energy of that building.

The Meanings of House Numbers

Now let's focus on the meaning of your house or apartment number. You can use the meanings of house numbers for your apartment number as well, although a house will vibrate more strongly to its number because it stands alone rather than within a building as an apartment might be. Once you've got the base number of your house or apartment, you can begin to understand the numerology of your home.

The Number 1 House

This is a house for independent, self-reliant people. The 1 house will encourage individuality, courage, determination, and integrity for those who live there. It's an excellent house for a person who wants to undertake an individualistic creative venture. If you want to follow your own instincts, this is the house for you.

The 1 house will foster leadership and solo undertakings. If you've been unduly weighted down with caretaking of others, this 1 house would be a good choice—if you're ready to be number 1 again.

The Challenge of a 1 House

You might feel isolated or alone in this house, even if there are others in the house. If you are the dependent type, a 1 house can be very challenging: It will require you to become independent. Also, learning to be patient might present a challenge living here. You've got to want to be independent in a 1 house. Patience might present a challenge living here. Another challenge might be: In this 1 house, there are all CEOs and no employees!

Key aspects fostered in a 1 house:

Courage	Independence
Honesty	Innovation
Much activity	Individuality
New beginnings	Leadership

The Number 2 House

The 2 house is a quiet house, excellent for two people who want to share space. In fact, this is a house for sharing anything, because a strong desire for peace and harmony pervades this home. An aggressive, impatient person won't do well in this house, because the 2 house demands patience and encourages sensitivity and gentleness. In addition, it will require attention to detail and a willingness to cooperate.

Easy as 1-2-3

When a person lives in a 2 house, he or she begins to grow in awareness of the subtle, small aspects of life. Sensitivity is heightened here, and this is a great house to develop your intuition and psychic abilities, and to pay attention to the subtle energies of gardens, art, music, and magic.

People who live in a 2 house can be very connected because they will become strongly tuned in to their energy and feelings. This is a good house for the growth of a partnership or marriage—it's not a house for someone who wants to live alone. The 2 is at its best with companionship.

The Challenge of a 2 House

There might be a tendency in a 2 house to collect things—too many things. How many seashells or salt shakers does any one house need, after all? Also, any form of conflict or discord will challenge those who live under the vibration of this house. At its extreme, the 2 vibration can find people nitpicking or being critical (after all, the 2 pays attention to detail, right?). A 2 house insists on balance in relationships.

Key aspects fostered in a 2 house:

Patience	Attention to details
Cooperation	Sensitivity
Warmth	Resolution of dualities
Tact	Harmony

The Number 3 House

Here's a fun house where you can feel positive about your life, because enthusiasm and charm permeate the 3 house. We would expect to find abundant creativity here. This house encourages expression of oneself: communication, creativity, and emotions. This is a home where you expand your vision for life.

Here you'll find a natural affinity for the positive, which naturally leads to positive results. A 3 house is conducive to generating creative, sexual, and spiritual energy.

Your social life is going to expand in this 3 house. Romance flourishes in a 3 house but expects truth and loyalty.

The Challenge of a 3 House

The challenge here has to do with getting *too* excited, *too* enthusiastic, and having *too* many friends: The challenge of the 3 house is to not scatter your energies. A 3 house is sometimes messy, which might be called "creative chaos." This house will drive a person with strong 4 energy nuts. You'd better expect to live with lightheartedness in this house!

Sixes and Sevens

There's a tendency with the 3 to play now and pay later, so a keen eye on finances will be necessary. Remember, all that entertaining can add up fast! In addition, spontaneous, impulsive action can be a challenge with the 3 house as well.

Key aspects fostered in a 3 house:

Creativity	Radiance
Openness	Friendships
Optimism	Imagination
Happiness	Enjoyment of life

The Number 4 House

This is the house to have if you want security and stability: A 4 house brings wholeness, down-to-earth living, and practicality. It's a good place to build a solid foundation for your future, because this house wants order and economy.

The 4 house lends itself to steady employment for those who live there. In addition, people or groups who are working toward a common goal will find the 4 house a good match as well.

This is a house to build toward something, and, if you're interested in gardening or earthiness, the 4 house is for you. Family matters and the affairs of relatives will demand that you use common sense and practical management if you live here. Last, a 4 house has a serious kind of vibration, and so will be a haven for those who aren't afraid of hard work and discipline.

Easy as 1-2-3

People who live in a 4 house will find it easier to be steady, loyal, well-respected, and grounded. This is a great home for planting your roots—and seeding your dreams.

The Challenge of a 4 House

Sometimes, living in a 4 house can feel like life is too much work. There might be a tendency to hoard at this house, or to become rigid and inflexible. Loosen up—you've got other numbers in your life to help you out. How about a perky little 3 car? Or a 3 phone number? One might want to be cautious in moving into a 4 home, and should accurately assess the amount of work it will require to maintain this particular house. The 4 is about hard work, after all, and under the 4, it's just not going to go away.

Key aspects fostered in a 4 house:

Stability

Plans for the future

Order

Discipline

Groundedness

Frugality

Hard work

The Number 5 House

If you feel stuck, this is the house for you. The 5 house is one of activity, movement, and change. There will be a lot of out-of-town trips, a constantly ringing phone (the 5 is the number of sales and networking), and the hustle and bustle of an extremely busy schedule.

The 5 house is a hub of activity. It lends itself to stimulating communication and the gathering of experiences and information—especially about ethnic cultures.

Routine is hard to establish and hold in a 5 house, and change is the constant. The coming and going of many people, as well as sudden or unexpected changes, will keep life anything but dull.

A 5 house encourages resourcefulness, enterprise, and promotion of oneself. Variety is the norm here—which sometimes leads to chaos and hectic living. Conditions rarely remain the same over a long period in this house. Many a romantic fling takes place in a 5 house, because people who live here will have enhanced magnetism, impulsiveness, enthusiasm, and will be more talkative and possibly more competitive. It would not surprise anyone who knows numbers to find a fast-talking, enthusiastic salesperson living here.

The Challenge of a 5 House

Life can sometimes feel like a chaotic whirlwind in this home. More than likely, there will be a tendency to make snap decisions here, but because your instincts will be sharpened, your decisions could be right on. Even so, you might want to slow down and deliberate before you make that decision. It may be hard to feel rested in this house, and if you're planning to be celibate—move on—this house isn't for you. Last, because of the pervasive element of change, this 5 house may have a high turnover in occupants.

Key aspects fostered in a 5 house:

Nonconformity	Gregariousness
Change	Sales
Variety	Publishing
Movement	Risk taking
Personal magnetism	

The Number 6 House

Nesting and family interests mark this house, so this is a great house for raising a family. Love of children, pets, animals, and family traditions are classic for this house number, and it's also good for those wanting to develop their artistic abilities.

Money, comfort, and good things are attracted to this house when life is lived out of good will and a humanitarian spirit. In addition, this is an excellent home for homeschooling or for a counselor who works at home, because the energy of a 6 house is warm, caring, and nurturing. Close, loving relationships will come to life in this house.

Easy as 1-2-3

The 6 house is the home of the gardener, especially for one who loves to beautify the home and grounds with lots of flowers. Make this a place of beauty and love, for that's the natural vibration of the 6.

The Challenge of a 6 House

The idea of giving and nurturing can get out of balance here: You could give too much to others and too little to yourself, trapping you in a sacrificing role. This is not balanced and under a 6 vibration, you will be challenged to correct the situation. Duty and responsibility will be ever present in a 6 house, so if you rebel at responsibility, this isn't going to be your first choice for a house. However, the 6 house will teach the lessons of responsibility—so maybe you should stick around after all.

Key aspects fostered in a 6 house:

Beautifying and creativity	Domesticity
Children	Teaching and counseling
Balance	Home-based business
Love	Service
Nurturing and nesting	Responsibility

The Number 7 House

The 7 house is a retreat, a sanctuary for those who need to rest, recuperate, contemplate, or do inner work. For those reasons, it's a perfect house for someone who wants to be alone, meditate, and seek divine inspiration. Education, learning, and research profit here, too, and the 7 house will be enjoyable for the writer, scientist, or student, because this house lends itself to focused investigation.

Sixes and Sevens

If partners are to live together in a 7 house, both should expect a lot of aloneness and aloofness. However, pairs of contemplative, introspective souls will do very well here.

Success in this house is attained through knowledge, skill, and specialization. The 7 vibration enhances intuition, dreams, telepathic communication, spiritual development, and metaphysical studies. This is the house for a very private person and the perfect house number for a retreat center.

The Challenge of a 7 House

This is not the home for those who want to attain material wealth or advancement in the business world. It's also a difficult home for marriage, partnership, or roommates. The 7 wants to be alone, basically, so this isn't the house for someone who can't live alone or wants to entertain regularly.

Key aspects fostered in a 7 house:

The inner life	Specialization
Solitude	Privacy
Analysis	Eccentricity
Contemplation	Study or research
Recuperation	

The Number 8 House

If you're ready to get the material side of your life in order, move into an 8 house. This house will encourage organization, vision, and management of financial matters, and through discipline and problem solving, you can achieve a position of power while living in an 8 house.

The 8 brings recognition and respect in the community for your good work, and success and financial abundance are possible under this house's vibration. Good judgment will be called for, as well as strength and decisiveness.

This is not a truly domestic home, but instead is often a place of business activity. People of authority, money, businesslike minds, and success will be attracted to an 8 house, because power, money, and success are the three hallmarks of the number 8. The 8 is also the number of self-mastery, so in this house, you may find that your spiritual beliefs enhance your material achievement. This house number almost always suggests that it is expensive to live here.

The Challenge for an 8 House

Under the 8 vibration, money goes out as money comes in. Usually, there are big expenses in an 8 home—no wonder you need to attract big money! The challenge is to stay focused and organized as you work toward abundance. Careful management of finances, honesty, and integrity, as well as justice, are all called for as you learn to live under the powerful vibration of the 8. This is not the house for the spendthrift—poor financial management under this vibration may bring disaster.

Key aspects fostered in an 8 house:

Material prosperity	Business
Authority	Good judgment
Leadership	Achievement
Self-mastery	Sound money management

The Number 9 House

This is a home for the compassionate and the tolerant, a great space for the humanitarian. If you are not racially or socially prejudiced (or if you are, you will be learning a lot of lessons in this arena), are philanthropic, or have a burning desire to help the world, this is the house for you. The 9 vibration allows you to see the possibilities, to see beyond limitations and oppression. This is a home for broadminded thinkers. You'll find rewards for past efforts in this house.

Easy as 1-2-3

Did we mention that business addresses work the same way as house and apartment numbers? Why not figure out the number for where you work, and then look to the building number for its meaning?

The 9 house is a good place to complete something, heal a wound, or pass on your deep understanding to others. Intuition, dreams, healing, spiritual pursuits, the arts, drama, philosophy, and even metaphysical teachings will all be sources of inspiration to those who live at this 9 house. When you live in a 9 house, you'll find people and money drawn to you for your humanitarian outlook, your compassion, and your wisdom.

The Challenge of a 9 House

Passionate, dramatic emotions may be fully expressed in the 9 house. Because 9 rules intense feelings that usually run to the extreme, we might expect to see this intensity unleashed in a passionate display of emotions. A marriage or relationship may experience difficulties if it's too limiting. The 9 also signifies detachment and impersonal love, because the energy is focused on the larger picture. In an effort to see the greatest good for the greatest number, you may fail to see the individual you're living with. The 9 is a very powerful number that exacts powerful feelings and lessons for those under its influence.

Key aspects fostered in a 9 house:

Selflessness	The arts
Completions and endings	Passionate feelings
Philanthropy	International interests
Tolerance	Good fortune
Wisdom	

More Numbers in Your Life

There are three other numbers you will want to consider. They are your P.O. Box number, town or state number, and your phone number. When you are considering a change, these three are numbers you can be aware of and consciously choose for your life.

We want to caution you against getting too concerned about all the numbers that surround your life. Some are more important than others. Your zip code, serial number on your car, and gym locker number aren't very significant in the scheme of things because their vibratory influence isn't strong enough to make a difference. It's the things close to you, things you interact with regularly, that will add or detract from your vibratory field (which is, numerically speaking, your Core Number energies). Ideally, we would want you to be surrounded by compatible, harmonious energy, and you can make that happen wherever you have a choice over the numbers involved. Here are three numbers you might want to choose carefully.

Your P.O. Box

P.O. boxes have numbers, too, and the number on your post office box is just one more number your life vibrates to. If you don't like what's going on, change the number!

Here's an example. Kay lives on an island and has a P.O. address numbered 1031. We add these numbers together: 1 + 0 + 3 + 1 = 5. So Kay has a "5" mailbox— good for communication, publication, and promoting herself. So naturally, she'd love to hear from you.

This is just one of the numbers Kay wants to be aware of. If a number, such as this 5, is repeated in her phone number, house address, or office number, she would want to take note of this influence. Does this number enhance or present a challenge to her five Core Numbers? Too much of any one number can be hard to live with.

Your Hometown

By now you've probably figured out that cities or towns have their own name numbers, too, that can tell you what to expect to find there. Think of the possibilities: If you're planning a move, you might want to consider the number of the name for city, town, or state you're looking at. What can this city offer you? Can you live up to its requirements? What will you have to give up or gain in this city, town, or state?

You could also use these numbers to find out if the number of your hometown resonates with who you are. Or you could find out a city or state's number before you plan your vacation, depending on what kind of vacation you want. No matter what you need, the energy's in the numbers!

Each city or town name has its own vibration as shown by its numbers. Some of the questions to ask after finding out the number for your hometown's name include these:

◆ Does your city name number match any of your personal numbers in your Numerology Profile?

◆ Is the city name's number one of your karmic lessons?

◆ Is the number of this town's name the same as your Life Path Number? You will have good success when your environment is the same number as your Life Path Number.

◆ Is the number the same as your Destiny Number, Soul Number, or Maturity Number?

If any of these numbers match your numbers, then this is probably a good place for you to be. After all, life will be easier for you if you harmonize where you live with your natural energy.

How does your hometown match up with your five Core Numbers?

Easy as 1-2-3

The name of the state where you reside also has a number, and so does your town or city. It pays to be aware of the influence these place name numbers have on your life.

We're not suggesting you move if your town, city, or state number doesn't match one of your Core Numbers! However, by discovering these numbers, you will know the requirements and demands that are placed on your life by living where you do. Is your town compatible with you? The town, city, or state number tells if the energy there supports you, allows you to grow, fosters your success, or is just a start-up town for you.

Most metaphysical folks would say you're living where you are for a reason. Figure the numbers to learn the answer—and see if you agree.

For an example, let's look at the state of Washington to find its number:

W A S H I N G T O N

5 1 1 8 9 5 7 2 6　5 = 49 = 13 = 4

This 4 number tells us that if you live in the state of Washington, you can expect to find people who are hardworking, practical, honest, serious, realistic, determined, and cautious. They might also be a bit stubborn, rigid, and security conscious. Risk taking is not their favorite thing.

If you were to live in this state, you would want to know this information. Because Kay is from the state of Washington and she just happens to have a 22/4 Life Path Number, we'd say she is living in the right place for her natural energy. But if 4 isn't your number and if you are the party type and like the laid-back life, you might want to relocate!

Your Phone Number

As with other numbers in your environment, your phone number has meaning that should be heeded. When calculating your phone number, you'll be using only the three-digit prefix and the last four digits, not the area code. For example, to figure the phone number 371-3381, add all the numbers together and then reduce your sum to a single-digit number. The total number here is 26 so we reduce it to 8.

This 8 phone number brings an attraction for money and authority! It also means that in some way it's expensive to have this number. You can refer to The Meaning of Numbers Quick Reference Guide in Chapter 3, or go to Part 2 for an in-depth look at any of the numbers.

The last four digits have the most significance. Add together these last four digits
to find a single number. Let's look again
at our example:

Easy as 1-2-3

Numbers in your environment, such as your address and phone number, have meaning. Understanding those meanings can help you move through life smoothly and wisely and help you to live in sync with all aspects of your life.

- 3381 are the last four digits

- 3 + 3 + 8 + 1 = 15

- Reduce to a single digit: 1 + 5 = 6

There are two layers to consider in examining the last four digits of your phone number:

1. **The reduced root number.** Checking out the meaning of the reduced number 6 from our example reveals that this phone number will bring responsibility for caring and nurturing of others, as well as advising and problem solving. It may also bring a lot of family issues handled over this phone number, or it might be about a service business. The person at 371-3381 may find that many of the phone calls are about family (6 is the total of the last four digits) and money (8 is the total of all seven digits). *[707*

2. **The individual numbers.** Our sample number, 3381, has two 3s, an 8, and a 1. On this phone number, there will be a lot of communication, possibly emotional discussions (3s). There will also be challenging moments with those you consider to be in authority (8), as you express yourself and establish your own sense of power (3 and 8). On the other hand, you might squander your power by engaging in gossip or trivial conversations—the choice is up to you. The 8 and the 3 in combination also suggest that you might have a tendency to be extravagant and spend money over the phone. (Cut up those charge cards now!) The 1 here reveals that you will be given opportunities to stand up for yourself and be self-reliant. All of this while you work with the family, responsibility, and service issues of the 6!

And you thought choosing a phone number was no big deal!

What about the other numbers in the phone number? Here's the scoop:

♦ **The area code**. This is a widespread collective number shared by all of the people in your area. Because it's widespread, its effect is general, unlike the specific set of four numbers, unique to you, and which you can choose for your phone number. For this reason, the area code is not used to calculate your phone number meaning.

Sixes and Sevens

When calculating your phone number, use *only* the three-digit prefix and the last four digits, *not* the area code!

♦ **The prefix**. This number refers to your local area and, again, has only general significance. While the three-digit prefix is part of your phone number and is figured in, the number that counts most is found in adding together the last four digits. The prefix is used in figuring the total vibrational force of your phone number.

Speaking of choosing a phone number: Yes, you can choose one. You have more control over your phone number than you do over a house or apartment number. You can pick your number or choose an alternate; however, some phone companies charge a fee for this service. Just ask for the bank of numbers available at this time, then take a few minutes and figure the numbers. It's worth the effort. Remember, it's the last four digits that count most.

It's in the Numbers

In this book, we've tried to show how you can live harmoniously by knowing what your numbers' energy reveals about you, those around you, and the places and things you surround yourself with. The rest is up to you. May your numbers guide you to greater wisdom and purpose, and we wish you much joy and happiness—by the numbers!

The Least You Need to Know

- ◆ Your house number tells about your house's energy.

- ◆ The numbers of your apartment can help you understand the influence of where you live.

- ◆ Your city or town's number can help you align with your own natural energy.

- ◆ You can add up your phone number to see if it rings true.

Appendix A

Further Reading

There are literally hundreds of books about numerology out there. Here are some that Kay recommends:

Adrienne, Carol. *The Numerology Kit*. New York: Penguin, 1988.

———. *Your Child's Destiny: A Numerology Guide for Parents*. New York: Penguin, 1994.

Arnold, Margaret. *Love Numbers*. St. Paul: Llewellyn, 1997.

Balliett, Dow. *How to Attain Success Through the Strength of Vibration*. Santa Fe: Sun Publishing, 1905.

Bishop, Barbara J. *Numerology: Universal Vibrations of Numbers*. St. Paul, Minnesota: Llewellyn, 1990.

Blyth, Laureli. *The Numerology of Names*. Kenthurst, Australia: Kangaroo Press, 1995.

Bruce-Mitford, Miranda. *The Illustrated Book of Signs and Symbols*. New York: DK Publishing, 1996.

Campbell, Florence. *Your Days Are Numbered*. Marina Del Rey, California: DeVorss & Co., 1931.

Crawford, Saffi, and Geraldine Sullivan. *The Power of Birthdays, Stars, and Numbers.* New York: Ballantine, 1998.

Deaver, Korra. *The Master Numbers.* Alameda, California: Hunter House, 1993.

Decoz, Hans. *Numerology: The Key to Your Inner Self.* Garden City Park, New York: Avery Publishing, 1994.

Delorey, Christine. *Life Cycles.* Randolph, Massachusetts: Osmos Books, 2000.

DiPietro, Sylvia. *Live Your Life by the Numbers.* New York: Penguin, 1991.

Drayer, Ruth. *Numerology: The Power in Numbers.* Mesilla, New Mexico: Jewels of Light Publishing, 1994.

Goodwin, Matthew. *Numerology: The Complete Guide, 2 v.* North Hollywood, California: Newcastle Publishing, 1981.

Heline, Corinne. *Sacred Science of Numbers.* Marina Del Rey, California: DeVorss & Co., 1991.

Hitchcock, Helyn. *Helping Yourself with Numerology.* West Nyack, New York: Parker Publishing, 1972.

Houston, Helen, and Juno Jordan. *Two Guides to Numerology.* North Hollywood, California: NewCastle Publishing, 1982.

Javane, Faith, and Dusty Bunker. *Numerology and the Divine Triangle.* Rockport, Massachusetts: Para Research, 1981.

Jeanne. *Numerology: Spiritual Light Vibrations.* Salem, Oregon: Your Center for Truth Press, 1987.

Jordan, Juno. *Numerology: The Romance in Your Name.* Marina Del Rey, California: DeVorss & Co., 1966.

———. *Right Action Number.* Marina Del Rey, California: DeVorss & Co., 1979.

Jordan, Juno, and Helen Houston. *Two Guides to Numerology.* North Hollywood, California: Newcastle Publishing, 1982 (out of print).

Line, Julia. *Discover Numerology*. New York: Sterling Publishing, 1993.

Linn, Denise. *Sacred Space*. New York: Ballantine Books, 1995.

Miller, Dorcas S. *Stars of the First People*. Boulder, Colorado: Pruett Publishing, 1997.

Millman, Dan. *The Life You Were Born to Live*. Tiburon, California: HJ Kramer, 1993.

Montrose. *Numerology for Everybody*. Chicago: Nelson-Hall, 1945.

Newmont, Nick. *Newmerology*. San Diego, California: Jodere Group, 2003.

Pierson, George. *What's in a Number?* New York: Abbeville Press, 1996.

Pond, Lucy, and David Pond. *The Metaphysical Handbook*. Port Ludlow, Washington: Reflecting Pond Publications, 1994.

Roguemore, Kathleen. *It's All in Your Numbers: The Secrets of Numerology*. San Francisco: Harper & Row, 1975.

Schimmel, Annemarie. *The Mystery of Numbers*. New York: Oxford University Press, 1993.

Tognetti, Arlene, and Lisa Lenard. *The Complete Idiot's Guide to Tarot, 2nd ed.* Indianapolis: Alpha Books, 2003.

The following books are good resources for related information:

Angeles, Arrien. *The Four Fold Path*. San Francisco: HarperCollins, 1993.

Bethards, Betty. *The Dream Book*. Rockport, Massachusetts: Element Books, 1995.

Hesse, Hermann. *Demian*. New York: Harper & Row, 1965.

Hillman, Laurence, and Donna Spencer. *Alignments*. New York: Lantern Books, 2002.

Marooney, Kim. *Angel Blessings*. Carmel, California: Merrill-West Publishing, 1995.

Your Numerology Profile

Figuring a Numerology Profile

REMEMBER

All double digit numbers
(except master numbers)
are reduced to a single digit.
For example, 17 = 1 + 7 = 8

Letter Conversion Grid

1	2	3	4	5	6	7	8	9
A	B	C	D	E	F	G	H	I
J	K	L	M	N	O	P	Q	R
S	T	U	V	W	X	Y	Z	

WORKSPACE

Record each
number
in its own star

Add vowel numbers together. Write numbers for vowel letters above the name.
Vowels:

START
HERE

= ___ total = ___ (reduce it) = Soul Number

Full Name _____

Write letters' numbers here. Add all numbers together.

= ___ total = ___ (reduce it) = Destiny Number

Consonants:
Add consonant numbers together. Write numbers for consonant below the name.

= ___ total = ___ (reduce it) = Personality Number

Date of Birth _____ _____ _____ = ___ total = ___ (reduce it)
Month   Day   Year
(use all four numbers)

= Life Path Number

Remember, if you have a master number don't reduce it!

Destiny Number ___ + Life Path Number ___ = ___ total = ___ (reduce it)

= Maturity Number

Major Cycles	Ages
1st Cycle _____ _____ Month of Birth	
2nd Cycle _____ _____ Day of Birth	
3rd Cycle _____ _____ Year of Birth	

MAJOR CYCLES CHART

Life Path	End of 1st Cycle Start of 2nd Cycle	End of 2nd Cycle Start of 3rd Cycle
1	26-27	53-54
2	25-26	52-53
3	33-34	60-61
4 and 22	32-33	59-60
5	31-32	58-59
6 and 33	30-31	57-58
7	29-30	56-57
8	28-29	55-56
9	27-28	54-55

Your Birthday Number is _____   (the day you were born) and reduced it is _____

YOUR NUMEROLOGY CHART

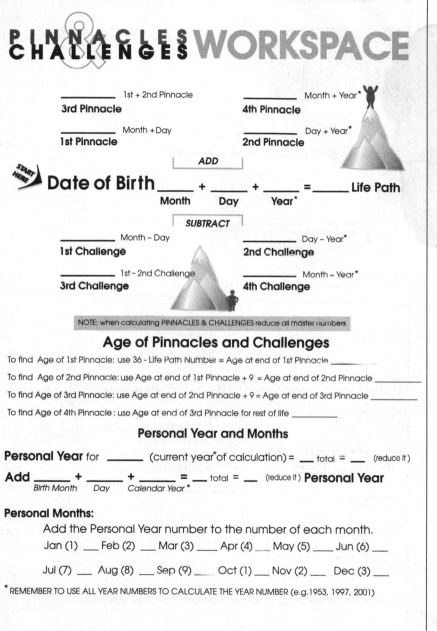

PINNACLES & CHALLENGES WORKSPACE

_____ 1st + 2nd Pinnacle
3rd Pinnacle

_____ Month + Year*
4th Pinnacle

_____ Month + Day
1st Pinnacle

_____ Day + Year*
2nd Pinnacle

ADD

Date of Birth _____ + _____ + _____ = _____ **Life Path**
            Month   Day   Year*

SUBTRACT

_____ Month − Day
1st Challenge

_____ Day − Year*
2nd Challenge

_____ 1st − 2nd Challenge
3rd Challenge

_____ Month − Year*
4th Challenge

NOTE: when calculating PINNACLES & CHALLENGES reduce all master numbers

Age of Pinnacles and Challenges

To find Age of 1st Pinnacle: use 36 − Life Path Number = Age at end of 1st Pinnacle _____

To find Age of 2nd Pinnacle: use Age at end of 1st Pinnacle + 9 = Age at end of 2nd Pinnacle _____

To find Age of 3rd Pinnacle: use Age at end of 2nd Pinnacle + 9 = Age at end of 3rd Pinnacle _____

To find Age of 4th Pinnacle: use Age at end of 3rd Pinnacle for rest of life _____

Personal Year and Months

Personal Year for _____ (current year*of calculation) = __ total = __ (reduce it)

Add _____ + _____ + _____ = __ total = __ (reduce it) **Personal Year**
     Birth Month   Day   Calendar Year*

Personal Months:

Add the Personal Year number to the number of each month.

Jan (1) ___ Feb (2) ___ Mar (3) ___ Apr (4) ___ May (5) ___ Jun (6) ___

Jul (7) ___ Aug (8) ___ Sep (9) ___ Oct (1) ___ Nov (2) ___ Dec (3) ___

* REMEMBER TO USE ALL YEAR NUMBERS TO CALCULATE THE YEAR NUMBER (e.g.1953, 1997, 2001)

Every number has a specific meaning. Here are keywords for each of the 9 numbers, to help you understand what these meanings are.

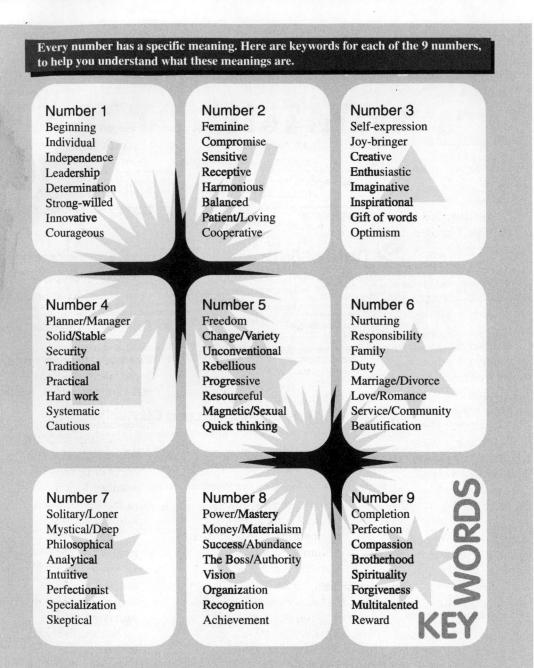

Number 1
Beginning
Individual
Independence
Leadership
Determination
Strong-willed
Innovative
Courageous

Number 2
Feminine
Compromise
Sensitive
Receptive
Harmonious
Balanced
Patient/Loving
Cooperative

Number 3
Self-expression
Joy-bringer
Creative
Enthusiastic
Imaginative
Inspirational
Gift of words
Optimism

Number 4
Planner/Manager
Solid/Stable
Security
Traditional
Practical
Hard work
Systematic
Cautious

Number 5
Freedom
Change/Variety
Unconventional
Rebellious
Progressive
Resourceful
Magnetic/Sexual
Quick thinking

Number 6
Nurturing
Responsibility
Family
Duty
Marriage/Divorce
Love/Romance
Service/Community
Beautification

Number 7
Solitary/Loner
Mystical/Deep
Philosophical
Analytical
Intuitive
Perfectionist
Specialization
Skeptical

Number 8
Power/Mastery
Money/Materialism
Success/Abundance
The Boss/Authority
Vision
Organization
Recognition
Achievement

Number 9
Completion
Perfection
Compassion
Brotherhood
Spirituality
Forgiveness
Multitalented
Reward

KEY WORDS

Index

HOW TO ORDER

Numerology Profile Chart

Kay Lagerquist, Ph.D.
* www.numerology-insights.com * insights@whidbey.com

To order a complete numerology chart, photocopy this page and send the following information. We will send you a 24-page report analyzing your numbers.

Current Name: _____

Address: _____

City: _____ State: _____ Zip: _____ Country: _____

Phone: ( ) _____

To order your chart, fill in your Birth Name and Birth Date—please print.

Complete Numerology Chart

$40.00 (plus tax and shipping)

Your chart information: Please fill in the requested information.

Name on Birth Certificate (exact spelling) (Print please.)

_____

Date of Birth: Month _____ Day _____ Year _____

Gift Chart Information

Fill in the requested information about the person you are ordering a numerology chart for.
Gift Numerology Chart: $40.00 (plus tax and shipping)

Name on Birth Certificate: _____

(exact spelling)

Date of Birth: Month: _____ Day: _____ Year: _____

Fill in Mailing Address (Print please.)

Deliver Numerology Profile to:	Send Gift Profile directly to:
Name _____	Name _____
Address _____	Address _____
City _____ State/Zip _____	City _____ State/Zip _____
Day Phone _____	Day Phone _____
Evening Phone _____	Evening Phone _____

Consultations

Interpretation of your numerology chart is available in person or by phone.

$195. (1.5 hours, taped) Chart report included.
Other consultations: Name change, Life Purpose, Personal Year analysis.
Coaching for Personal Growth, and Spiritual Development also available.
Call for fees and appointment information   360-221-2696

Postage and Handling Charges

	U.S.	Canada	Mexico	All Other International
Each Numerology Profile	7.00	8.00	9.00	15.00

Payment made in U.S. funds.

#	Profiles		Price each
	Name: _____		
	Name: _____		
	Name: _____		

Numerology Profiles **Total $** _____

Chart Consultation **Total $** _____

For WA residents only **Tax 8.6% $** _____

***Shipping** (see shipping table above) **$** _____

Grand Total $ _____

Payment:
Pay by check or money order. Checks must have name, address, and phone printed on check. Make checks payable to Kay Lagerquist.

Our Mailing Address:
Mail this form and check or money order to:
Insights—Kay Lagerquist, Ph.D.
P.O. Box 1031
Langley, WA 98260
Phone: 360-221-2696
E-mail: insights@whidbey.com

Allow three weeks for delivery. Prices and availability subject to change without notice.